EATING DISORDERS IN THE 21ST CENTURY

COGNITIVE THERAPY OF EATING DISORDERS ON CONTROL AND WORRY

EATING DISORDERS IN THE 21ST CENTURY

Additional books in this series can be found on Nova's website
under the Series tab.

Additional E-books in this series can be found on Nova's website
under the E-books tab.

EATING DISORDERS IN THE 21ST CENTURY

COGNITIVE THERAPY OF EATING DISORDERS ON CONTROL AND WORRY

SANDRA SASSAROLI
AND
GIOVANNI MARIA RUGGIERO
EDITORS

Nova Science Publishers, Inc.
New York

For permission to use material from this book please contact us:
Telephone 631-231-7269; Fax 631-231-8175
Web Site: http://www.novapublishers.com

Additional color graphics may be available in the e-book version of this book.

LIBRARY OF CONGRESS CATALOGING-IN-PUBLICATION DATA

Cognitive therapy of eating disorders on control and worry / editors, Sandra Sassaroli, Giovanni Maria Ruggiero.
p. ; cm.
Includes bibliographical references and index.
ISBN 978-1-60876-617-8 (hardcover)
1. Eating disorders--Treatment. 2. Cognitive therapy. I. Sassaroli, Sandra. II. Ruggiero, Giovanni Maria.
[DNLM: 1. Eating Disorders--therapy. 2. Cognitive Therapy--methods. 3. Eating Disorders--psychology. WM 175 C6767 2009]
RC552.E18.C627 2009
616.85'26--dc22

2009041968

Published by Nova Science Publishers, Inc. + New York

CONTENTS

INTRODUCTION

1. CORE PSYCHOLOGICAL FACTORS IN THE CAUSAL PROCESS OF EATING DISORDERS

As the title suggests, this book privileges the exploration of two psychological factors correlated with eating disorders (ED): a cognitive belief, which is the need of and the desire of control, and a cognitive/emotional process, which is worry. Control and worry are "core" psychological factors, which means that they are general psychological attitudes which predispose individuals to develop an ED and contribute to maintain it, while they are less directly linked to the preoccupation with eating and body shape. For example, the dependence of self-esteem on the control of body weight in the first cognitive model of bulimia by Fairburn (1981) was not a core factor, but a causal process which links a core factor (self-esteem) and symptoms together.

Actually, need of control and worry are far from exhausting the whole set of core psychological and emotional factors correlated with ED. A rapid overview of the set of the most frequently studied core factors of ED should start from maladaptive perfectionism, either in the form of self-oriented and socially prescribed anxiety about performance (Bastiani, Rao, Weltzin, & Kaye, 1995; Pratt, Telch, Labouvie, Wilson, & Agras 2001) or in the form of concern over mistakes, interpreted as equivalent to failure (Bulik et al., 2003; Halmi et al., 2000). The second factor in order of relevance is a lowered self-esteem of individuals with ED conceived as a global negative view of themselves and not narrowed on the inability to control eating, shape and weight. This negative self-judgment is autonomous and independent of performance and is seen as part of a unconditional and permanent negative identity. In turn, this negative self-view plausibly depends on a submissive attitude, perceived lower rank, a pervasive need of approval from others linked to deep emotion of shame and a fear of being intruded upon or disconfirmed by others (Guidano & Liotti, 1983). Data from human sufferers of anorexia nervosa and bulimia nervosa are consistent with the presence of submissive behaviors and perceived low social rank (e.g. low self-esteem, helplessness, and feelings of shame) (Troop, Allan, Treasure, & Katzman, 2003; Troop, Allan, Serpell, & Treasure, 2008).

Another general emotional process of patients with ED is mood intolerance. This term refers to an inability to cope appropriately with intense emotional states, such as anger, anxiety or depression, and in some cases there is intolerance even of positive emotions, like excitement (Fairburn, Cooper, & Shafran, 2003). Instead of accepting changes in mood and dealing appropriately with them, patients with ED would tend to fear any emotional change and judge it as a catastrophic signal of sufferance (Claes, Vandereycken, & Vertommen, 2001; Holderness, Brooks-Gunn, & Warren, 1994; Paul, Schroeter, Dahme, & Nutzinger, 2002). Binge eating, self-induced vomiting and intense exercising may also be used as forms of mood control behaviors.

Also interpersonal processes are factors which contribute to the maintenance of ED. Among the problematic interpersonal situations which may influence the severity of ED the more frequent are family tensions and adverse interpersonal events (Fairburn, Cooper, & Shafran, 2003). Family tensions often intensify resistance to eating, which is in turn a intensification of their need for a sense of control displaced onto dietary self-control (Fairburn, Shafran, & Cooper, 1999). Adverse interpersonal events commonly precipitate episodes of binge eating and the severity of bulimia nervosa (Steiger, Lehoux, & Seguin, 1999).

Generally, the trait of impulsivity has been found only in bulimic subjects (Claes, Vandereycken, & Vertommen, 2002; Diaz-Marsa, Carrasco, & Saiz, 2000) but not in anorexics. However, rather than reflecting an enduring personality trait, impulsivity may depend on the erratic dietary patterns and emotional instability of patients with bulimia. In fact, impulsivity decreases following reductions in binge eating and purging (Ames-Frankel et al., 1992).

Linked to impulsivity is sensation seeking. Sensation seeking is defined as a need for novel, and complex sensations and experiences and the willingness to take physical and social risks for the sake of such experiences (Zuckerman, 1979). Bingeing and purging behaviors are frequently associated with measures of sensation seeking (Rossier, Bolognini, Plancherel, & Halfon, 2000; Steiger, Jabalpurwala, Champagne, & Stotland, 1997). On the other hand, this is not true for dietary restriction (Steiger et al., 1997).

There are also some data about narcissism. Narcissism is more characteristic of individuals with ED than in other psychiatric disturbances (i.e., anxiety, affective, and adjustment disorders), suggesting that it may be a unique risk factor for ED (Steiger et al., 1997). In addition, narcissism seems to persist after remission from bulimia. This finding suggests that it may be a characteristic personality trait in individuals with bulimia (Lehoux, Steiger, & Jabalpurlawa, 2000).

Sociotropy is a personality style characterized by concern with acceptance and approval from others, whereas autonomy is a personality style oriented towards independence, control, and achievement. Heightened vulnerability for an ED may be associated with a sociotropy–autonomy conflict. That is, individuals with EDs may strive to maintaing independence, but also rely on interpersonal relationships for validation and self-esteem (Narduzzi & Jackson, 2000). Two studies using non-clinical university samples suggest that low self-esteem may mediate the relationship between autonomy and disordered eating (Frederick & Grow, 1996), whereas ambivalence over emotional expression may mediate the relationship between sociotropy and disordered eating (Krause, Robins, & Lynch, 2000). That is, women characterized by high sociotropy may be reluctant to express emotions that may threaten their interpersonal relationships (e.g., anger), but suppression of these emotions may make them vulnerable to ED symptomatology.

Neuroticism is characterized by a predisposition towards emotionality, hypersensitivity, anxiety, worry, moodiness, and depression (Eysenck & Eysenck, 1985). Individuals with EDs score higher on neuroticism than controls (Diaz-Marsa et al., 2000; Ghaderi & Scott, 2000;

Podar, Hannus, & Allik, 1999). Neuroticism is also positively correlated with ED symptomatology in female university samples (Brookings & Wilson, 1994; Geissler & Kelly, 1994; Janzen, Saklofske, & Kelly, 1993), and community samples (Cervera et al., 2003; Gual et al., 2002), and with bulimic symptomatology in a small male university sample (Finlayson, Kelly, & Saklofske, 2002).

In conclusion, anorexia and bulimia seem both consistently characterized by perfectionism, obsessive-compulsiveness, neuroticism, negative emotionality, harm avoidance, low self-directedness, low cooperativeness, and traits associated with avoidant personality. Consistent differences that emerge between the two disorders are high constraint and persistence and low novelty seeking in anorexia and high impulsivity, sensation seeking, novelty seeking, and traits associated with borderline personality in bulimia (Cassin & von Ranson, 2005).

In sum, research suggests that ED are characterized by perfectionism, narcissism, sociotropy, and autonomy, whereas impulsivity and sensation seeking are more typical of disorders characterized by bingeing. To our opinion, control and worry are overlooked. This book is an attempt to narrow this conceptual gap.

2. Control and Worry as Core Psychological Factors of Eating Disorders: A Hypothesis

Although control was a psychological variable frequently quoted in the papers of the great first theorists of ED, the interested about this psychological factor faded away when the era of empirical research about ED begun. This is astonishing, because any clinician knows that individuals with ED engage in extreme restricted eating and purging behaviors essentially to control their world and make their life more manageable and controllable. In fact, individuals with ED feel a lack of capacity to control personal relationships, internal reactions and general events. This is their way to satisfy their human need for control. The hypothesis of this book is that individuals with ED perceive control as a general attitude involving not only eating and body weight and shape but external events and internal feelings as well.

The key feature of worry is the predominance of negatively oriented thoughts, which means that the worrying individual tends to have negative expectations, to judge negatively events and situations. Worry is a core factor of anxiety, but from our viewpoint it plays a role also in ED. We assume that individuals with ED worry and think a lot about weight, fat, and body shape because they predict and fear a long chain of negative consequences related to such factors. These negative consequences would affect interpersonal problems, sense of self-efficacy, and fear of being blamed or disparaged by parents, peers, etc. In short, ED subjects may worry like anxiety disordered subjects. In our view worry is associated with ED symptoms.

3. General Overview of the Book

The aim of this book is to illustrate a variant of the standard cognitive treatment for ED. This therapy is based on the principle that assessing and treating the patient's process of worry and sense of control fosters greater understanding of the psychopathology of the eating disorder and increases the efficacy of cognitive treatment. We call this therapy the control and worry-focused treatment of eating Disorders (CWT-ED). This therapy is based on the principle that assessing and treating the patient's process of worry and sense of control fosters greater understanding of the psychopathology of the eating disorder and increases the efficacy of cognitive treatment. CWT-ED therapy is innovative in that it assumes that biased beliefs and processes in the domains of control and worry are among the relevant cognitive distortions of eating disorders and should be added to other factors, such as clinical perfectionism, mood intolerance, and low self-esteem, as the targets of cognitive-behavioral therapy for eating disorders.

The book is an edited collection of chapters that discuss the psychopathological roles played by control and worry in ED, and provide a detailed description of the therapeutic protocol, which primarily focuses on the treatment of the cognitive factors of control and worry as core factor of a psychotherapy of ED. In addition, the book has contributions from other theorists in the field who have investigated the role of worry, preoccupation, and control, or who explore the connections between worry, control, and other cognitive factors underlying eating disorders, such as perfectionism, self-esteem, and impulsivity. The treatment section of the book includes not only the CWT-ED protocol, but also guidelines for treatments with different orientations, such as psychodynamic and family therapy, and a discussion of the differences and similarities to the CWT-ED protocol.

Chapter 1 deals with the hypothesis of control and worry in ED, their psychopathological role and the theoretical background which suggested to focus our attention on these two aspects of negative thinking. The chapter is written from a purely cognitive-behavioral viewpoint. A special section of the chapter focuses on the problem of the relationship between control and stress, a factor which frequently decreases the degree of perceived control of individuals with ED. For this reason, stress often is a precipitating event in the development of ED. The authors are Sandra Sassaroli (Studi Cognitivi, Post-graduate Cognitive Psychotherapy School, Milano, Italy) and Giovanni M. Ruggiero (Psicoterapia Cognitiva e Ricerca, Post-graduate Cognitive Psychotherapy School, Milano, Italy).

Chapter 2 reconsider the theme of control from a constructivistic viewpoint. The two authors, David A. Winter (University of Hertfordshire, UK) and Eric J. Button (Leicester University) are tow respected theorists of kellian personal construct theory. Still in the 1980s Eric Button described anorexia nervosa as a quest for control.

Chapter 3 describes in details the procedures of the control and worry-focused treatment of eating disorders. It is written by Sassaroli and Ruggiero again.

Chapter 4 explores the role of control in a particular type of ED: the binge eating disorder. The Authors are Piergiuseppe Vinai, Silvia Cardetti, Noemi Ferrato and Paola Vallauri of Studi Cognitivi and of the research group "Gnosis" (Cuneo, Italy).

Chapter 5 explores the developmental ground of control and perfectionism: criticism in the relationship with parents. In addition, the link between perceived criticism and two possible correlates like sense of responsibility and humiliation is explored. It is written by Sassaroli and Ruggiero. The authors are: Marina Apparigliato, Francesca Fiore, Giovanni M. Ruggiero, Clarice Mezzaluna, Carmelo Lamela and Sandra Sassaroli.

Chapter 6 reports emerging evidence suggesting that some individuals with anorexia nervosa, like those with autism spectrum disorders, display "weak central coherence", a cognitive style characterized by a tendency to focus on detail at the expense of seeing the overall gestalt. This excessive attention to detail can seriously compromise these patients' psychological well-being and overall quality of life. It can also shape some of the symptoms and personality features that maintain the illness. This chapter addresses the history, concept and measurement of central coherence, and presents converging evidence from neuropsychological and clinical sources in relation to coherence problems in anorexia. Importantly, the chapter also describes how such evidence can be usefully translated into clinical practice and how weak central coherence and central beliefs concerning control may interact with each other. The authors are Eva Kemps (Flinders University, Adelaide, Australia) and Carolina Lopez and Kate Tchanturia (both of the King's College of London, UK).

Chapter 7 discusses the complex inter-relationship between personality disorders and impulsivity in ED. In addition, the authors discuss impulsivity and control are opposite poles of a pathological domain. The authors are J. Hubert Lacey and Kate Webb, both of the St George's Hospital Eating Disorders Service in London, UK.

Chapter 8 describes a group intervention model based on cognitive behavioral therapy principles that has been carried out for the past several years in an adolescent inpatient department for ED. Daniel Stein (Tel Aviv University, Israel), Eynat Zubery (Tel Aviv University, Israel), and Yael Latzer (Haifa University, Israel) deals with to the difficulties inherent in the application of CBT to this population, describe our model, highlight our findings with several vignettes, and discuss the implications of our findings in the overall management of patients with ed.

Chapter 9 Zubery, Latzer and Stein describes a family-based therapeutic program focused on parents in outpatient ED care which combines a cognitive behavioral methods with a psychodynamic approach in group settings.

Chapter 10 Yael Latzer, Tamar Peretz (Rambam Medical Center, Haifa, Israel), Sarit Kreutzer (Rambam Medical Center, Haifa, Israel), Eynat Zubery and Danny Stein aim to describe an alternative treatment model for bulimia nervosa, integrating cognitive behavioral and short-term dynamic therapies. Referred to as conflict-oriented Cognitive Behavioral Therapy (CO-CBT), this model focuses on the underlying emotional and dynamic aspects of bulimia more than does traditional cognitive-behavioral therapy.

The final chapter 11 is a concise review of the pharmacological treatment of ED. The authors are Ruggiero, La Mela and Sassaroli.

References

Ames-Frankel, J., Devlin, M. J., Walsh, B. T., Strasser, T. J., Sadik, C., Oldham, J. M., & Roose, S. P. (1992). Personality disorder diagnoses in patients with bulimia nervosa: Clinical correlates and changes with treatment. *Journal of Clinical Psychiatry, 53*, 90–96.

Bastiani, A. M., Rao, R., Weltzin T., & Kaye W. H. (1995). Perfectionism in anorexia nervosa. *International Journal of Eating Disorders, 17*, 147-152.

Brookings, J. B. & Wilson, J. F. (1994). Personality and Family-Environment Predictors of Self-Reported Eating Attitudes and Behaviors. *Journal of Personality Assessment, 63*, 313-326.

Bulik, C. M., Tozzi, F., Anderson, C., Mazzeo, S. E., Aggen, S., & Sullivan, P. F. (2003). The relation between eating disorders and components of perfectionism. *American Journal of Psychiatry, 160*, 366-368.

Cassin, S. E., von Ranson, K. M. (2005). Personality and eating disorders: a decade in review. *Clinical Psychological Review, 25*, 895-916.

Cervera, S., Lahortiga, F., Martınez-Gonzalez, M. A., Gual, P., de Irala-Estevez, J., & Alonso, Y. (2003). Neuroticism and low self-esteem as risk factors for incident eating disorders in a prospective cohort study. *International Journal of Eating Disorders, 33*, 271–280.

Claes, L., Vandereycken, W., & Vertommen, H. (2003). Eating disordered patients with and without self-injurious behaviours: A comparison of psychopathological features. *European Eating Disorders Review, 11*, 379-396

Díaz-Marsá, M., Carrasco, J. L., & Sáiz, J. (2000). A study of temperament and personality in anorexia and bulimia nervosa. *Journal of Personality Disorders, 14*, 352-359.

Eysenck, H. J., & Eysenck, M. W. (1985). *Personality and individual differences: A natural science approach.* New York: Plenum.

Fairburn, C. G., Cooper, Z., & Shafran, R. (2003). Cognitive behaviour therapy for eating disorders: a "transdiagnostic" theory and treatment. *Behaviour Research and Therapy, 41*, 509-528.

Fairburn, C. G., Shafran, R., & Cooper, Z. (1999). A cognitive behavioural theory of anorexia nervosa. *Behaviour Research and Therapy, 37*, 1–13.

Finlayson, R. A., Kelly, I. W., & Saklofske, D. H. (2002). Bulimic symptomatology, body-image, and personality characteristics of university men. *Psychological Reports, 91*, 496-502.

Frederick, C. M., & Grow, V. M. (1996). A mediational model of autonomy, self-esteem, and eating disordered attitudes and behaviors. *Psychology of Women Quarterly, 20*, 217-228.

Geissler, T., & Kelly, I. W. (1994). Bulimic symptomatology and personality factors in a non-clinical sample: A replication. *Psychological Reports, 75*, 224-226.

Ghaderi, A., & Scott, B. (2000). The Big Five and eating disorders: a prospective study in the general population. *European Journal of Personality, 14*, 311-323.

Gual, P., Perez-Gaspar, M., Martinez-Gonzalez, M. A., Lahortiga, F., de Irala-Estevez, J., & Cervera, S. (2002). Self-esteem, personality, and eating disorders: Baseline assessment of a prospective population-based cohort. *International Journal of Eating Disorders, 31*, 261–273.

Guidano, V. F., & Liotti, G. (1983). *Cognitive Processes and Emotional Disorders*. New York, The Guilford Press.

Halmi, K. A., Sunday, S. R., Strober, M., Kaplan, A., Woodside, D. B., Fichter, M., Treasure, J., Berrettini, W. H., & Kaye, W. H. (2000). Perfectionism in Anorexia Nervosa: Variation by Clinical Subtype, Obsessionality, and Pathological Eating Behavior. *American Journal of Psychiatry, 157*, 1799-1805.

Holderness, C. C., Brooks-Gunn, J., & Warren, M. P. (1994). Eating disorders and substance use: A dancing vs. a nondancing population. *Medicine and Science in Sports and Exercise, 26*, 297-304.

Janzen, B. L., & Saklofske, D. H., & Kelly, I. W. (1993). Personality and bulimic symptomatology. *Journal of Clinical Psychology, 49*, 649-53

Krause, E. D., Robins, C. I., & Lynch, T. R. (2000). A mediational model relating sociotropy, ambivalence over emotional expression, and disordered eating. *Psychology of Women Quarterly, 24*, 328-335.

Lehoux, P. M., Steiger, H., & Jabalpurlawa, S. (2000). State/trait distinctions in bulimic syndromes. *International Journal of Eating Disorders, 27,* 36-42.

Narduzzi, K. J., & Jackson, T. (2000). Personality differences between eating-disordered women and a nonclinical comparison sample: A discriminant classification analysis. *Journal of Clinical Psychology, 56*, 699-710.

Paul, P., Schroeter, K., Dahme, B., & Nutzinger, D. O. (2002). Self-injurious behavior in women with eating disorders. *American Journal of Psychiatry, 159*, 408-411.

Podar, I., Hannus A., & Allik J. (1999). Personality and Affectivity Characteristics Associated With Eating Disorders: A Comparison of Eating Disordered, Weight-Preoccupied, and Normal Samples. *Journal of Personality Assessment, 73*, 133-147.

Pratt, E. M., Telch, C. F., Labouvie, E. W., Wilson, G. T., & Agras, S. W. (2001). Perfectionism in women with binge eating disorder. *International Journal of Eating Disorders, 29*, 177-186

Rossier, V., Bolognini, M., Plancherel, B., & Halfon, O. (2000). Sensation seeking: a personality trait characteristic of adolescent girls and young women with eating disorders? *European Eating Disorders Review, 8*, 245-252.

Steiger, H., Jabalpurwala, S., Champagne, J., & Stotland, S. (1997). A controlled study of trait narcissism in anorexia and bulimia nervosa. *International Journal of Eating Disorders, 22*, 173-178.

Steiger, H., Lehoux, P. M., & Seguin, L. (1999). Impulsivity, dietary control and the urge to binge in bulimic syndromes. *International Journal of Eating Disorders, 26*, 261 – 274.

Troop, N. A., Allan, S., Serpell, L., & Treasure, J. L. (2008). Shame in women with a history of eating disorders. *European Eating Disorders Review, 16*, 480-488

Troop, N. A., Allan, S., Treasure, J. L. & Katzman, M. (2003). Social comparison and submissive behaviour in eating disorders. *Psychology and Psychotherapy: Theory, Research and Practice, 76,* 237-249.

Zuckerman, M. (1979). *Sensation Seeking: Beyond the Optimal Level of Arousal.* New Jersey, USA: Erlbaum Hillsdale.

In: Cognitive Therapy of Eating Disorders…
Editors: S. Sassaroli and G.M. Ruggiero
ISBN: 978-1-60876-617-8

Chapter 1

THE NEED OF AND THE COMPULSION TO CONTROL AND THE TENDENCY TO WORRY IN EATING DISORDERS

Sandra Sassaroli[1] and Giovanni Maria Ruggiero[2]
[1] "Studi Cognitivi" Cognitive Psychotherapy School, Milano, Italy
[2] "Psicoterapia Cognitiva e Ricerca" Cognitive Psychotherapy School, Milano, Italy

ABSTRACT

The first chapter deals with the hypothesis of control and worry in eating disorders (ED), their psychopathological role and the theoretical background which suggested to focus our attention on these two aspects of negative thinking. The chapter is written from a purely cognitive-behavioral viewpoint. From a cognitive viewpoint, the symptomatology of ED can be reduced to an exaggerated preoccupation with the theme of perfection, self-esteem and control and to a peculiar link between such cognitive beliefs and eating behaviours. Individuals affected with ED often look for control (Bruch, 1973, 1982). The sense of control is often obtained by the continuous monitoring of a certain parameter, such as bodily perception in panic, intrusive thought in obsessionality, and so on. In the case of ED, such a parameter appears as concerns over eating and body weight and shape (Fairburn & Harrison, 2003). As explained by Slade (1982), dietary restrictions enhance the subjective sense of being in control. In additi0on, Control, perfectionism and low self-esteem are all forms of a neurotic tendency to negative thought. Hence, it is natural to wonder whether in worry, which is the most typical form of negative thinking, is present in ED. A special section of the chapter focuses on the problem of the relationship between control and stress, a factor which frequently decreases the degree of perceived control of individuals with ED. For this reason, stress often is a precipitating event in the development of ED.

1. CONTROL IN COGNITIVE MODELS

The belief of the need for control comes from the more general psychological concept of control, which has been defined as the feeling of a relationship between a intentional state and an external or internal outcome (Seligman, 1975). Skinner (1996) called it sense of control and referred it to the individual's assessment of the level of control available in a context.

In the cognitive clinical model, the theme of control is related with either the self-regulatory skill of internal states and the capacity to influence external events. The feeling of being in control is associated with a psychological healthy status (Steptoe & Appels, 1989), while the failure to exert cognitive and emotional control is a fundamental factor contributing to emotional disorders. In his famous paper, Langer (1975) showed that people not affected by an emotional disorder tend to overestemimate their degree of exerted control on events and situations, frequently judging to have a good control even of situation actually governed by chance.

Thompson (1999) underlines that there are some factors that encourage a judgement of increased control. This hypothesis is supported by a fascinating set of studies. For example, Langer (1975) has shown that people tend to reject the chance to exchange a personally chosen ticket, even if exchaging the ticket would plausibly increase the odds of winning. Probably, the action of personally choosing the ticket is linked to a feeling of control that is emotionally appealing and convincing. On the other hand, a not personally chosen ticket lacks this emotional quality, even if it is more prominsing to win, from a purely rational viewpoint.

However, people do not show a indiscriminate tendency to overestimate their perceived control. In fact, individuals are likely to consider their exerted control higher in settings that are characterized by personal involvement, familiarity, foreknowledge of the desired outcome, and a focus on success than in other circumstances. Personal involvement refers to situations in which individuals are active agents and not passive spectators. For example, personally driving a car could stimulate a higher feeling of control as opposed to being a passenger in an aircraft. Familiarity means that when circumstances are well known and not new to the agent, the individual can easily feel a higher control of events. Foreknowledge of the desired outcome stresses that it is important to have a clear idea of the desired outcome during tasks. This clarity of outcome generates a higher sense of control in individuals. Finally, focus on success as opposed to focus on loss and failure. If the task is aimed at gaining a success instead of avoiding a damage, the feeling of control is higher.

All these mentioned factors are crucial in understanding why in many emotional disorders there is a typical feeling of insufficient control. For example, people affected by emotional disorders tend to underestimate their capacity to control events and feelings. Actually, at least in the case of depression it would be more correct to say that depressed individuals tend to show a realistic estimation of their control on external events, while non depressed individuals would rather tend to overestimate their control (Alloy & Abramson, 1979). This results suggest that there is a healthy need to overestimate control in particular conditions, which are: a familiar situation; a strong focus on success; when the desired outcome is already well-known; and when people are tacking action for themselves. In these conditions, the overestimation of control is tendencially convenient and reasonable from a pragmatic viewpoint, even if not rationally correct. On the other hand, depressed individuals fail to detach themselves from a realistic pessimism even when it is detrimental.

Depressed individuals are not alone in their pessimistic feeling of insufficient control. Anxious people can perceive the same discomfortable feeling. In their case, the lack of control is coloured with the anxiety of the possible consequences of the loss fo control. In fact, there is a logical link between cognitive beliefs of insufficient control and feelings of anxiety. Anxious individuals show many of the factors listed by Thompson (1999) in her paper. They focus their feeling of control on loss, avoidance, danger, and damage rather than on success. In addition, they show a low sense of personal involvement in anxiety related situations, and confused ideas about the outcome of feared events (Barlow, 2002). Many theoretical models and empirical research have conceptualized and explored anxiety as a perception of lack of control. Anxiety-disordered subjects would judge the world as dangerous and themselves as vulnerable because they consider their level of exerted control on external events or internal reactions as insufficient (Barlow, 2002; Basoglu & Mineka, 1992; Foa, Zinbarg, & Olasov-Rothbaum, 1992; Mineka & Zinbarg, 1996; Rapee, Craske, Brown, & Barlow, 1996; Shapiro & Astin, 1998, pp. 23). Barlow (2002) suggests that a perceived lack of control over "external" threats (i.e., events, objects, or situations that are fear producing for an individual) and/or control over negative "internal" emotional and bodily reactions are central factors for the experience of anxiety problems. In fact, to have control over external reality and internal states is a basic human need. When this need is not satisfied, people experiences feelings of fear and anxiety (Bandura, 1977; Deci & Ryan, 1985).

2. From Lack of Control to Desire of Control

A possible criticism against the control-centered model of anxiety would be that this theory focuses only on the feeling of lack of control. In fact, a perceived lack of control may lead to avoidance behavior, as in the case of some anxiety disorders. Anxiety is related with the beliefs that anxiety-related events and sensations are uncontrollable. However, individuals may vary with respect to their reaction to a perceived loss of control. It is true that a perceived lack of control tends to generate anxiety and avoidance, desire to fly. However, it is true as well that a judgement of insufficient control may generate not avoidance, but a desire to increase control or an obsessive compulsion to regain control.

On the other hand, some individuals may add to this anxious perception a high committment to being in charge of every situation which they encounter. This attitude may generate the exact opposite of avoidance and flight, which is a quest for absolute control and the belief that a sort of absolute and total control is achievable. These individuals may believe that their degree of control is insufficient but also believe that control is possible, achievable, and compulsory. Thus, not only an anxious feeling of insufficient control, but also a desire of control. This belief can be related with a compulsion to control (Sassaroli & Ruggiero, 2002). This belief is as much distorted as the anxious belief that control is totally absent, and is 'desire of control' or 'desirability of control' (Burger & Cooper, 1979). Actually, the desire of control is generally positively related to the percepetion of control (Burger, 1992). However, there is theoretical and empirical evidence that when an individual's perceived level of control does not reach that which they desire, they may experience negative psychological consequences, (Burger, 1992; Conway, Vickers, & French, 1992; Garant & Alain, 1995; Wilkinson & Camove, 1992). In our opinion, this desire of control generates not only anxiety, but also compulsive behaviours aimed at retrieving control. Thus, we propopse that desire of control is related not only with anxiety, but also with obsessionality.

Moulding & Kyrios (2006) are the scholars who have assessed that there is a significant correlation between desire of control, obsessive symptomatology and obsessive related beliefs like sense of responsibility. Besides, the experimental manipulation of the sense of responsibility increases the degree of desire of control. These results are suggestive of a possible aetiological role for destre of control in leading to obsessive beliefs and behaviours. Perception of control may be a determining factor in the motivation to act out compulsions and increase an obsessive sense of personal responsibility and individuals who attempt to control a situation may be more likely to judge themselves as responsible for the outcomes of their actions (Moulding, Kyrios, & Doron, 2007).

This desire of control seems to be a uni-dimensional variable. However, Burger and Cooper (1979) initially articulated the desire of control in the subdomains of the desire to make one's own decisions, the desire to take preventive actions to ensure that situations do not get out of hand, the desire to avoid situations in which others have control, and the desire to control others and constructed a scale to assess this cognitive variable. Consequently, they proposed a psychometric instrument, the Desirability of Control Scale, which would have replicated this three-dimensional structure. However, in following studies factorial analysis did not confirm these subdomains. Thus, Burger (1992) concluded that it is justifiable to regard desire for control as a unidimensional construct.

In 2002 Gebhardt and Brosschot renowned the attempt to propose a three-dimensional definition, and actually found a three-factorial structure in the instrument of Burger and Cooper. The three dimensions were: 1) 'Control others', which measures the desire to be in charge of and control others and emphasizes dominance, active coping, and psychological adjustment; 2) 'Control self', which measures the desire to control one's own life and is mainly related to self-sufficiency and independence; and 3) 'Relinquish control', which measures the desire to leave others in control and is associated with passive coping and poor psychological adjustment. 'Control others' and 'Control self' were both negatively related to avoidance strategies and to depressive reaction patterns. In contrast, 'Relinquish control' was positively related to avoidance strategies and a depressive reaction pattern. In conclusion, the three dimensions of Gebhardt and Brosschot's desire of control add some details to the definition of desire of control. However, in terms of clinical significance the uni-dimensional definition seems still sufficient. In fact, the total score of the instrument of Gebhardt and Brosschot provide results not different from those of the three subscales.

3. Control in Eating Disorders

From a cognitive viewpoint, the symptomatology of ED can be reduced to an exaggerated preoccupation with the theme of perfection, self-esteem and control and to a peculiar link between such cognitive beliefs and eating behaviours. In 1981 the first report concerning the use of cognitive-behavior therapy to treat eating disorders (ED) was published (Fairburn, 1981). Since then, the role of non-adaptive cognitive beliefs in ED has been widely recognized and the usefulness of targeting them for modification in therapy in order to produce change has been prominent. In scientific literature, perfectionism and low self-esteem are generally considered as the most important non-adaptive beliefs in ED. However, a possible third cognitive factor underlying eating disorders could be the so-called need of control.

In the field of ED studies, the belief of control has been the object of theoretical reflections. Individuals affected with ED often look for control (Bruch, 1973, 1982). The sense of control is often obtained by the continuous monitoring of a certain parameter, such as bodily perception in panic, intrusive thought in obsessionality, and so on. In the case of ED, such a parameter appears as concerns over eating and body weight and shape (Fairburn & Harrison, 2003). As explained by Slade (1982), dietary restrictions enhance the subjective sense of being in control. Hence, ED could be described as disorders of the sense of self-esteem and self-worth which are, without remedy, pervasively negative, if not lacking in such subjects. It is absolutely no coincidence that ED have often been defined as a psychopathology of control (Bruch, 1973, 1982; Button, 1985; Katzman & Lee, 1997). Smith (2002) speculated that, when control is taken away as in prison and the body of female prisoners become the objects of external forces, food is experienced not only as part of the disciplinary machinery, but also as a powerful source of pleasure, resistance and rebellion.

Actually, the fate of the belief of control in the history of the studies about ED has been rather odd and bizarre. Control and pursuit of control were psychological variables frequently present in the papers of the great first theorists of ED, like Hilde Bruch (1973, 1982), Arthur Crisp (1967, 1995), Garfinkel and Garner (1982), and Mara Selvini-Palazzoli (1974). However, such popularity did not lead to empirical research about the role played by the need for control in ED. Perfectionism and Self-Esteem surpassed the popularity of the old clinical conceptualization of control in the boom era of empirical studies about ED in the 1980s. This study not only provides empirical evidence for such a role, but also clarifies the psychopathological influence of Control. According to our analysis, control is both directly linked to and influences Drive for Thinness via the moderation effect.

Still in the 1980s Eric Button, a clinician and theorist coming from the field of Kellian personal construct theory, described anorexia nervosa as a quest for control (Button, 1985). According to Button, ED individuals engage in extreme restricted eating and purging behaviors essentially to constrict their world. The perspective of ED people on the world has become narrowed. Issues of relationships, work, play and even life and death tend to come second place to the bigger issues of weight, size, fat, food, and eating. "Although the sufferers may have a job, be engaged in study or bringing up a family, they are generally more preoccupied with trying to fend off the temptation of food" (Button, 2005, p. 199). The more plausible explanation for such extremes of constriction may be because this constriction makes life more manageable and controllable. ED individuals feel a lack of capacity to control personal relationships, internal reactions and general events. To gain a feeling of control, to achieve some degree of predictability, ED people are ready to restrict their lives to a narrowed experience centered on eating and body size. This is their way to satisfy their human need for control. However, while managing eating and body size initially offers the attraction of some degree of controllability, it eventually drives them into an isolated and unhealthy existence (Button, 1985; 2005).

More recently, Eiber, Mirabel-Sarron, and Urdapilleta (2005) argued that the maintenance of anorexia nervosa initially shows an extreme need to control eating which is supported by low self-esteem. Such hypothesis is interesting, but considers control as strictly linked to dietary restriction (Masheb & Grilo, 2002; Shearin, Russ, Hull, Clarkin, & Smith, 1994). In our view, for individuals with ED, the perception of control is a general attitude involving not only eating and body weight and shape but external events and internal feelings as well. Generally speaking, control is a complex construct, linked not only to eating and body aspect but to life in general (Rotter, 1966; Shapiro & Astin, 1998). This view agrees with previous theories that considered controlling behavior to be a general attribute of the ED personality (Button, 1985; Katzman & Lee, 1997).

We come across such an ample conceptualization in only one paper by Surgenor, Horn, Plumridge, and Hudson (2002), who stressed that psychological control plays a central role in the etiology and maintenance of anorexia nervosa. Surgenor et al. stress that the construct of control shows multiple meanings. For example, in Bruch (1973, 1982) the anorexic girl is both the predominant controlling agent and the victim of a controlling other, often the mother. Bruch (1973, 1982) and Crisp (1967, 1995) favored the notion of competence, effectiveness, personal autonomy, and even asceticism as means to achieve a sense of control. Orbach (1978, 1986) suggested that control is placed outside of the individual with ED and that the most powerful sources of external control are sociopolitical.

Dieting is an important tool by which control is attained. Control can be conceptualized as a coping belief regarding the need to obsessively control the unpredictable events and the threats of external world. In addition, control can be thought as a failure in self-regulatory abilities to manage negative emotions. In fact, research has suggested that the failure to exert efficacious cognitive and emotional control is a fundamental factor contributing to disorders such as anorexia nervosa. Many studies have shown that anorectic subjects have maladaptive attentional strategies when they are confronted with weight and body related stimulation (Fassino et al., 2002; Sackville et al., 1998). Such maladaptive strategies would imply intense appraisal of fear and anxiety related to body and food stimulation. Anorexic subjects, terrified by their negative uncontrollable emotions, desperately seek to balance their emotional sufferance by exerting a material control on external parameters, such as the amount of eaten food or their body weight and shape.

Until now, to our knowledge, there has been little research about the role of the need of control as a cognitive belief in ED. The vast majority of the studies considered control as strictly linked to dietary restriction (Shearin, Russ, Hull, Clarkin, & Smith, 1994; Masheb & Grilo, 2002). Serpell, Treasure, Teasdale, & Sullivan (1999) have shown that gaining a sense of control and pride in one's ability to control one's eating combats the feeling of being taken over by thoughts of food or of lacking control of one's thoughts, eating, and weight. Williams, Chamove, & Millar (1990) and Williams et al. (1993) have empirically shown that ED individuals perceive themselves as highly controlled by family and society. It is possible that there is a correlation between the sense of perceived control and the cognitive belief of control. Waller (1998) has shown that in ED individuals a reported history of sexual abuse was linked to a lower level of perceived personal control, while a more external locus of control was associated with more severe eating psychopathology among abused women, particularly if the abuse was more severe.

4. Loss of Control and Stress in the Development of Eating Disorders

Conceptually, stress and the cognitive psychopathology of the fear of loss of control are strictly linked with each other. In fact, research reports that among the major psychological consequence of a stressful situation is the uprising of an appraisal of lowered control in persons. According to Baum, Cohen, and Hall (1993), the disorganizing effect of persistent feelings of loss of control after a traumatizing experience of violation of expectations for regulating aspects of one's life normally under control is a condition of chronic stress. When individuals perceive a loss of control during a stressful situation, they may interpret this situation of lack of control as evidence that they have little control over their lives in general. Davidson, Baum, and Collins (2006) found that persons reporting more loss of control have more stress-associated symptoms than does subjects not experiencing as many control-related problems. A further confirmation of the link between stress and loss of control comes from Folkman, Chesney, Pollack, and Coates (1993), who found that stress appraised as controllable is associated with involvement coping, which in turn is associated with diminished depressive mood, while stress associated with detachment is associated with increased depressive mood and is also directly associated with increased depressive mood.

The relationship between stress and loss of control is plausibly present also in eating disorders (ED). Stressful situations and major life events negatively affect eating in both human and animal models (Fairburn & Harrison, 2003; Connan & Treasure, 1998). Coping and crisis support are important aspects of dealing with stress, and a study by Troop, Holbrey, and Treasure (1998) showed that women with ED have less effective stress-coping mechanisms. Raffi, Rondini Grandi, and Fava (2000) found that the prodromal phase of bulimia nervosa is characterized by stressful life events. In addition, Fryer, Waller, and Kroese (1997) assessed the relationship between stressors and disturbed eating attitudes among adolescent females.

As known, low self-esteem and perfectionism are two of the most frequently observed risk factors in the development of common eating disorders (ED) (Halmi et al, 2000; Vohs et al., 1999). With regards to the relationship between stress, perfectionism, and self-esteem in ED, one hypothesis is that, in a perfectionistic personality, stressful situations could trigger abnormal eating, or even ED. Similarly, in individuals with ED, perfectionism could increase their distress at the events that develop as their condition continues (Hewitt, Flett, & Ediger, 1995; Hewitt & Flett, 1993). In a stressful performance situation, a perceived failure in a perfectionistic individual with poor self-esteem could unmask a parallel tendency to worry about and feel dissatisfied with perceived eating mistakes and imperfections in body shape and weight.

A number of research of our team (Ruggiero, Ciuna, Levi, & Sassaroli, 2003; Sassaroli & Ruggiero, 2005; Sassaroli et al., 2005; Ruggiero et al, 2008) explored the interaction between stress and cognitive correlates of ED using university exams as a quasi-experimental stress situation in non clinical university students. A university exam is a good example of a potentially invalidating stress situation. An exam affects one's own perception of personal competence and efficacy. Research has shown that perfectionism is related to perceptions of greater course difficulty and higher anxiety prior to the examination (Brown et al., 1999).

The studies showed that in non-clinical female individuals, stress brings out a previously absent association between some psychological predisposing factors for ED, and an actual desire or plan to lose weight. In a more recent study, the authors found that the dimensions of pathological perfectionism, low self-esteem, and perceived stress are related to an increase in dieting thoughts and dissatisfaction with body aspect in non-clinical women during a performance that could potentially challenge the perception of their self-esteem. The stressful situation seemed to induce a psychological and behavioural organization in non-clinical women that overlaps with a frank ED, while the non-stressful situation shows only a partial and mild resemblance to ED. The stressful situation can be interpreted as an experience of invalidation, which could explain the connection between cognitive constructs and behaviors related to eating disorders. Summing up, these findings suggest that stress may stimulate behaviours related to ED in a predisposed personality (Ruggiero et al., 2008). From a clinical viewpoint, such results suggest that the dimensions of pathological perfectionism and low self-esteem, in conjunction with a state of stress, stimulate an increase in thoughts of dieting and dissatisfaction with body aspect in non-clinical women during a performance that could potentially challenge their perception of their self-esteem.

Summing up, these results support the hypothesis that, during a stress situation, the degree to which a subject experiences concern over mistakes and perceived stress affects their drive for thinness and body dissatisfaction and that, in non-clinical females, a stressful situation may induce thoughts of dieting. Summing up, the results suggest that stress may be a central factor in transforming a vague insecurity into a pervasive desire to lose weight.

The hypothesis of stress acting as a turning point in the development of ED calls to mind George Kelly's definition of a psychological disorder (Kelly, 1969; Button 1996), which is any personal construction that is used repeatedly despite consistent invalidation. Both stress and invalidation are explicative concepts that indicate, from either a cognitive or a biological viewpoint respectively, situations in which a constructs architectural rigidity is tested and, if present, revealed. Human behaviour can be interpreted as cycles of experimentation, always ending with an outcome that either validates or invalidates the anticipations that the action-probe was designed to test.

The constructivist interpretation of the interplay of concern over mistakes and stress in ED is that the person tends to have a tight, impermeable, and rigid construct which encompasses perfectionism, self-esteem, avoidance of mistakes, dieting, control of weight, and body shape. An experimental situation in which the person's skills are tested could reveal a relationship between fear of mistakes, control, and invalidation (i.e., failure or fear of failure of the performance), and the emergence of symptomatological attitudes related to ED.

A stress situation could be considered a situation in which the person experiences a lack of control. In perfectionism, the over-prediction of threatening events is linked to a highly intense fear of failure in important performances. Eating disorders could be described as disorders of self-esteem combined with the need for illusory compensation (i.e., a need to feel in control of life), which gets displaced onto controlling eating (Fairburn, Shafran, & Cooper, 1999). Thus, it is no coincidence that eating disorders are often defined as a psychopathology of control (Bruch, 1973; Button, 1985, 2005; Katzman & Lee, 1997). As shown by Slade (1982), dietary restrictions enhance a subjective sense of being in control. Individuals with ED engage in extremely restrictive eating and purging behaviours. Their essential goal is to constrict their world, making life more manageable and controllable. Issues of relationships, work, play, and even life and death, tend to be judged as less important than the bigger issues of weight, body size, fat, food, and eating.

In conclusion, eating disorders could be the displacement of invalidations suffered in life onto the narrowed domains of eating, body, and weight. Such displacement would permit individuals with ED to maintain their rigid and impermeable constructs (Sassaroli, Lorenzini, & Ruggiero, 2005).

5. The Interplay Between Perfectionism, Self-Esteem, and Need for Control in Eating Disorders

In conclusion, control, low self-esteem and perfectionism are a set of plausible cognitive factor for eating disorders. However, little is known about their interplay in the pathological process. A possible answer starts from the observation that all of the three above mentioned cognitive factors are clearly related to anxiety and to a worrying cognitive style. In fact, perfectionism could be defined an over-prediction of threatening events related to mistakes, a highly intense and anxious fear of failure after important performances. Pathological perfectionists never feel anything is done completely enough or well enough and always experience feelings of self-criticism and a sense of ineffectiveness. The concern over mistakes dimension of perfectionism is relevant to individuals with eating disorders because they would tend to interpret any perceived shortfall and any bodily or weight imperfection as catastrophic failures of their strong desire for a faultless, impeccable, and dazzling social and self-image. This condition does not allow the person to display imperfections or to admit difficulties (Hewitt & Flett, 1991).

The hypothesis that perfectionism is rooted in anxiety and that in turn anxiety has common features with ED is supported by studies of the fear response. Such studies in patients with anorexia nervosa have been shown to involve serotonin levels in the mesiotemporal lobe. Specific to the mesiotemporal lobe is a reduction in serotonin receptor binding (Frank et al., 2002), thought to be a protective mechanism in response to serotonin hyperactivity in the mesiotemporal lobe. Researchers have suggested that high levels of serotonin would result in high levels of anxiety and control found in anorectics (Kaye et al, 2000; Strober, 2004).

The anxiety hypothesis is also applicable to the belief of control. In fact, according to many important authors (e.g., Barlow, 2002; Basoglu & Mineka, 1992; Hoyer, Becker, and Roth, 2001; Rapee, Craske, Brown, & Barlow, 1996) anxiety is concerned with one's control over the threat. The future-directed thinking present in anxiety mainly addresses the assessment of the probability and size of the threat, and one's own ability to cope with it. Feeling in control over the threat means not only to be able to predict the threat, but also being able to respond to the feared threat in a way that reduces or eliminates it. In the case of ED, the need for control tends to be narrowed to the themes of fat, body shape and eating (Sassaroli & Ruggiero, 2005).

Other studies have explored the direct link between sense of control and perfectionism. Mor, Day, Flett, and Hewitt (2006) found that perfectionism and low feeling of personal control were associated with greater anxiety. Soenens et al. (2005) found that parents' psychological control plays a role in the intergenerational transmission of perfectionism. Mediation analyses show that maladaptive perfectionism is a significant intervening variable between parental psychological control and ED symptoms (Soenens et al., 2008). Analytic theorists have emphasized the importance of perfectionism as a means of attaining control over their environment by people with obsessive compulsive disorder (Mallinger, 1984; Salzman, 1968; Straus, 1948).

There is a relationship also between lowered self-esteem and anxiety (Silverstone, 1991). In individuals with anxiety disorders there is a tendency to judge themselves as temperamentally weak, uncapable to tolerate negative states of mind and prone to lose control over external events and internal states (Guidano & Liotti, 1983). This correlation between low self-esteem and control is plausible also in eating disorders. In fact, also individuals with eating disorders suffer of mood intolerance and fear of losing control which may generate negative self judgment.

An empirical study has shown that there are interaction effects between control, self-esteem, and perfectionism (Sassaroli, Gallucci, & Ruggiero, 2008). The study clarifies that these three constructs are tightly interwoven. Summing up, the study confirms that perfectionism has a direct effect on eating disorders, but its effect is moderated by sense of control and lowered self-esteem.

From a clinical viewpoint, the findings of the study suggest that perfectionism alone (i.e., without a general sense of lack of control and low self-esteem) is unable to generate eating disorders. Thus, symptoms may be an attempt to retrieve a personal sense of control and self-esteem via the pursuit of perfection, at least in the narrow domain of eating, weight, and body shape. Severely biased levels of perception of control and self-esteem would influence the effect of perfectionism on eating disorders.

6. The Psychopathology of Worry in Eating Disorders

Control, perfectionism and low self-esteem are all forms of a neurotic tendency to negative thought. Hence, it is natural to wonder whether in worry, which is the most typical form of negative thinking, is present in ED. Worry is a mental process widely studied in cognitive research as a main feature of anxiety (Borkovec, Ray, & Stober, 1998) and it is the central feature of generalized anxiety disorder as defined by DSM-IV (APA, 1994). The key feature of worry is the predominance of negative thoughts, that means that worrying people think a lot about possible negative events they are afraid of (Borkovec, 1993). Both worriers and anxiety disordered people have much richer predictive networks of negative and even catastrophic events than non worriers and nonanxious people (Vasey & Borkovec, 1992).

Although worry is generally thought as strictly linked to anxiety, actually it is found across diverse clinical conditions including affective disorders, anxiety disorders, insomnia, psychosis and also eating disorders (ED). Thus, worry may be a transdiagnostic process. In fact, as direct comparisons between different disorders have generally revealed more similarities than differences, it is argued that worry is characterized by the same process across disorders (Ehring & Watkins, 2008).

To our knowledge, there is not a large body of research devoted to the association between worry and ED. Up until now, there are only five studies that assumed that worry may play a role in the psychopathological process of ED and investigated the relationship between worry and ED. Wadden, Brown, Foster, and Linowitz (1991) investigated different kinds of worry in nonclinical adolescents and found that girls showed higher worry levels about weight and food than boys. Kerkhof et al. (2000) administered the Penn State Worry Questionnaire to ED subjects and control people and found higher scores in the clinical sample. Scattolon and Nicky (1995) found that food consumption in a nonclinical sample of chronic dieters was triggered by social-evaluative/school-related worry. Sassaroli and Ruggiero (2005) found that in a stress situation worry is related to the Eating Disorders

Inventory's subscales in nonclinical subjects. Sassaroli et al. (2005) have definitely shown the association between worry and ED.

In addition, there are two studies regarding rumination in ED. The term rumination indicates a variant of worry present in depression and in other mood disorders, and has been studied mostly by Nolen-Hoeksema (2000). Rumination is related to past negative events, while worry is a preoccupation with future negative events. According to Troop and Treasure (1997), the onset of bulimia is associated with rumination in response to life events. Hart and Chiovari (1998) have shown that dieters show significant more rumination about eating and food than non dieters. Nolen-Hoeksema et al (2007) have shown that rumination predicted future increases in bulimic symptoms as well as onset of binge eating. The results suggest that rumination may contribute to the etiology of bulimic pathology.

Another stream of research which supports the presence of worry in ED is the body of works which has explored the relationship between neuroticism and ED. In the theory of Eysenck and Eysenck (1985), neuroticism is a personality attitude which encompass worry. In fact, neuroticism is characterized by a predisposition towards emotionality, hypersensitivity, anxiety, worry, moodiness, and depression (Eysenck & Eysenck, 1985). Many works have shown that individuals with EDs score higher on neuroticism than controls (Diaz-Marsa et al., 2000; Ghaderi & Scott, 2000; Podar, Hannus, & Allik, 1999), that neuroticism is also positively correlated with ED symptomatology in female university samples (Brookings & Wilson, 1994; Geissler & Kelly, 1994; Janzen, Saklofske, & Kelly, 1993), and community samples (Gual et al., 2002; Wade et al., 2000), and with bulimic symptomatology in a small male university sample (Finlayson, Kelly, & Saklofske, 2002).

All these studies suggest that worry is present and may play a role in ED. Also the DSM supports this viewpoint. In fact, in DSM-IV, the fear of fatness criterion of anorexia nervosa refers to that: even though underweight, the anorexic individual is intensely afraid of gaining weight or of becoming fat and a criterion of bulimia nervosa in DSM-IV refers to that: The self-evaluation of bulimic subjects is excessively influenced by their body shape and weight. These DSM definitions suggest that fear of fatness in anorexic individuals and body dissatisfaction in bulimic individuals may be worries about possible future negative events, such as gaining weight and becoming fat. Plausibly, the above mentioned DSM criteria of anorexia and bulimia nervosa suggest that individuals with ED worry and think a lot about weight, fat, and body shape because they predict and fear a long chain of negative consequences related to such factors. These negative consequences would affect interpersonal problems, sense of self-efficacy, and fear of being blamed or disparaged by parents, peers, etc. In short, ED subjects may worry like anxiety disordered subjects. In our view worry is associated with ED symptoms.

Sassaroli et al. (2005) have definitely shown that worry is present in ED and plays a psychopathological role. To our knowledge, this is one of the first studies that investigate the association between worry levels and ED and the first one that has clearly shown the strength of such association. In fact, Sassaroli and Ruggiero (2005), Scattolon and Nicky (1995), and Wadden et al. (1991) studied the relation between worry and ED in nonclinical subjects. Actually, only Kerkhof et al. (2000) studied worry in ED subjects.

Basically, the study of Sassaroli et al. (2005) supports and extends the findings by Kerkhof et al. (2000). They found that worry is significantly higher in ED subjects than in a control group and is clearly associated with the ED symptomatology. This association was found for each of the symptoms of ED. On the other hand, the data from the EDI (eating disorders inventory) did not completely replicate these associations. In fact, worry is related to drive for thinness and body dissatisfaction, but not to bulimia. Therefore, the study suggests that pervasive worry is related to ED symptoms but the EDI suggests that this may be not totally true at least for some aspects of bulimic symptomatology. A possible explanation for the different results from SCID and EDI assessments of symptoms may be that the former is based on clinical judgment, whereas the latter is based on patient self-report. Could the patients themselves erroneously evaluate of even conceal their bulimic behaviors? Or could they pay more attention on weight and body image than on bingeing and purging?

Given the association between worry and ED, what presumably is the psychopathological role played by worry? Is worry a psychological factor underlying ED symptoms or, alternatively, is worry only a side effect of catastrophic cognitive beliefs that underlie the origin and the maintenance of ED? It may be that worry influences the etiology and the pathogenesis of ED by the same mechanism identified in generalized anxiety disorder by Vasey and Borkovec (1992)? Actually, there is a feature of worry that is crucial for understanding its role in psychopathology. This feature is that worry is predominantly verbal and abstract, as opposed to visual imagery and concrete thought (Borkovec & Inz, 1990). Verbal thought about emotional material elicits much less cardiovascular response then does visual imagery (Vrana, Cuthbert, & Lang, 1986). The verbal system is relatively isolated from emotions, giving the human mind a capability to inhibit spontaneous reactions and to plan complex responses. Subsequently, people tend to use verbalization as a strategy for gaining emotional self-control. However, worrying people do not plan complex responses to overwhelming events, but tend to repeat to themselves that things will get worse. In other words, worry is a fallacious strategy to solve problems.

A possible hypothesis is that worry operates via metacognitive processes. Metacognition focuses on any knowledge involved in thought processes, appraisal and beliefs of cognition itself (Flavell, 1979; Nelson & Narens, 1990). According to Ardovini (2002) experiences of adequate quality promote metacognitive functions, namely a set of mental processes whose role is to protect the individual from psychopathological suffering and construct and articulate a sense of self. Another way to interpret metacognition is the ability to make inferences about others' mental states has been termed 'theory of mind'. It underlies the ability to engage in complex social interaction. However, according to Tchanturia et al. (2004) there was no evidence of any selective impairment of theory of mind in anorexic sufferers. However, according to Adrian Wells (2000), although worrying is used as a means of coping with anticipated threats, it becomes the object of negative beliefs and appraisals. Pathological worry is maintained by positive and negative metacognitive beliefs concerning the advantages and the dangers of worrying. In turn, these beliefs become object of worry. This particular kind of worry is called by Wells (2000) 'meta-worry'.

To our knowledge there no studies about the role of meta-worry as a psychological factor underlying ED. In addition, little is known about the interaction of meta-worry with cognitive beliefs and worry in ED. In a recent study Sassaroli and Ruggiero (2009) have used the Metacognition Questionnaire (MQ) (Cartwright-Hatton & Wells, 1997), an instrument that measures several domains of metacognitions. The questionnaire generates scores for the following five sub-scales: Positive Beliefs About Worry, that measures the belief that worry helps people to cope with reality; Negative Beliefs About Worry, Controllability And Danger, that measures negative beliefs about worry, the controllability of thoughts, and possible negative consequences; Meta-Cognitive Efficiency And Confidence, that measures doubts about cognitive and mental efficiency; General Negative Beliefs, that measure the belief that worry and thoughts should be controlled, and includes sense of responsibility, punishment, and superstition; Cognitive Self-Consciousness, that measures the tendency to monitor mental activity.

The results of the study have provided the demonstration that ED subjects have higher levels of meta-worry than control people and have supported the hypothesis that in ED the worry about fat, weight and eating in turn becomes the object of negative beliefs and appraisals. When worrying is appraised as dangerous, the degree of preoccupation with food, weight, and fat increases and it is difficult for the ED individual to obtain an internal state signalling that it is safe to stop worrying. The basic hypothesis is that in ED the worry about fat, weight and eating becomes the object of metacognitive beliefs and appraisals.

However, the study failed to provide empirical evidence that this high level of meta-worry is able to predict the symptomatology of ED. This means that basically metacognitive beliefs focused on worry are present in ED, but also that they may not play an additional role in the psychological process that maintain high the severity of ED. In conclusion, worry is a phenomenon present in ED and plausibly plays a role in maintaining the disorders, but the mechanism of its psychopathological action is still unclear.

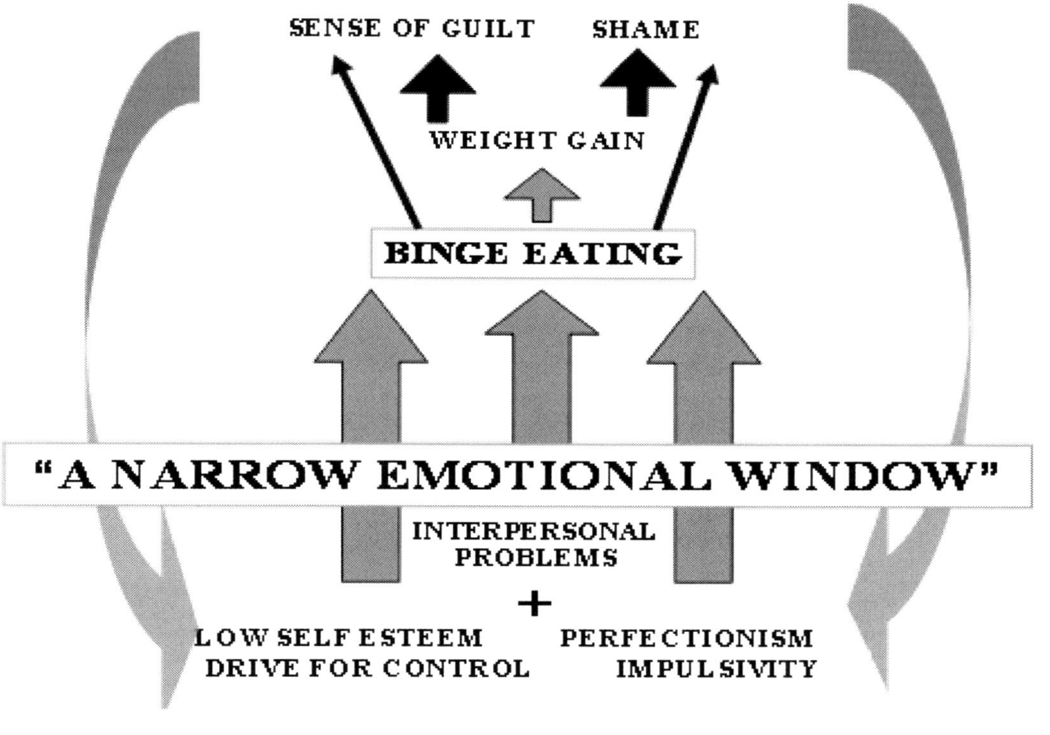

Figure 1.

REFERENCES

Alloy, L. B., & Abramson, L. Y. (1979). Judgment of contingency in depressed and nondepressed students: Sadder but wiser? *Journal of Experimental Psychology: General, 108*, 441-485.

APA, American Psychiatric Association (1994). *Diagnostic and Statistical Manual of Mental Disorders (DSM-IV)*. Washington DC: American Psychiatric Press.

Ardovini, C. (2002). Attachment theory, metacognitive functions and the therapeutic relationship in eating disorders. *Eating and Weight Disorders, 7*, 328-31.

Bandura, A. (1977). *Social Learning Theory*. Englewood Cliffs, NJ: Prentice-Hall.

Barlow, D. H. (2002). *Anxiety and its disorders: The nature and treatment of anxiety and panic.* (2nd ed.). New York: Guilford Press.

Basoglu, M., & Mineka, S. (1992). The role of uncontrollable and unpredictable stress in post-traumatic stress responses in torture survivors. In M. Basoglu (Ed.), *Torture and Its Consequences: Current Treatment Approaches*. Cambridge: Cambridge University Press, pp. 182-225.

Baum, A., Cohen, L., & Hall, M. (1993). Control and intrusive memories as possible determinants of chronic stress. *Psychosomatic Medicine, 55*, 274-286.

Borkovec, T. D. (1993). The nature, functions, and origins of worry. In G. Davey, F. Tallis (Eds.), *Worrying: Perspectives on Theory, Assessment and Treatment*. Chichester, England: Wiley, pp. 5-33

Borkovec, T. D., & Inz, J. (1990). The nature of worry in generalized anxiety disorder: A predominance of thought activity. *Behaviour Research and Therapy, 28*, 153-158.

Borkovec, T. D., Ray, W. J., & Stöber, J. (1998). Worry: A cognitive phenomenon intimately linked to affective, physiological, and interpersonal behavioral processes. *Cognitive Therapy and Research, 22*, 561-576.

Brookings, J. B., & Wilson, J. F. (1994). Personality and family-environment predictors of self-reported eating attitudes and behaviors. *Journal of Personality Assessment, 63*, 313–326.

Brown, E. J., Heimberg, R. G., Frost, R. O., Makris, G. S., Juster, H. R., & Leung, A. W. (1999). Relationship of perfectionism to affect, expectations, attributions and performance in the classroom. *Journal of Social and Clinical Psychology, 18*, 98-120.

Bruch, H. (1973). *Eating disorders: Obesity, Anorexia Nervosa and the Person Within*. New York: Basic Books.

Bruch, H. (1982). Anorexia nervosa: Theory and therapy. *American Journal of Psychiatry, 139*, 1531-1538.

Burger, J. M. (1992). *Desire for Control: Personality, Social, and Clinical Perspectives*. New York: Plenum.

Burger, J. M., & Cooper, H. M. (1979). The desirability of control. *Motivation and Emotion, 3*, 381–393.

Button, E. J. (1985). Eating disorders: A quest for control? In E. J. Button (Ed.), *Personal Construct Theory and Mental Health*. London: Croom Helm, pp. 153-168.

Button, E. J. (2005). Eating disorders. In D. Winter & L. L. Viney (Eds.), *Personal Construct Psychotherapy*. London: Whurr Publishers, pp. 199-212.

Cartwright-Hatton, S., Wells, A. (1997). Beliefs about worry and intrusions: the Meta-Cognitions Questionnaire and its correlates. *Journal of Anxiety Disorders, 11*, 279-296.
Connan, F., & Treasure, J. (1998). Stress, eating and neurobiology. In H. W. Hoeck, J. L. Treasure, & M. Katzman (Eds.), *Neurobiology in the Treatment of Eating Disorders*. Chichester, UK: Wiley, pp. 211-236.
Conway, T. L., Vickers, R. R., French, J. R. P. (1992). An application of person-environment fit theory: Perceived versus desired control. *Journal of Social Issues, 48*, 95–107.
Crisp, A. H. (1967). Anorexia nervosa. *Hospital Medicine, 1*, 713-718.
Crisp, A. H. (1995). *Anorexia Nervosa: Let Me Be*. Hove: Lawrence Erlbaum Associates Ltd.
Davidson, L. M., Baum, A., & Collins, D. L. (2006). Stress and control-related problems at three mile island. *Journal of Applied Social Psychology, 12*, 349-359.
Deci, E. L., & Ryan, R. M. (1985). *Intrinsic Motivation and Self-Determination In Human Behavior*. New York: Plenum.
Diaz-Marsa, M., Carrasco, J. L., & Saiz, J. (2000). A study of temperament and personality in anorexia nervosa and bulimia nervosa. *Journal of Personality Disorders, 14*, 352–359.
Ehring, T., & Watkins, E. R. (2008). Repetitive negative thinking as a transdiagnostic process. *International Journal of Cognitive Therapy, 1*, 192–205.
Eiber, R., Mirabel-Sarron, C., Urdapilleta, I. (2005). Les cognitions et leur évaluation dans les troubles des conduites alimentaires [Cognitions in eating disorders and their assessment]. *L'Encephale, 31*, 643-652.
Eysenck, H. J., & Eysenck, M. W. (1985). *Personality and Individual Differences: A Natural Science Approach*. Plenum Press: New York.
Fairburn, C. G. (1981). A cognitive behavioural approach to the management of bulimia. *Psychological Medicine, 11*, 707–711.
Fairburn, C. G., & Harrison, P. J. (2003). Eating disorders. *The Lancet, 361*, 407-416.
Fairburn, C. G., Shafran, R., & Cooper, Z. (1999). A cognitive behavioural theory of anorexia nervosa. *Behaviour Research and Therapy, 37*, 1–13.
Fassino, S., Piero, A., Daga, G., Leombruni, P., Mortara, P., & Rovera, G. (2002). Attentional biases and frontal functioning in anorexia nervosa. *International Journal of Eating Disorders, 31*, 274-283.
Finlayson, R. A., Kelly, I. W., & Saklofske, D. H. (2002). Bulimic symptomatology, body-image, and personality characteristics of university men. *Psychological Reports, 91*, 496–502.
Flavell, J. H. (1979). Metacognition and cognitive monitoring: a new area of cognitive developmental inquiry. *American Psychologist, 34*, 906-911.
Foa, E. B., Zinbarg, R., & Olasov-Rothbaum, B. (1992). Uncontrollability and unpredictability in post-traumatic stress disorder: an animal model. *Psychological Bulletin, 112*, 218-238.
Folkman, S., Chesney, M., Pollack, L., & Coates, T. (1993). Stress, control, coping, and depressive mood in human immunodeficiency virus-positive and -negative gay men in San Francisco. *Journal of Black Psychology, 30*, 78-105.
Frank, G. K., Kaye, W. H., Meltzer, C. C., Price, J. C., Greer, P., McConaha, C., & Skovira, K., (2002). Reduced 5-HT2A receptor binding after recovery from anorexia nervosa. *Biological Psychiatry, 52*, 896-906.
Fryer, S., Waller, G., & Kroese, B. S. (1997). Stress, coping, and disturbed eating attitudes in teenage girls. *International Journal of Eating Disorders, 22*, 427 – 436.

Garant, V., & Alain, M. (1995). Perception de contrôle, désir de contrôle et santé psychologique [Perception of control, desire of control and psychological health]. *Revue Canadienne des Sciences du Comportement, 27*, 251–267.

Garfinkel, P. E., & Garner, D. M. (1982). *Anorexia Nervosa: A Multidimensional Perspective*. New York: Brunner Mazel.

Gebhardt, W. A., & Brosschot, J. F. (2002). Desirability of control: Psychometric properties and relationships with locus of control, personality, coping, and mental and somatic complaints in three Dutch samples. *European Journal of Personality, 16*, 423–438.

Geissler, T., & Kelly, I. W. (1994). Bulimic symptomatology and personality factors in a non-clinical sample: A replication. *Psychological Reports, 75*, 224–226.

Ghaderi, A., & Scott, B. (2000). The big five and eating disorders: A prospective study in the general population. *European Journal of Personality, 14*, 311–323.

Gual, P., Perez-Gaspar, M., Martinez-Gonxalez, M. A., Lahortiga, F., de Irala-Estevez, J., & Cervera-Enguiz, S. (2002). Self-esteem, personality, and eating disorders: Baseline assessment of a prospective population-based cohort. *International Journal of Eating Disorders, 31*, 261–273.

Guidano, V. F., & Liotti, G. (1983). *Cognitive Processes and Emotional Disorders*. New York, The Guilford Press.

Halmi, K. A., Sunday, S. R., Strober, M., Kaplan, A., Woodside, D. B., & Fichter, M. (2000). Perfectionism in anorexia nervosa: Variation by clinical subtype, obsessionality, and pathological eating behavior. *American Journal of Psychiatry, 157*, 1799–1805.

Hart, K. E., & Chiovari, P. (1998). Inhibition of eating behavior: negative cognitive effects of dieting. *Journal of Clinical Psychology, 54*, 427-430.

Hewitt, P. L., & Flett, G. L. (1991). Perfectionism in the self and social context: Conceptualization, assessment, and association with psychopathology. *Journal of Personality and Social Psychology, 60*, 456-470.

Hewitt, P. L., & Flett, G. L. (1993). Dimensions of perfectionism, daily stress, and depression: A test of the specific vulnerability hypothesis. *Journal of Abnormal Psychology, 102*, 58-65.

Hewitt, P. L., Flett, G. L, & Ediger, E. (1995). Perfectionism traits and perfectionistic self-presentation in eating disorder attitudes, characteristics, and symptoms. *International Journal of Eating Disorders, 18*, 317-326.

Hoyer, J., Becker, E. S., & Roth, W. T. (2001). Characteristics of worry in GAD patients, social phobics, and controls. *Depression and Anxiety, 13*, 89-96.

Janzen, B. L., Saklofske, D. H., & Kelly, I. W. (1993). Personality and bulimic symptomatology. *Journal of Clinical Psychology, 49*, 649–653.

Katzman, M. A., & Lee, S. (1997). Beyond body image: the integration of feminist and transcultural theories in the understanding of self starvation. *International Journal of Eating Disorders, 22*, 385-394.

Kaye, W., Klump, K., Frank, G., & Strober, M. (2000). Anorexia and Bulimia Nervosa. *Annual Review Medical, 51*, 299-313.

Kelly, G. A. (1969). Ontological acceleration. In B. Maher (Eds.). *Clinical Psychology and Personality. The Selected Papers of George Kelly*. New York, Wiley, pp. 7-45.

Kerkhof, A., Hermas, D., Figee, A., Laeremans, I., Pieters, G., & Aardema, A. (2000). De Penn State Worry Questionnaire en de Worry Domains Questionnaire: eerste resultaten bij Nederlandse en Vlaamse klinische en poliklinische populaties [The Penn State Worry

Questionnaire and the Worry Domains Questionnaire: First results in Dutch and Flemish in- and outpatient groups]. *Gedragstherapie, 33*, 135-145.

Langer, E. J. (1975). The illusion of control. *Journal of Personality and Social Psychology, 32*, 311-328.

Mallinger, A. E., (1984). The obsessive's myth of control. *Journal of American Academy of Psychoanalysis, 12*, 147-165.

Masheb, R. M., & Grilo, C. M. (2002). On the relation of flexible and rigid control of eating to body mass index and overeating in patients with binge eating disorder. *International Journal of Eating Disorders, 31*, 82-91.

Mineka, S., & Thomas, C. (1999). Mechanisms of change in exposure therapy for anxiety disorders. In T. Dalgleish & M. Power (Eds.), *Handbook of Cognition and Emotion.* Chichester, UK: John Wiley and Sons, Ltd. pp. 613-636.

Mor, S., Day, H. I., Flett, G. L., & Hewitt, P. L. (1995). Perfectionism, control, and components of performance anxiety in professional artists. *Cognitive Therapy and Research, 19*, 207-225.

Moulding, R., & Kyrios, M. (2006). Anxiety disorders and control related beliefs: the exemplar of Obsessive–Compulsive Disorder (OCD). *Clinical Psychology Review, 26*, 573-583.

Moulding, R., Kyrios, M., & Doron, G. (2007). Obsessive-compulsive behaviours in specific situations: The relative influence of appraisals of control, responsibility and threat. *Behaviour Research and Therapy, 45*, 1693-1702.

Nelson, T. O., & Narens, L. (1990). Metamemory: a theoretical framework and new findings. In G. Bower (Ed.), *The Psychology of Learning and Motivation*. New York: Academic Press, pp. 26-45.

Nolen-Hoeksema, S. (2000). The role of rumination in depressive disorders and mixed anxiety/depressive symptoms. *Journal of Abnormal Psychology, 109*, 504-511.

Nolen-Hoeksema, S., Stice, E., Wade, E., & Bohon, C. (2007). Reciprocal relations between rumination and bulimic, substance abuse, and depressive symptoms in female adolescents. *Journal of Abnormal Psychology, 116*, 198–207.

Orbach, S. (1978). *Fat is a Feminist Issue*. London: Paddington Press.

Orbach, S. (1986). *Hunger Strike - The Anorectic's Struggle as a Metaphor for Our Age*. London: Faber & Faber.

Podar, I., Hannus, A., & Allik, J. (1999). Personality and affectivity characteristics associated with eating disorders: A comparison of eating disordered, weight preoccupied, and normal samples. *Journal of Personality Assessment, 73*, 133–147.

Raffi, A. R., Rondini, M., Grandi, S., & Fava, G. A. (2000). Life events and prodromal symptoms in bulimia nervosa. *Psychological Medicine, 30*, 727-731.

Rapee, R. M., Craske, M.G., Brown, T.A., & Barlow, D.H. (1996). Measurement of perceived control over anxiety-related events. *Behavior Therapy, 27*, 279-293.

Rotter, J. B. (1966). Generalized expectancies for internal versus external control of reinforcement. *Psychological Monographs, 80*, 609.

Ruggiero, G. M., Bertelli, S., Boccalari, L., Centorame, F., Ditucci, A., La Mela, C., Scarinci, A., Vinai, P., Scarone, S., & Sassaroli, S. (2008). The influence of stress on the relationship between cognitive variables and measures of eating disorders (in healthy female university students): a quasi-experimental study. *Eating and Weight Disorders, 13*, 142-148.

Ruggiero, G. M., Levi, D., Ciuna, A., & Sassaroli S (2003). Stress situation reveals an association between perfectionism and drive for thinness. *International Journal Eating of Disorders, 34*, 220-6.

Sackville, T., Schotte, D., Touyz, S., Griffiths, R., & Beumont, P. J. V. (1998). Conscious and Pre-Conscious Processing of Food, Body Weight and Shape, and Emotion-Related Words in Women with Anorexia Nervosa. *International Journal of Eating Disorders, 23*, 77-82.

Salzman, L. (1968). The Obsessive Personality: Origins, Dynamics and Therapy. New York: Aronson.

Sassaroli, S., & Ruggiero, G. M. (2002). I costrutti dell'ansia: obbligo di controllo, perfezionismo patologico, pensiero catastrofico, autovalutazione negativa e intolleranza dell'incertezza [The constructs of anxiety: Compulsion to control, pathological perfectionism, catastrophic thought, negative self-evaluation, and intolerance of uncertainty]. *Psicoterapia Cognitiva e Comportamentale, 8*, 45-60.

Sassaroli, S., & Ruggiero, G. M. (2009). Autostima, metarimuginio, perfezionismo, responsabilità e rimuginio nei disturbi alimentari [Self-esteem, meta-worry, perfectionism, responsibility and worry in eating disorders]. *Ricerca in Psicoterapia/Research in Psychotherapy, 12*, 21-36, available http://www.spr-italia.it/pdf/spr_volume_12.pdf

Sassaroli, S., & Ruggiero, G. M. (2005). The role of stress in the association between low self-esteem, perfectionism, and worry, and eating disorders. *International Journal of Eating Disorders, 37*, 135-141.

Sassaroli, S., Bertelli, S., Decoppi, M., Crosina, M., Milos, G., & Ruggiero, G. M. (2005). Worry and eating disorders: A psychopathological association. *Eating Behaviors, 6*, 301-307.

Sassaroli, S., Gallucci, M., & Ruggiero, G. M. (2007). Low perception of control as a cognitive factor of eating disorders. Its independent effects on measures of eating disorders and its interactive effects with perfectionism and self-esteem. *Journal of Behavior Therapy and Experimental Psychiatry, 39*, 467-488.

Sassaroli, S., Lorenzini, R., & Ruggiero, G. M. (2005). Kellian invalidation, attachment, and the construct of 'control'. In D. Winter & L. L. Viney (Eds.), *Personal Construct Psychotherapy*. London, Whurr Publishers, pp. 34-42.

Sassaroli, S., Mezzaluna, C., Amurri, A., Bossoletti, R., Ciccioli, T., Perrotta, A., Romualdi, A., Stronati, A., Urbani, S., Valenti, V., Milos, G., & Ruggiero, G. M. (2005). Stress plays a role in the association between cognitive constructs and measures of eating disorders in male subjects. *Eating and Weight Disorders, 10*, 117-124.

Scattolon, Y. S., & Nicky, R. M. (1995). Worry as an inhibitor of dietary restraint. *Behavioural and Cognitive Psychotherapy, 23*, 25-33.

Seligman, M. E. P. (1975). *Helplessness: On Depression, Development, and Death*. San Francisco: W.H. Freeman.

Selvini-Palazzoli, M. S. (1974). *Self Starvation: From the Intrapsychic to the Transpersonal Approach*. London: Chaucer.

Serpell, L., Treasure, J., Teasdale, J., & Sullivan, V. (1999). Anorexia nervosa: Friend or foe? *International Journal of Eating Disorders, 25*, 177-186.

Shapiro, D. H., & Astin, J. A. (1998). *Control Therapy: An Integrated Approach to Psychotherapy. Health, and Healing*. New York: John Wiley.

Shearin, E. N., Russ, M. J., Hull, J. W., Clarkin, J. F., & Smith, G. P. (1994). Construct validity of the Three-Factor Eating Questionnaire: flexible and rigid control subscales. *International Journal of Eating Disorders, 16*, 187-198.

Silverstone, P. H. (1991). Low self-esteem in different psychiatric conditions. *British Journal of Clinical Psychology, 30*, 185–188.

Skinner, E. (1996). A guide to constructs of control. *Journal of Personality and Social Psychology, 71*, 549-570.

Slade, P. (1982). Toward a functional analysis of anorexia nervosa and bulimia nervosa. *British Journal of Clinical Psychology, 21*, 167-179.

Smith, C. (2002). Punishment and pleasure: women, food and the imprisoned body. *The Sociological Review, 50*, 197-214.

Soenens, B., Elliot, A. J., Goossens, L., Vansteenkiste, M., Luyten, P., & Duriez, B. (2005). The intergenerational transmission of perfectionism: Parents' psychological control as intervening variable. *Journal of Family Psychology, 19*, 358-366.

Soenens, B., Vansteenkiste, M., Vandereycken, W., Luyten, P., Sierens, E., & Goossens, L. (2008). Perceived parental psychological control and eating disordered symptoms: Maladaptive perfectionism as a possible intervening variable. *Journal of Nervous and Mental Disease, 196*, 144-152.

Steptoe, A., & Appels, A. (1989). *Stress, Personal Control and Health*. Chichester: JohnWiley & Sons, Ltd.

Straus, E. W. (1948). On obsession: A clinical and methodological study. *Nervous and Mental Disease Monograph*, 78.

Strober, M. (2004). Pathologic fear conditioning and anorexia nervosa: on the search for novel paradigms. *International Journal of Eating Disorders*, 35, 504-508.

Surgenor, L-J., Horn, J., Plumridge, E.W., & Hudson, S.M. (2002). Anorexia nervosa and psychological control: a reexamination of selected theoretical accounts. *European Eating Disorders Review*, 10, 85-101.

Tchanturia, K., Happé, F., Godley, J., Treasure, J., Bara-Carril, N., & Schmidt, U. (2004). 'Theory of mind' in anorexia nervosa. *European Eating Disorders Review, 12*, 361 - 366.

Thompson, S. C. (1999). Illusion of control: How we overestimate our personal influence. *Current Directions in Psychological Science, 8*, 187-190.

Troop, N. A., Holbrey, A., & Treasure (1998). Stress, coping, and crisis support in eating disorders. *International Journal of Eating Disorders*, 24, 157-166.

Vasey, M. W. & Borkovec, T. D. (1992). A catastrophizing assessment of worrisome thoughts. *Cognitive Therapy and Research, 16*, 1-16.

Vohs, K. D., Bardone, A. M., Joiner, T. E. Jr., Abramson, L. Y., & Heatherton, T. F. (1999). Perfectionism, perceived weight status, and self-esteem interact to predict bulimic symptoms: a model of bulimic symptom development. *Journal of Abnormal Psychology, 108*, 695-700.

Vrana, S. R., Cuthbert, B. N., & Lang, P. J. (1986). Fear imagery and text processing. Psychophysiology, 23, 247-253.

Wadden, T. A., Brown, G., Foster, G. D., & Linowitz, J. R., (1991). Salience of weight-related worries in adolescent males and females. *International Journal of Eating Disorders, 10*, 407-414.

Waller, G. (1998). Perceived control in eating disorders: Relationship with reported sexual abuse. *International Journal of Eating Disorders, 23,* 213 – 216.

Wells, A. (2000). *Emotional Disorders and Metacognition: Innovative Cognitive Therapy*. Chichester, UK: Wiley.

Wilkinson, E. J., & Camove, A. S. (1992). Anxiety and desire for control. *New Zealand Journal of Psychology, 21*, 71–73.

Williams, G. J., Chamove, A. S., & Millar, H.R. (1990). Eating disorders, perceived control, assertiveness and hostility. *British Journal of Clinical Psychology, 29*, 327-335.

Williams, G. J., Power, K. G., Millar, H. R., Freeman, C. P., Yellowlees, A., Dowds, T., Walker, M., Campsie, L., MacPherson, F., & Jackson, M.A. (1993). Comparison of eating disorders and other dietary/weight groups on measures of perceived control, assertiveness, self-esteem, and self-directed hostility. *International Journal of Eating Disorders, 14*, 27-32.

In: Cognitive Therapy of Eating Disorders...
Editors: S. Sassaroli and G.M. Ruggiero
ISBN: 978-1-60876-617-8

Chapter 2

A PERSONAL CONSTRUCT PERSPECTIVE ON CONTROL IN EATING DISORDERS

David A. Winter[1] and Eric J. Button[2]
[1]University of Hertfordshire and Barnet, Enfield and Haringey Mental Health NHS Trust
[2]Leicestershire Partnership NHS Trust
United Kingdom

ABSTRACT

In this chapter we shall apply George Kelly's (1955) personal construct theory to the topic of control in eating disorders. We shall commence with a brief introduction to the theory, followed by consideration of how control is viewed from a personal construct theory perspective. We shall then review the personal construct theoretical and research literature relating to control in eating disorders. Finally, Eric Button will describe the personal construct psychotherapeutic approach that he has developed for clients with eating disorders and the ideas concerning the development and change of these disorders on which this is based.

1. PERSONAL CONSTRUCT THEORY

Personal construct theory was the forerunner of constructivist approaches to psychology and psychotherapy, and remains the best elaborated such approach. It views the person as a scientist, who is centrally concerned with the anticipation of his or her world, formulating hypotheses, or constructions of events, testing these out, and, if he or she is functioning optimally, revising them if they are invalidated. The building blocks of this process consist of a system of bipolar personal constructs, which is hierarchically organised, such that some constructs (e.g. 'attractive – unattractive') are superordinate to others (e.g. 'thin – fat'). Although there may be some commonality of construing between individuals, particularly within the same cultural group, every person's construct system is unique. Central to intimate relationships is the attempt to construe the other person's construction processes, or 'sociality'.

Kelly viewed emotions as representing an awareness of transitions in construing, as by experiences of validation or invalidation of one's constructions. For example, he considered that people feel threatened when they are aware of an imminent comprehensive change in their core structures, those superordinate aspects of their construing that are central to their identities. Similarly, guilt, for Kelly, was the experience of dislodgement from one's core role, one's characteristic mode of interacting with others. Habitual introverts may, for example, experience guilt if they catch themselves behaving gregariously. Anxiety, in personal construct theory terms, is the awareness that one's constructs do not enable one to predict the events with which one is confronted. For example, the person who has a well elaborated system of constructs concerning Western dining and cuisine may feel anxious on his or her first visit to a Japanese restaurant.

The person may adopt various strategies to avoid invalidation or anxiety. For example, he or she may constrict the world to those events that are predictable (for example, only visiting Western restaurants). Conversely, he or she may 'dilate', opening up to a range of new experiences in the hope that this will enable the development of a system of constructs to apply to the formerly unpredictable events. Another contrasting pair of strategies is loosening, in which the person's predictions become so vague as to be invulnerable to invalidation, and tightening, in which predictions are very precise. Optimally, there is a cyclical interplay of such contrasting strategies, but in psychological disorder the use of the strategies tends to be imbalanced: for example, habitually loose construing has been observed in people diagnosed as thought disordered schizophrenics and tight construing in those diagnosed with anxiety and depressive disorders (Winter, 1992, 2003). In general, disorders involve the repeated use of constructions despite repeated invalidation.

2. Control in Personal Construct Theory

2.1. Personal Construct Processes and Control

The notion of control is central to personal construct theory since, for Kelly (1955), an individual's constructs are the means by which he or she controls and predicts the world. For example, he stated that a person may control his or her destiny 'to the extent that he can develop a construction system with which he identifies himself and which is sufficiently comprehensive to subsume the world around him' (p. 126). Within the person's construct system, control is also provided by the hierarchical relationships in which superordinate constructs subsume those which are subordinate.

Although the person's constructs offer control, they also place restrictive controls upon him or her in that they determine the pathways of movement that are available. Being bipolar, each construct offers a choice of direction of movement, and the particular direction that is chosen on a construct will be that which appears to give greater opportunities for extension or definition of the construct system. Viewed in this way, even the most apparently self-destructive choices may be comprehensible. For example, Fransella (1972) provided evidence that a person may 'choose' to stutter because this carries more implications, and possibilities for anticipating the world, than does fluency.

A more specific consideration is given to control in personal construct theory as the final stage of the decision-making process that Kelly (1955) referred to as the Circumspection-Preemption-Control (CPC) Cycle. In the 'Circumspection' phase of this cycle, the person considers all of the issues, or constructs, involved in a decision. For example, in deciding whether to eat, the person might take into account whether or not he or she is hungry, how food is likely to affect his or her weight, or how appetising the food appears to be. In the 'Preemption' phase, the person effectively selects a particular construct (e.g. 'hungry – not hungry') as being the only one on which it is relevant to focus. Finally, in the 'Control' phase, the person chooses to apply one pole of this construct (e.g. 'I am hungry') and may then act (e.g. eating) accordingly. As Dunnett (1985) notes, achieving control does not necessarily mean that action will occur immediately, or at all, on the basis of the chosen pole of the pre-empted construct as the person may first consider the superordinate and subordinate implications of this construct within his or her system.

While pre-emption, the ruling out of certain constructs in construing a situation, is thus a central aspect of control, so may be the process, discussed above, that Kelly termed constriction, the ruling out of certain elements of the situation (e.g. only being concerned with food and not with interpersonal aspects of a situation). Dunnett (1985) considers that constriction may take the place of both the Circumspection and Pre-emption phases of the CPC Cycle, and that this may occur when there are 'mutually incompatible superordinates warring amongst themselves' (p. 42).

Sassaroli, Lorenzini, and Ruggiero (2005), who view control as 'the absolute certainty of avoiding all the threatening events continuously predicted by anxious, worrying and perfectionistic people' (p. 36), relate it to tight construing, as well as to 'impermeability' and 'literalism'. Impermeability refers to a construct's inapplicability to new elements of the person's experience. For example, the person who construes fish in terms of whether it is fried or grilled will not readily be able to apply this construct to a plate of raw fish. Literalism is 'a way of thinking, feeling, or doing which implies the restricted and absolute interpretation of an event or relationship' (Landfield, 1980, p. 315), and in particular is characterised by either very tight or very loose relationships between the feeling, value and behaviour aspects of a person's constructs.

2.2. Faulty Control

When a person is unable to communicate the construct under which he or she is operating, his or her behaviour tends to be seen as uncontrolled, but, for Kelly (1955), 'to say that something is out of control is merely to say that we have given up trying to explain it' (p. 127). It may be, for example, that we have misunderstood the person's construct system or wrongly predicted the alternatives that he or she chose. If one person's behaviour seems more controlled than that of another, who appears to be impulsive, this, in Kelly's view, is because the former person engages in long-cycle, and the latter in short-cycle, experiments. However, the behaviour of the person who performs long-cycle experiments may appear no less baffling than that of the impulsive person if the superordinate constructs that underlie these experiments are not understood.

For Kelly, therefore, all behaviour could be seen as controlled, but he did nevertheless consider that control could be faulty. Indeed, he stated that 'all disorders of construction are disorders which involve faulty control' (Kelly, 1955, p. 927). 'Disorders of control' may be viewed in terms of difficulties with the various phases of the CPC Cycle. For example, impulsivity may be associated with a foreshortening of the Circumspection phase of this cycle, the person, as in many of those who engage in parasuicidal behaviour (Winter, 2005), quickly seeing a problem in terms of only one dimension. This may be because he or she has a 'one-track mind', but may be an attempt to avoid the anxiety associated with viewing the problem in terms of several apparently incompatible dimensions. Whatever the reason, it is very much the opposite of the situation of the ruminative person, who circumspects endlessly, constantly considering the issues involved in the problem without being able to pre-empt one of these. Kelly (1955) also describes how impulsivity may occur as a result of difficulty with the Preemption phase of the CPC Cycle, the person being unable to choose an issue because it is more superordinate than any other but instead doing so because he or she can act upon it. Finally, impulsivity may arise from difficulty in the Control phase of the cycle, as when the person, having made a choice on the pre-empted issue, acts upon this choice without considering the appropriate time or place to do so.

As we have seen, in addition to the CPC Cycle, control may be achieved by various other processes, and each of these may be reflected in a disorder. For example, constriction may serve to reduce anxiety by minimising 'apparent incompatibilities' and limiting the person's world to events that are predictable. However, it may also be manifested in a disorder since 'it may let issues accumulate which will eventually threaten a person with insurmountable anxiety' (Kelly, 1955, p. 908). Kelly also indicated that tight construing, which Sassaroli et al. (2005) linked with control, may lead to a 'collapse' into anxiety when the person, whose predictions are very precise, is faced by a changing world. In addition, Landfield (1980) has described how literalism in the 'functional relatedness of feeling, value, and behavior' is related to problems involving both over- and under-control.

3. Control in Eating Disorders: A Personal Construct View

While anorexia has been viewed as a person's attempt to attain a feeling of control (Bruch, 1973), bulimia might at first sight appear to be a manifestation of a lack of control. However, from a personal construct perspective, each of these types of eating disorder may be viewed as 'a quest for control' (Button, 1985, p. 153). Kelly (1955) made a similar point in relation to sexual behaviour, stating that:

> 'Whereas one person may impulsively seek to perform the sex act, another may just as impulsively seek to avoid it. The person who avoids it is not showing more control; his control is simply exercised in another direction' (p. 931).

It might not be unexpected, therefore, if the construct systems of people diagnosed as bulimic and anorexic, in addition to those with other types of eating disorders, share some similar features. For example, it may be that the system of constructs that best allows them to predict and control their world relates to issues such as eating and weight. Such a view has been suggested by case studies using the repertory grid (the principal assessment method derived from personal construct theory) of clients with eating disorders in which there are indications of a relationship between resistance to change and the importance of weight to the individual (Crisp & Fransella, 1972; Fransella & Crisp, 1970; Mair & Crisp, 1968). In Fransella's (1970) terms, eating and its control may constitute the eating disordered person's 'way of life', whereas other areas of their construing are much less well elaborated and therefore provide less of a basis for anticipating the world. Websites and media attention devoted to eating disorders are likely to elaborate even further this way of life. An indication of the possible effect of the media on attitudes towards weight was provided by the finding of Riaz and Winter (2008) that, in females of South Asian origin, those who preferred Hollywood to Bollywood films were more likely to construe skinny people as sexually attractive.

There is some research evidence, at least with anorexics, for the view that an eating disorder may offer more meaning than life at normal weight in that the self at one's thinnest has been found to be construed much more extremely by such individuals than the self at normal weight (Button, 1983). A high level of meaningfulness of constructs associated with the self at normal weight has also been associated with better weight maintenance in anorexics (although not in obese people) (Fransella & Button, 1983). In addition, in anorexics, low meaningfulness of the construct 'anorexic – not anorexic' at discharge from hospital, and a decrease in the meaningfulness of the construct 'thin – fat' between second and third follow-up assessments, has been related to good outcome (Button, 1983).

Despite such indications of the importance of weight- and eating-related constructs in anorexics, particularly those who are more resistant to treatment, there is some evidence that such constructs, while more evident in bulimics than in anorexics, may be no more prominent in female clients with eating disorders than in those with other clinical problems (Button, 1993). It is also at first sight surprising that anorexics have been found to construe normal weight more favourably than being thin. However, this has been viewed as reflecting the 'if only syndrome', associated with resistance to change, in which the anorexic considers that if only normal weight were attained his or her life would be perfect (Button, 1983; Fransella & Crisp, 1979).

In terms of the CPC Cycle, both the anorexic and the bulimic may be considered to show impulsivity, quickly pre-empting eating as the issue on which to focus, choosing a position on this issue, and acting, often without considering whether the time or place is right. Clearly, the difference between the two extreme types of eating disorder is in the particular choice that is made in relation to eating. In personal construct theory terms, the basis for this choice is the extent to which possibilities for extension and definition of the construct system are elaborated. Thus, the anorexic will anticipate more such possibilities by not eating and the bulimic by eating.

Eating disorders can also be viewed in terms of the other processes of construing that, as we have seen, may be involved in control. For example, the person with an eating disorder may be considered to have constricted his or her world to the area of eating or not eating, perhaps in an attempt to avoid the anxiety and unpredictability faced in other areas of his or her life, such as the interpersonal world. Indeed, Button (2005) considers constriction to be the personal construct concept that is the most useful in understanding eating disorders as an attempt to make life more manageable, in contrast to the lack of control and invalidation experienced in relationships with other people.

Within the constricted world relating to eating and weight, the anorexic, in contrast to the bulimic, might be viewed as constricting even further, control of eating also allowing avoidance of conflictual or unpredictable issues such as sexuality. The theme of constriction may also be apparent in other areas of the person's life. For example, Eleanor, who had received personal construct psychotherapy, described how 'constriction is still a strong thread in my life, not just in my diet but at work [always taking a safe option so as not to fail], in relationships [seeking people who do not expect too much, but who also give too little] and at play [at one point I hardly left my house for six months, preferring to be alone rather than risk forming bonds with others]' (Button, 2005, p. 206). Button (1993) relates the more pronounced constriction in anorexics than in bulimics to findings that while both types of client, like other clinical groups, show negative self-construing (Batty & Hall, 1986; Mottram, 1985; Munden, 1982; Ryle & Evans, 1991), anorexics have a more favourable view of themselves when younger (Weinreich, Doherty, & Harris, 1985). This suggests that the anorexic may be particularly prone to constriction in an attempt to avoid the greater invalidation experienced in the adult, than in their childhood, world. The ultimate constriction, and one of which anorexics put themselves at risk, is death, and there is some evidence using personal construct methodology that such individuals may be characterised by high levels of death threat (Warren & Beumont, 2000).

Anorexics and bulimics might also appear to be at opposite poles on the dimension of tight versus loose construing. Evidence for this view has been provided by research indicating more unidimensional construing in anorexics than in bulimics and normal and clinical control groups, as well as the use of fewer constructs in anorexics than in normal controls (Button, 1993). Furthermore, there is evidence that the tighter the anorexic's construing, the poorer the likely outcome of his or her treatment (Button, 1983). Tight construing has also been observed in other studies of anorexics (Mottram, 1985), restrained eaters (Neimeyer & Khouzam, 1985), and female students showing disordered eating (Heesacker & Neimeyer, 1990), but not in a mixed sample of anorexic and bulimic students (Batty & Hall, 1986). That tight construing in eating disorders is not necessarily specific to anorexics was indicated by Coish (1990), who found bulimics to be characterised by lack of construct differentiation on some, but not all, of the repertory grid measures that she used. However, in common with most of the research in this area, she failed to use a non-eating disordered clinical control group, and was therefore unable to demonstrate that the construing of bulimics was tighter than that of any other clinical group. In a sample of bulimic clients, Dimcovic and Winter (2007) have found greater severity of eating disorder in those whose construing was tighter and more polarised.

The use of tight, undifferentiated construing as a strategy for controlling anxiety in people with eating disorders has been related to insecure attachment patterns deriving from the person's childhood relationships (Heesacker & Neimeyer, 1990). This position is consistent with the constructivist view of eating disorders proposed by Guidano and Liotti (1983) and the attempt by Lorenzini and Sassaroli (1995) to integrate personal construct theory with attachment theory. The latter workers regard insecure attachment as 'a context in which the child tends to conceive any invalidation as a threatening event' (Sassaroli, Lorenzini, & Ruggiero, 2005, p. 38), and consider that in eating disorders 'the person tends to have a tight, impermeable and rigid link between 'perfection' and 'absence of mistakes', and between 'self-esteem' and 'avoidance of mistakes'' (p. 39). In support of such views, they have found that, in female students, on a stressful day (when they received their examination results) constructs of perfectionism and parental criticism were significantly associated with dissatisfaction with the body and a drive for thinness, but that this was not the case on unstressful days (Ruggiero et al., 2003). Associating stress with a perceived lack of control, they assume that in relating perfectionism with a drive for thinness the students were attempting to regain control in the area of eating and weight. They also consider that 'perfectionistic over-concern for mistakes' is particularly apparent in people with eating disorders. A repertory grid study by Mottram (1985) of anorexic clients has provided some evidence for this view in that these clients' perfectionist tendencies were considered to be reflected in their tendency to construe their ideal selves as different from other people. Tatham and Winter (2007), as well as finding women with eating disorders to show more insecure attachment patterns than their non-eating disordered sisters, investigated parents' construing of their daughters. Daughters with eating disorders were found to be viewed more negatively than their non-eating disordered sisters as adults, but not retrospectively as children. There were also indications of differences in the content of the constructs applied to the two sisters, such as examples of the eating disordered, compared to the non-eating disordered, sister being construed as more obedient as a child and more perfectionistic as an adult.

4. A Personal Construct Psychotherapeutic Approach for Eating Disorders

4.1. Historical Reflections

I (EB) first became interested in the concept of control in eating disorders whilst conducting my PhD on anorexia nervosa during the 1970s in London's Royal Free Hospital. I was supervised by Fay Fransella, who has been at the forefront of the promotion of personal construct theory. She had paved the way for my work by her preliminary studies on anorexia nervosa with the late Arthur Crisp (Fransella & Crisp, 1970; Crisp & Fransella, 1972).

One of the main ideas which was to emerge from my PhD (Button, 1980) was that people with anorexia nervosa were deficient in person-construing, i.e. they were relatively rigid and impoverished in their ability to construe people. In many ways, this was similar to ideas expressed by Bannister and others about schizophrenia (e.g. Bannister & Salmon, 1966). In the case of anorexia nervosa, I argued that the disorder emerged in a context of negative experience with other people, which they responded to by a narrowing of focus on to the area of weight and eating. In personal construct theory terms, this involved the processes of 'preemption' (weight is *the* issue) and 'constriction'. In other words, by focussing on what weight they are (with a preference on lower/thinner) as the key issue in defining themselves, they have set a very narrow agenda for themselves in which little else is important. Progress through the disorder narrows the focus further and further and the person becomes less and less in touch with other people, typically restricting themselves to home and immediate family and less involved with the wider social world. There was some support for this position in my thesis, in that a longer duration of the disorder was associated with fewer personal constructs for construing people.

In *Personal Construct Theory and Mental Health* (Button, 1985, pp. 153-158) I first put forward the argument that eating disorders represent 'A Quest for Control'. It seems to me that all of us want control of our lives, or at least the *illusion of control.* Faced with many things we have little or no control over (e.g. mortality, who our parents are, the weather, terrorism), human beings seek out areas of at least temporary predictability and control. If we are lucky, our childhood years may be reasonably predictable, with adequate meals at regular intervals, the knowledge that our parents will always be there, etc. Of course, not everyone is so fortunate and major adversity may strike from an early age, but often the major challenges to this predictability occur during adolescence/early adulthood, which perhaps uncoincidentally is the peak time for the onset of eating disorders. As children emerge into the adult world, things become far less predictable (at least for a while) and complex, a prospect which can be exciting but scary.

Since completing my PhD, I have had almost three decades of clinical experience of working with people with eating disorders, which has given me ample opportunity to test out and develop these ideas in the real world of clinical practice. I will attempt to put more flesh on the bones of this during the next few pages.

4.2. Development of an Eating Disorder

Eating disorders often emerge in the context of the transition from childhood to adulthood. There are likely to be a number of reasons why this might be so, including: the biological changes of puberty; the challenges and competitiveness of forming sexual relationships; the need for greater autonomy and less dependence on parents; the tensions between seeking a unique identity and the desire for social acceptance by one's peers. There are also cognitive changes of the sort highlighted by Piaget and the potential realisation of one's own mortality and the fragility of what may have previously been taken for granted. The individual's view of the world ('personal construct system') is likely to be severely challenged by a rapid escalation and diversification of possibilities, expectations and points of view. Faced with a potentially bewildering array of possibilities (particularly in today's rapidly developing electronic age), a young person may be highly vulnerable to invalidation. This is particularly likely in interactions with their peers, who in their own struggle for identity can be remarkably insensitive to others. Such invalidation can lead to low self-esteem, lack of confidence and low mood. The person may also feel that their life is out of control and one way of trying to deal with this is by finding an area of greater control. It is hardly surprising that weight and size may become a target, given the media emphasis on slimness as an ideal, particularly for females who also happen to represent at least 90% of people who present with eating disorders to specialised clinics. Thus initially, the person may hypothesise that the reason for their difficulties is that they are too fat (even when they are not objectively obese). They may thus have a personal construct system in which much of their construing of others (particularly girls and young females) is based on size, with the assumption that in order to be liked, popular and confident they need to be slim or have the perfect figure. This is put to the test by dieting and/or other strategies, which may be successful in the short-term in that praise, envy and increased attentions from the opposite sex may follow. Such shallow and limited thinking, however, is unlikely to be successful in the longer term, given that only the most superficial of relationships can be sustained on such a basis. Longer-term relationships require a much wider understanding of people - further invalidation seems likely if they rely primarily on weight as the primary or sole dimension of self-evaluation.

Faced with such massive invalidation, two broad possibilities seem open. Operating like a true scientist, one might conclude that weight is not the issue and that getting slim is not after all the Holy Grail. This is probably what happens to most young people who try dieting and/or other such conformist behaviour. They develop new avenues, new ways of looking at themselves and others and hopefully gradually develop a wider understanding of people and themselves. The chances are that such individuals take an early exit from the road to an eating disorder (much as do most young people who dabble in drugs). Some, however, dig their heels in and hang on desperately to the same construct, which at least gives them some tenuous sense of control over events and their lives. They thus try even harder, maybe seeking further and further weight loss and this gradually becomes the central focus of their everyday life. They almost give up on trying to control other people and their range of interactions with other people may become increasingly narrowed. As their focus becomes primarily on trying to control what and when they eat, they increasingly avoid social contact around food, for fear of loss of control. Once this spiral is well in train, it can be very difficult to get out of it and their behaviour is likely to lead to them being construed by others as having an eating disorder. At this point, any sense of control they may have will once again be put in jeopardy as they face pressures from others to seek medical or psychological help.

4.3. To Change or Not to Change?

Facing the possibility that one is ill, particularly from a mental health standpoint, can be a very threatening experience and confront one with an immense sense of loss of control. The clinician who first encounters a person presenting with an eating disorder must be aware of this and be prepared to help them manage the emotions associated with the prospect of major change. Experienced clinicians will be aware of how to handle this and help the patient or client feel sufficient trust and safety in order to be able to contemplate and eventually embark on the process of change.

In terms of control, the person may particularly fear what may happen if they let go of their control of their eating. Typically, they fear that their weight will spiral out of control in an upwards direction and that they may become fatter and fatter. In the case of anorexia nervosa, recovery inevitably necessitates considerable weight gain and there is no way round this bitter pill. Nevertheless, this does not have to be rapid and in most cases it does not lead to obesity or ever-escalating weight gain as feared. The therapist's aim will be to create a therapeutic climate in which the patient becomes prepared initially to test the water and hopefully gradually to extend both the range and quantities of food eaten. In many ways this is akin to the kind of behavioural treatment that is typically used with phobic disorders. Nowadays, this type of intervention can usually be achieved at out-patient level, but in very severe and intractable cases, intensive and lengthy in-patient or day-patient treatment may be required. As with all psychotherapy, it is likely that the relationship between therapist/s and patient is a key element to the process of change.

Similar issues of letting go of control of eating also apply to bulimic disorders. Commonly, the patient severely restricts their eating during the day, but succumbs to binge-eating in the evening. It has been extensively demonstrated (e.g. Polivy et al, 1984) that restrained eating and starvation is a major cause of binge-eating, so that at an early stage the sufferer needs to relax their control by aiming for something like three decent and regular meals plus snacks per day. When presented with this evidence, many patients will see the wisdom of this and be prepared to give it a go, being pleasantly surprised when the urges to binge-eat decrease. They may still fear loss of control of their weight, but in most cases they will learn that their weight does not necessarily change when they eat normally.

The fear of loss of control of *weight* is of central importance, but it is by no means the only matter to be confronted. From a personal construct theory point of view, I have argued that in the longer-term the key issue is whether or not the person can develop a wider range of constructs for construing people in more psychological terms and not solely in terms of their body size or shape. This applies to both their construing of other people and themselves. One of my favourite therapeutic lines goes something like this: "There are thousands of people out there who weigh 8 stone (112 lbs/51kg), but only one of them is you". Hopefully at this stage in the development of mankind, we are able to see people in more than stereotypical terms, in spite of the fun that we all get at times by comments like "he's a typical man"! Most of my patients are young women and my aim is to help them discover who they are and who they can become if they are prepared to experiment and respond to their natural inclinations and preferences. I would particularly aim to help them identify and build on self-constructions which they regard as positive (e.g. I have a good sense of humour and enjoy listening to others). Such broadening and enhancement of their self-image is very important and I have shown that more positive self-construing is associated with a significantly better outcome (e.g. Button & Warren, 2002).

Having a more positive and multi-dimensional self-image is probably necessary for recovery from an eating disorder. Just as important, however, is how one views or construes other people and one's relationship to them. Man is a social animal and we are all dependent on other people to some degree. The ability to understand and get on with a reasonably wide range of people is essential if one is to survive and thrive. I have placed person construing at the centre of my theory of eating disorders and in my therapeutic work I place considerable emphasis on the development of patients' construing of other people. This can be very challenging as people are highly varied and complex and they are also capable of behaving very differently, depending on context and mood. Many patients react badly to change in moods of people they interact with and may often assume that a negative mood in another (e.g their partner) means they have done something wrong or they are unliked/unloved *themselves.* It may be necessary to invest considerable time in the exploration of other people's view of the world, which may be very different from ours. Such exploration can take many different forms, ranging from asking people to try techniques such as fixed role therapy (Kelly, 1955), in which one experiments with or acts out the role of an imaginary person for a fixed period. It can be illuminating to put oneself in someone else's shoes, to try and look at the world from another's perspective. In this way, the patient hopefully begins to discover that other people don't necessarily mirror their own construing. For example, if my patient does not turn up for an appointment, I might assume that this means they don't like me, when it's actually because they couldn't face asking their boss for time off, in case they think badly of them. One very important aspect of this is learning how to anticipate people's moods and the signs that they are preoccupied with some issue, which may have no bearing on you.

Reconstruing of other people may sometimes need to give particular focus to a key individual in a person's life, such as an abuser or other negatively construed figure. In some cases, it is difficult for a person to move on until they have made sense of or come to terms with such a person and/or their behaviour. Indeed, making sense of bad or unwelcome behaviour in another may be essential to the understanding of such tendencies in ourselves and there are often useful parallels to be drawn between the two perspectives. This type of work can be highly challenging, but rewarding if it shifts the person away from repetitive, negative patterns of construing of others.

So what does this all have to do with control? Having some sense of control over our interpersonal world is likely to be a central plank of our psychological well-being. This does not mean directly controlling others (such as by force or by power relationships), but being in a position where one can broadly predict other people's behaviour and not be constantly intimidated or thrown by other people. It also means being in a position where one can engage in relationships with other people, in which one can be close to someone, but not fear losing one's self. In terms of recovery from an eating disorder it means putting weight and eating into their appropriate contexts rather than being constantly at centre stage.

This form of 'personal construct psychotherapy' which I have outlined for eating disorders (Button, 1993) has not been subject to controlled trials for the treatment of eating disorders in the way that cognitive-behavioural therapy (CBT) has (see National Institute for Clinical Excellence, 2004), but other outcome studies (Metcalfe, Winter, & Viney, 2007; Viney, Metcalfe, & Winter, 2005; Watson & Winter, 2005) suggest that for general psychological problems personal construct psychotherapy may be at least as effective as CBT. A focus on the personal constructions which under-pin issues of control may thus prove to be a fruitful line of approach in helping someone move on from a life dominated by weight and eating.

References

Bannister, D., & Salmon, P., (1966). Schizophrenic thought disorder: specific or diffuse? *British Journal of Medical Psychology, 39*, 215-9.

Batty, C., & Hall, E. (1986). Personal constructs of students with eating disorders: Implications for counselling. *British Journal of Guidance and Counselling, 14*, 306-13.

Bruch, H. (1973). *Eating disorders: Obesity, anorexia nervosa and the person within.* New York: Basic Books.

Button, E. J. (1980). *Construing and clinical outcome in anorexia nervosa.* Unpublished Ph.D. thesis, University of London.

Button, E. J. (1983). Construing the anorexic. In J. Adams-Webber & J. Mancuso (Eds.), *Applications of Personal Construct Theory*. Toronto: Academic Press, pp. 305-16.

Button, E. J. (1985). Eating disorders: A quest for control? In E. J. Button (Ed.), *Personal Construct Theory and Mental Health*. London: Croom Helm, pp. 153-168.

Button, E. J. (1993). *Eating Disorders: Personal Construct Therapy and Change.* Chichester Wiley.

Button, E. J. (2005). Eating disorders. In D. Winter & L. L. Viney (Eds.), *Personal Construct Psychotherapy*. London: Whurr Publishers, pp. 199-212.

Button, E. J., & Warren, R.I. (2002). Self-image in anorexia nervosa 7.5 years after initial presentation to a specialized eating disorder service. *European Eating Disorders Review, 10*, 399-412.

Coish, B. J. (1990). *A personal construct theory of bulimia.* Unpublished Ph.D. thesis, La Trobe University.

Crisp, A. H., & Fransella, F. (1972). Conceptual changes during recovery from anorexia nervosa. *British Journal of Medical Psychology, 45*, 395-405.

Dimcovic, N., & Winter, D.A. (2007). *The mystery of bulimia. What lies behind the symptom?* Manuscript in preparation.

Dunnett, G. (1985). Construing control in theory and therapy. In D. Bannister (Ed.), *Issues and Approaches in Personal Construct Theory*. London: Academic Press, pp. 37-46.

Fransella, F. (1972). *Personal Change and Reconstruction.* London: Academic Press.

Fransella, F., & Button, E. J. (1983). The "construing" of self and body size in relation to the maintenance of weight gain in anorexia nervosa. In P. I. Darby (Ed.), *Anorexia Nervosa: Recent Developments in Research*. New York: Liss.

Fransella, F., & Crisp, A. H. (1970). Conceptual organisation and weight change. *Psychosomatics and Psychotherapy, 18*, 176-85.

Guidano, V. F., & Liotti, G. (1983), *Cognitive processes and emotional disorders.* New York, The Guilford Press.

Heesacker, R. S., & Neimeyer, G. J. (1988). Assessing object relations and social cognitive correlates of eating disorder. *Journal of Counseling Psychology, 37*, 419-26.

Kelly, G. A. (1955). *The Psychology of Personal Constructs.* New York: Norton.

Landfield, A. W. (1980). The person as persepctivist, literalist, and chaotic fragmentalist. In A. W. Landfield & L. M. Leitner (Eds.), *Personal Construct Psychology: Psychotherapy and Personality*. New York: Wiley, pp. 289-320.

Lorenzini, R., & Sassaroli, S. (1995). Attachment as an informative relationship. *International Journal of Personal Construct Psychology, 3*, 239-48.

Mair, J. M., & Crisp, A. H. (1968). Estimating psychological organization, meaning and change in relation to clinical practice. *British Journal of Medical Psychology, 4*, 15-29.

Metcalfe, C., Winter, D., & Viney, L. (2007). The effectiveness of personal construct psychotherapy in clinical practice: A systematic review and meta-analysis. *Psychotherapy Research, 17*, 431-442.

Mottram, M. A. (1985). Personal constructs in anorexia nervosa. *Psychiatric Research, 19*, 291-5.

Munden, A. (1982). *Eating problems amongst women in a university population.* Unpublished manuscript, Department of Psychiatry, University of Southampton.

Neimeyer, G. J., & Khouzam, N. (1985). A repertory grid study of restrained eaters. *British Journal of Medical Psychology, 58*, 365-8.

Polivy, J., Herman, C. P., Olmsted, M. P., & Jazwinski, C. M. (1984). Restraint and binge eating. In R. C. Hawkins, W. Fremouw & P. F. Clement (Eds.), *The Binge-Purge Syndrome: Diagnosis, Treatment and Research.* New York: Springer, pp. 104-122.

Riaz, A., & Winter, D. A. (2008). *The effects of Hollywood and Bollywood media and place of birth on the body image perception of South Asian females*. Manuscript in preparation.

Ruggiero, G. M., Levi, D., Ciuna, A., & Sassaroli S. (2003). Stress situation reveals an association between perfectionism and drive for thinness. *International Journal Eating of Disorders, 34*, 220-6.

Ryle, A., & Evans, C. D. H. (1991). Some meanings of body and self in eating-disordered and comparison subjects. *British Journal of Medical Psychology, 64*, 273-83.

Sassaroli, S., Lorenzini, R., & Ruggiero, G. M. (2005). Kellian invalidation, attachment, and the construct of 'control'. In D. Winter & L. L. Viney (Eds.), *Personal Construct Psychotherapy*. London, Whurr Publishers, pp. 34-42.

Tatham, M., & Winter, D. A. (2007). *Attachment and perceived parental treatment reported by siblings discordant for eating disorder pathology*. In preparation.

Viney, L. L., Metcalfe, C., & Winter, D. A. (2005). The effectiveness of personal construct psychotherapy: a meta-analysis. In D. A. Winter & L. L. Viney (Eds.), *Personal Construct Psychotherapy: Advances in Theory, Practice and Research*. London: Whurr, pp. 347-64.

Warren, B., & Beumont, P. V. J. (2000). The personal construction of death in anorexia nervosa. *British Journal of Medical Psychology, 73*, 53-65.

Watson, S., & Winter, D. A. (2005). A process and outcome study of personal construct psychotherapy. In D. A. Winter & L. L. Viney (Eds.). *Personal Construct Psychotherapy: Advances in Theory*, Practice and Research. London: Whurr, pp. 335-46.

Weinreich, P., Doherty, J., Harris, P. (1985). Empirical assessment of identity in anorexia and bulimia nervosa. *Journal of Psychiatric Research, 19*, 297-302.

Winter, D. A. (1992). *Personal Construct Psychology in Clinical Practice: Theory Research and Applications*. London: Routledge.

Winter, D. A. (2003). Psychological disorder as imbalance. In F. Fransella (Eds.), *International Handbook of Personal Construct Psychology*. Chichester: Wiley, pp. 201-209.

Winter, D. A. (2005). Deliberate self-harm and reconstruction. In D. A. Winter & L. L. Viney (Eds.), *Personal Construct Psychotherapy: Advances in Theory, Practice and Research*,(pp. 127-35).

In: Cognitive Therapy of Eating Disorders...
Editors: S. Sassaroli and G.M. Ruggiero
ISBN: 978-1-60876-617-8

Chapter 3

THE CONTROL AND WORRY-FOCUSED TREATMENT OF EATING DISORDERS (CWT-ED)

***Sandra Sassaroli*[1] *and Giovanni Maria Ruggiero*[2]**
[1] "Studi Cognitivi" Cognitive Psychotherapy School, Milano, Italy
[2] "Psicoterapia Cognitiva e Ricerca" Cognitive Psychotherapy School, Milano, Italy

1. ABSTRACT

The control and worry-focused treatment of eating disorders (CWT-ED) is not a new therapy. The CWT-ED is a variant of the standard cognitive treatment for eating disorders (ED) that assumes that the assessment and treatment of worry and of the belief of control will increase the understanding of the psychopathology of ED and the efficacy of cognitive treatment. The original model of cognitive therapy for ED considers low self-esteem and pathological perfectionism as the prominent distorted cognitions underlying ED and the most important targets of the psychological treatment (Fairburn, Cooper, & Shafran, 2003). The goal of cognitive-behavioral work that challenges and disputes pathological perfectionism and low self-esteem is to decrease an individual's pervasive fear of failure, and diminish self-criticism that arises from negative appraisals of his or her performance. The CWT-ED assumes that biased beliefs and processes in the domain of control and worry are also among the relevant cognitive distortions of ED and must be added to pathological perfectionism and low self-esteem as the targets of a cognitive-behavioural therapy for ED.

2. ASSESSMENT AND TREATMENT OF WORRY IN EATING DISORDERS

Some studies have shown either an association between worry and ED, or the presence of worry in ED (see chapter VI). As discussed in chapter VI, the key feature of worry is the predominance of negative thoughts (Borkovec, 1993; Vasey & Borkovec, 1992). The cognitive treatment of worry encompasses the following steps:

Step I: Assessing worry. The therapist evaluates the amount of time spent by the patient worrying about themes related and unrelated with body, eating, food, and weight. The worries related to body and the eating related worries of individuals with ED are linked with other worries regarding feelings of not being sufficiently qualified, competent, or suited to the demands of life, or with the themes of perfection and fear of mistakes, or with the theme of control.

Step II: Recognizing worry as an intentional state. In this step, the patient learns to consider worry not as an ungovernable state, but as an intentional attitude that is at least partially controllable.

Step III: Assessing the intentional goals of worry. In this phase, the therapist guides the patient to recognize the reasons and goals that underly the process of worry.

Step IV: Reframing the patient's attitude towards worry, and training him or her to stop worrying. The therapist guides the patient to find mental attitude alternatives to worry.

2.1. Session I: Assessing Worry

Usually, patients with ED do not reflect on their mental processes and habits. In their opinion, it is natural to spend a lot of time worrying about fat, eating, and weight. Given that, in patients with ED, worry is significantly associated with a drive for thinness, dissatisfaction with body, fear of fatness, eating, and overweight, it is plausible that patients with ED would spend a lot of time negatively judging their body aspect, weight, and fat (Sassaroli et al, 2005). Thus, the assessment of worry begins by asking how much time the patient thinks about his or her weight, fat, and body aspect.

> T. – How much time per day do you think about your fat, weight, or body?
>
> T. – Are these thoughts negative? Do you negatively judge your weight or your body aspect?

The negative judgment depends on negative mental associations that link fat and weight to repulsive body aspects, low self-esteem, and a sense of loss of control of life. In addition, the ideation of being perfect and faultless reinforces this mental association.

However, at this moment of the assessement process, the interviewer focuses on the process of worry and does not explore the whole chain of negative thoughts linked to body aspect, eating, fat, and weight in detail. The goal is rather to encourage the patient to become aware of his or her tendency to worry and of the amount of time each day spent worrying.

> T. – We agree that you negatively judge your body aspect, and/or your fat, and/or your weight for a number of reasons These reasons are basically fears and negative thoughts related to your self, self-esteem, and your ideas about how your life should or could be. Let's call 'worry' this bulk of negative thoughts. How much time do you spend worrying about your fat, weight, and/or body aspect? And how much time do you spend worrying about all your negative ideas linked to fat and overweight?

T. – Please rate your worry using the following scale:

1 ☐ = I never worry about dissatisfaction with my body, fear of fatness, eating, and being overweight and all the negative ideas and fears associated with fat and being overweight.

2 ☐ = I rarely worry about dissatisfaction with my body, fear of fatness, eating and overweight and all the negative ideas and fears associated with fat and being overweight. These worries are sometimes present in my mind, but not every day and the duration of these thoughts are very short, lasting no more than a few minutes. It is an unpleasant thought, but not really disturbing.

3 ☐ = I spend some time worrying about dissatisfaction with my body, fear of fatness, eating, and overweight and all the negative ideas and fears associated with fat and being overweight. This worry is present almost every day, and is really disturbing. However, I can manage it and even control it, although with some difficulty. This worry does not really negatively affect my life or some aspects of my life, such as my social life, work efficiency, etc. The duration of this worry can be significant, but it is never excessively prolonged. It may last more than few minutes, or go away and come back, but it never takes up hours and hours of my day.

4 ☐ = I spend a lot of time worrying about my dissatisfaction with my body, fear of fatness, eating, and overweight and all the negative ideas and fears associated with fat and being overweight. My worry is present every day and lasts for hours and hours. It is not only disturbing, but also pervasive and negatively affects some aspects of my life. For example, it decreases my concentration at work, or damages my social life.

5 ☐ = I always worry about my dissatisfaction with my body, fear of fatness, eating, and overweight and all the negative ideas and fears associated with fat and being overweight. This worry is the only thought I have. I can't do anything else but worry. It totally ruins my life.

2.2. Step II: Recognizing Worry as an Intentional State

The goal of this intervention is to make the patient more conscious of the reasons and the motives underlying his or her proneness to worry. Frequently, patients begin to worry in an automatic way; therefore, they consider worry as an unintentional impulse that begins by on its own when they are absent-minded, and never as the result of a voluntary deliberation. Items 1 and 2 in Table 1 are a short evaluation form of the nature of worry as an automatic impulse at the beginning of the treatment (see Table 1 at the end of section 2.6).

The therapist instructs the patient to recognize the very moment at which worrying begins and to explore the subjective reasons that explain and justify their worries. In short, the patient should recognize that worry is a state of preoccupation. It is true that worry is not a totally intentional state of mind. But this does not mean that worry is completely unintentional. Actually, worry is also a partially controllable condition. To some degree, we can increase or decrease our worries, and sometimes we can even stop it. Although it is difficult to directly and immediately stop severe worrying, we can use indirect ways to be in better command of it. For example, looking for an alternative thought, a distracter from worry, may erase the worry from the mind. Thus, we can partially control worry and we can always attempt to stop it. Or, we can decide not to stop worrying at all if we think it is worthy. In fact, worry can be useful when coping with a challenging situation. In short, it is possible to analyze worry in terms of intentional goals.

In this way, the person can increase his or her awareness that worry is not an unintentional impulse, but can be conceived as a conscious choice, a mental state aimed at a given goal. The therapist can help the patient using an open explanation of the partially voluntary nature of worry.

T. – Please, let us attempt to understand why you tend to worry. For a moment, consider that worrying is a totally voluntary attitude. Please, attempt to imagine that you can choose whether or not to worry, that all your preoccupations are a voluntary deliberation. A deliberation aimed at achieving an intentional goal. Can you imagine this? I do not deny that worry is also a kind of automatic attitude, something we start doing inadvertently when we are absent-minded. But, you will agree that worrying is not totally unintentional. It is also a voluntary state of mind. It is not an impulse, or an involuntary event like your heart beat. Thus, it is possible to ascertain the intentional goals of worry.

After some sessions devoted to this topic, it is possible to assess the change in the patient's belief that worry is an impulse, using item 3 in Table 1 (see Table 1 at the end of section 2.6).

2.3. Step III: Assessing the Intentional Goals of Worry

Worry can be conceptualized as an intentional state by means of which the person pursues a purpose. What are the goals of worry? What is the function of worry?

T. – Please do not consider worry as a kind of unintentional impulse. Consider it as a voluntary action, something you intentionally choose to do in order to achieve a given goal. What could this goal be? Why do you worry? What are the goals of your worry?

The therapist reports the capacity of the patient to consider worry as an intentional state using item 4 of Table 1 (see Table 1 at the end of section 2.6).

In cases where the patient is unable to examine and identify the goals of his or her worries, the therapist should propose a list of possible ideas to patients about the function of worrying drawn from the scientific literature. For example, Borkovec and Roemer (1995) found that anxious individuals think that worry facilitates general motivation, helps prevent negative events from occurring, prepares one for the negative consequences of possible life events, makes one feel that the negative event is less likely to occur (superstition), and helps to solve problems. In short, people rate motivation, preparation for the worst, superstition, avoidance/prevention of negative outcomes, and problem solving as the most typical reasons for their worries. Recent research suggests that holding such positive beliefs about worry could increase the frequency of worrying (Davey et al, 2005; Startup & Davey, 2001).

T. – Do you believe that worrying helps to solve your problems?

T. – Do you believe that worrying facilitates your motivation to cope with the problems and demands of life?

T. – Do you believe that worrying helps you to prevent negative events from occurring?

T. – Is it possible that worrying makes you feel as though negative events are less likely to occur?

T. – Do you believe that worrying prepares you for the negative situations that may occur in life?

T. – Do you believe that worrying may prepare you to be less shocked and experience less grief when negative life events occur?

T. – Do you believe that worrying protects you from negative emotions in the event that a negative situation occurs?

In addition, another possible goal of worrying is distraction from more emotionally laden topics (Borkovec & Roemer, 1995). This goal is more difficult to assess given that it implies a lack of awareness. Thus, it is important to provide a concrete example.

T. – Sometimes we tend to worry about an issue just to avoid worrying about other more laden topics. For example, I knew a person who tended to worry about dirt and contamination to avoid to worrying about the crisis of his/her marriage. May the same apply to you?

The therapist assesses the positive beliefs of the patient about worry using items 5, 6, 7, 8, 9, and 10 in Table 1 (see Table 1 at the end of section 2.6).

On the other hand, anxious individuals may also believe that worrying has negative consequences. The most frequent negative beliefs are that worrying disrupts effective performance, exaggerates the problem, and causes emotional discomfort (Davey, Tallis & Capuzzo, 1996). When negative beliefs about worrying are present, it is possible to start worrying about the supposed negative consequences of worrying. In short, the person begins to worry about worrying. Wells (1999) calls this particular kind of worry type II worry or meta-worry (worry about one's own thoughts and worry).

T. – What do you think about the fact that you spend a lot time worrying?
T. – Do you have any negative thoughts about worrying?
T. – What are your most frequent negative thoughts about worrying?
T. – Do you fear that worrying will disrupt effective performance?
T. – Do you fear that worrying could exaggerate the problem?
T. – Do you fear that worrying will cause emotional discomfort?

The therapist assesses the negative beliefs of the patient about worrying using items 11, 12, and 13 in Table 1 (see Table 1 at the end of section 2.6).

2.4. Step IV: Reframing the Patient's Attitude Towards Worry

Basically, people tend to worry because they feel they have good reasons to worry. It is even possible that the patient may fear stopping worrying, because he or she has many personal beliefs that justify worrying as a perfectly reasonable attitude. Thus, the therapist must reframe these beliefs.

The cognitive intervention is aimed at challenging the belief that worry is an adaptive attitude. The therapist encourages the patient to critically discuss all his or her positive assumptions about worry. Patients with ED need to learn how to recognize the right measures of worry. Basically, worry is an adaptive alarm signal that should trigger pragmatic management of problems. However, worry can easily generate senseless and prolonged mental ruminations. The wrong underlying assumption is "If I have a problem, worrying seems like the most rational stance to cope with the problem."

The acceptable degree of preoccupation is recognizable if it is not overwhelming, but emotionally manageable, and if it amplifies the intellectual capacity to generate positive solutions and the emotional capacity to accept partial, imperfect solutions (Lehay, 2002). Instead, pathological worrying generates poor, repetitive, and unproductive thinking that is not substantially aimed at generating practical solutions (Vasey & Borkovec, 1992; Sassaroli et al, 2005).

In addition, the therapist must stress the disrupting effects of worry. Negative thinking decreases coping skills. The patient is encouraged to believe that the negative effects of worry are a reason to stop worrying, not to reinforce it. In fact, it is possible that an awareness of the negative effects of worrying might generate a paradoxical increase in worrying by the patient rather than encouraging attempts to stop worrying. Thus, the patient may tend to worry about these possible negative consequences of worrying and add this second level of worry to the basic one. This is the above mentioned meta-worry; worrying about one's own thoughts and worrying.

As discussed earlier, the possible negative consequences feared by patients due to worrying are the disruption of effective performance, emotional discomfort, fear of losing mental control, and a negative self-evaluation of emotional weakness. The intervention by the therapist must involve both the challenge and disputation of the probability and severity of the supposed damage produced by worry and also the recognition that worrying actually creates damage. However, it is important to tell to the patient that this awareness must lead him or her to become determined to stop and avoid worrying, and not to add other levels of worry to the basic one.

Thus, patients need to be both reassured about their worst fears and encouraged to rid themselves of their tendency to worry. For example, the patient may fear that worrying may induce a severe mental disorder. In short, the patient may feel that he or she will become insane. In this case, a simple psycho-educational intervention can restore confidence. Otherwise, it is necessary to assess and test the catastrophic chain of the worrying ideations. On the other hand, we must confirm that worrying actually generates damage, and that it is necessary to decrease it.

The therapist assesses the disputation of beliefs underlying the patient's proneness to worry using items 14, 15, and 16 in Table 1 (see Table 1 at the end of section 2.6).

2.6. Step V. Training Patients to Stop Worrying

The following step is to discuss the belief that worrying is uncontrollable. Actually, worry is partially an automatic attitude. However, the therapist must stress that worry is automatic and poorly controlled in the beginning, but that maintaining worry is subject to voluntary control.

Table 1. Assessment of the phases of worry-focused treatment of ED

		Strongly agree	Agree	Neutral	Disagree	Strongly disagree
Assessment of worry as an impulse at the beginning of the treatment						
1	Does the patient describe worry as an automatic event?	☐	☐	☐	☐	☐
2	Does the patient describe worry as a kind of impulse?	☐	☐	☐	☐	☐
Assessment of the patient's change of belief that worry is an impulse						
3	Does the patient still describe worry as an automatic event after exploring the intentional components of worry?	☐	☐	☐	☐	☐
Assessment of the patient's capacity to consider worrying to be an intentional state						
4	The patient can consider worry as an intentional state provided with goals	☐	☐	☐	☐	☐
Assessment of the patient's positive beliefs about worry. The patient thinks that worry:						
5	Facilitates motivation *(motivation)*	☐	☐	☐	☐	☐
6	Helps to prevent negative events *(prevention)*	☐	☐	☐	☐	☐
7	Makes him or her feel as though negative events are less likely to occur *(superstition)*	☐	☐	☐	☐	☐
8	Helps to solve problems *(problem solving)*	☐	☐	☐	☐	☐
9	Distracts from more laden topics *(distraction)*	☐	☐	☐	☐	☐
10	Protects from negative emotions in the event of a negative situation *(emotional shield)*	☐	☐	☐	☐	☐
Assessment of the patient's negative beliefs about worry. The patient thinks that worry:						
11	Disrupts effective performance	☐	☐	☐	☐	☐
12	Exaggerates problems	☐	☐	☐	☐	☐
13	Causes emotional discomfort	☐	☐	☐	☐	☐
Assessment of the disputation of the beliefs underlying proneness to worry						
14	Worry does not induce severe damages, such as mental disorders	☐	☐	☐	☐	☐
15	Worry damages coping skills, performance, social life, self-esteem	☐	☐	☐	☐	☐
16	The negative consequences of worry are a good reason to stop worrying	☐	☐	☐	☐	☐
Assessment of the training to stop worrying						
17	The beginning of worries are uncontrollable, but the maintenance of worry is subject to voluntary mental control	☐	☐	☐	☐	☐
18	It is possible to manage, detach from, and stop worrying	☐	☐	☐	☐	☐
19	It is necessary to accept that worry tends to restart after that the patient has managed to stop it	☐	☐	☐	☐	☐

The patient should carefully monitor his or her initiation of worry and accept being involved with worry at its beginning. However, with time the patient could detach him or herself from analyzing the reasons for the worrying episode, assessing the possible pros and cons of this worry, and lastly, attempt to stop worrying by switching his or her attention from negative thoughts to positive elements.

Given that the start of a worry is a kind of automatism, it is true that after successfully stopping the patient will tend to inattentively begin worrying again. The therapist must tell the patient that he or she should appreciate a successful cessation of worry and accept without self-negative thoughts any new worrying episode. When the patient suddenly notices that he or she is again involved in a worrying episode, he or she should engage in another attempt to manage and stop worrying according to suggestions given above. Thus, it is necessary to encourage the patient to use this blend of acceptance of and opposition to worry.

Another possible intervention is to guide the patient to pursue emotional detachment from worry. The patient should attempt to emotionally disconnect him or her self from the state of preoccupation without attempting to stop the flow of negative thinking. To develop detachment from worry, the person must shift his or her focus from emotional sufferance to anything else. Segal, Williams, and Teasdale (2001) recommend focusing on particularly futile objects, like commonly overlooked body perceptions (for example, the tactile perception of contact between two toes of a foot). The futility of this object is aimed at decreasing the degree of emotional engagement and to train the patient to accept any kind of thought. Thus, the patient learns to stop looking for "important things," which usually generates anxious thoughts.

The last intervention is to look for better alternatives to worrying. The patient has developed a kind of addiction to worrying and is not used to conceiving of any different mental stance other than worrying. "What would I do if I did not worry?" is the question. It is necessary to guide the patient to learn that it is possible to look for explanations and answers in the absence of worries. The key idea is that a quiet approach to problems is actually more fruitful than a worrisome attitude.

The therapist assesses the training to stop the patient from worrying using items 17, 18, and 19 in Table 1 (see Table 1 at the end of section 2.6).

3. Assessment and Treatment of the Patient's Belief of Control in Eating Disorders

As written in chapter IV, the clinical concept of the anxious perception of lack of control is applicable to ED. In fact, the need for ED subjects to feel in control of their lives, which gets displaced by controlling eating, weight, and body shape, implies a pervasive perception of insufficient control. Subjects with anorexia nervosa often look for control (Bruch, 1973; Button, 1985) and their sense of control is often obtained by continuously monitoring their eating, body weight, and shape (Fairburn & Harrison, 2003; Slade, 1982).

In addition, research supports the idea that individuals with ED believe that control over either one's self or of reality is possible and compulsory (Sassaroli, Gallucci, & Ruggiero, 2008). This is not the anxious perception of lack of control, but it may be the active and obsessive desire for increased control (Moulding & Kyrios, 2006; Sassaroli & Ruggiero 2002).

Concerning the treatment of control issues, the therapist should develop a strategy that challenges the patient's belief that the degree of control exerted by the patient is insufficient (appraisal of control as insufficient) and the belief that only absolute control is acceptable (desire for and compulsion to control). The main characteristics of the treatment of control in ED are as follows:

1. *Step 1) Assessing the patient's belief of control.* We assume that in individuals with ED, maladaptive eating and purging behaviors are an attempt to gain a sense of control. For this reason, the therapist explores the patient's personal sense of control, his or her perception of sufficient/insufficent control, the desire for increased control, and the compulsion for absolute control.
2. *Step 2) Assessing the connection between control of eating, weight, and food and the patient's perception of general control of life.* The therapist assesses whether this sense of control involves not only eating and body, but the whole course of one's life and whether there is a conscious assumption that connects eating, weight, and/or body size with a sense of control over external events, others, the world, or one's self.
3. *Step 3) Reframing the patient's belief of insufficient control.* The therapist encourages the patient to question the belief that his or her control over life is insufficient, and to recognize that frequently a partial degree of control affords a reasonable degree of personal safety and emotional self-confidence. In addition, the therapist questions the connection between feelings of general control of life and the control of fat and weight.
4. *Step 4) Reframing the patient's compulsion for absolute control.* The therapist encourages the patient to question his or her rigid and dichotomous concept of control. According to the patient's cognitive bias, the only real and acceptable control is absolute control. Such extreme control would encompass not only eating and weight, but also the self and the external world. The therapist lists the domains other than eating in which the patient with an ED applies his or her compulsion to control, and proposes a plan to decrease controlling behaviors in each domain. The therapist analyzes and discusses the feelings and thoughts experienced by the patient during implementation of the program. The final aims are a smaller degree of exerted control, and the ability to judge a partial degree of control as being sufficient. In short, the therapist guides the patient to believe that he or she can achieve and tolerate a smaller degree of control. In addition, the therapist guides the patient with ED to engage in non-controlling behaviors, concerning not only eating and food, but also other domains.

3.1. Step 1: Assessing the Patient's Belief of Control

The assessment begins with the therapist asking the patient to explain his or her maladaptive eating behaviors and associated emotions in terms of thought. The therapist encourages the patient to adapt a critical attitude, and clarifies that each given behavior and/or emotion corresponds to an evaluation of the situation in terms of feelings and cognitive beliefs. In this way, the patient can conceive his or her behaviors and emotions as a conscious attitude and no longer as an uncontrollable impulse.

We assume that in patients with ED, maladaptive eating behaviors are an attempt to gain a sense of control over external events, of others and the world, and of self-control.

T. – How would you define your attitude toward food and eating?

In time, the therapist could repeat the question using a more directive formulation:

T. – Would you define your attitude toward food and eating a controlling attitude?
T. – Would you say that your eating habits have increased your feeling of being in control?

To further explore the meaning of this controlling attitude, the therapist will ask the patient what he or she fears if they give up control over eating habits.

T. – What would happen if you ate more than now?
T. – What would happen if you became fatter than now?
T. – What would happen if you gained weight?

Of course, the patients tend to control not only eating, fat, and weight, but also other domains of their lives.

T. – Do you control only eating, fat, and weight or do you also control other domains of your life?
T. – Do you aim to control others' judgment? Your feelings and emotions? The events of your daily life? Your performance at school, work, or elsewhere?

At this point, the therapist will ask what the patient fears if he or she lost control.

T. – What would happen if you lost control of the domains of your life other than eating, fat, and weight?

3.2. Step 2. Assessing the Connection between Control of Eating, Weight, and Food and General Control of Life

The patient links his feelings of control to the control of fat and weight. The therapist encourages the patient to explore and critically discuss this link.

T. – Do you think that controlling eating, fat, and weight makes you more able to control anything else?
T. – Do you really believe that controlling fat and weight will enable you to control anything else?

The therapist attempts to make the patient aware that his or her restricted eating behaviors are a way to maintain control over reality and the self. For this reason, the therapist asks whether there is an underlying assumption that connects eating, weight, and/or fat with the sense of control.

T. – Is it possible that you feel that gaining weight, eating more, and or becoming fatter would give you a perception of lacking control?

T. – Is it possible that you feel that via the control of weight, eating, and/or fat you could succeed in controlling everything?

If the patient accepts this assumption that connects eating, weight, and fat with control as true, is it possible to assess whether the sense of control is a core belief, an important goal of his or her life.

T. – Do you think that control is important?

T. – Is control an important goal to you?

T. – How much time during the day do you think or worry about your sense of control?

The therapist/interviewer evaluates the degree of involvement of the patient with the belief of control using items 1, 2, and 3 in Table 2 (see Table 2 at the end of section 3.5).

3.3. Step 3. Reframing the Patient's Belief of Insufficient Control

Basically, the belief of control is an anxiety belief. The patient fears that his or her degree of control over his or her self, emotions, and the world is insufficient. The questions to test and challenge this assumption basically regards the fear of losing the feeling of control over the self and the world (Lehay & Holland, 2000).

The first step is a critical discussion of the connection between the fear of losing ones control of eating, fat, and weight and the fear of insufficient control:

T.– You fear that if you stop controlling your weight and fat, you will lose your self-control and self-esteem and your capacity to control events and your life. Is this fear justified?

T.– Let's imagine a weight suitable to your height and age. Is it acceptable to you? Or would that weight imply a condition of insufficient control?

The second step is to critically discuss the fear of insufficient general control, challenging the following beliefs:

T.– Is it possible to have a sudden, total, and catastrophic lack of control? Which proofs and/or clues do you present to support your fear of losing control?

T.– If possible, how much is probable?

T.– If probable, to what degree will this lack of control be severe and unbearable?

T.– How could you remedy this lack of control?

T.– Could you tolerate this lack of control?

The therapist attempts to make the patient cognizant of his or her past episodes of decreased control. The goal of this intervention is to conceptualize a reformulation of a tragic fear of insufficient control into a less dramatic awareness that it is possible to tolerate a degree of decreased control.

> T.– Are you sure that you have never lost the sense of control over your life? T.– If so, what happened? How did you manage that situation of insufficient control?
>
> T.– What exactly did you feel when that event of decreased control occurred? Did you suffer emotional or material damages?

Comparison with other less controlling people could be useful.

> T.– Do you know anyone that accepts a lesser degree of control?

Another intervention is imagining the future. What if the patient lost control? What might happen? The therapist leads the patient to recognize that it is possible to tolerate a partial decrease in control, and that in our lifetimes we have had many past experiences in which we did not have total control, and so on.

> T.– Please imagine that you'll lose some control. What might happen? Are you sure that the consequences will be catastrophic? Could we imagine less catastrophic scenarios?

In the end, the therapist actively encourages the patient to accept decreased control.

> T. – In the past, you lost control. How did this happen? Can you imagine what happens when you lose control? I think you would survive.

The therapist can also encourage the patient to feel that the fear of insufficient control is manageable. This is possible not only by criticizing catastrophic thought, but also by emotional training aimed at learning to tolerate negative emotions.

> T.– To you, decreased control means a negative emotional state. However, we can attempt to tolerate our negative emotions. What does tolerating a negative state of mind mean? Are you sure that you would not be able to tolerate it?

Another therapeutic tool is to encourage the patient to feel that he or she can remedy the decreased control

> T.– As we know, you judge the lack of control as a catastrophe. Are you sure that you cannot find a concrete remedy that would make this lack of control more manageable?

At this moment, the therapist can evaluate the success of reframing the belief of insufficient control.

The therapist assesses the reframing of the belief of insufficient control using items 4, 5, 6, 7, 8, and 9 in Table 2 (see Table 2 at the end of section 3.5).

3.4. Step 4. Reframing the Patient's Belief of Compulsory Control

The drive for control is an option, a choice, a goal in our mind. Thus, it is possible to consider it from a critical viewpoint. The therapist must encourage the patient to assume an attitude of detached self-observation and self-distancing from the drive for control. It is something more than the simple perception of insufficient control. It is the belief that it is possible and necessary to control everything. It is an active and obsessive desire for total control. We can call it the desire for control (Moulding & Kyrios, 2006) or the drive for compulsory control (Sassaroli & Ruggiero, 2002).

T. - Do you believe that it is possible to control everything?
T. - Do you believe that you are capable of controlling everything?
T. -Do you believe that it is necessary to control everything?

The therapist should encourage the patient to test the evidence for and against his or her beliefs that absolute control is necessary.

T.– You desire absolute control. Moreover, you feel compelled to pursue absolute control. But why? Did you ever explore which of your own ideas make this desire for control so necessary and compulsory?

The therapist should ascertain the chain of fears that underlie the compulsion to control.

T.– What might happen if you did not control eveything?

Sometimes, the assumption underlying the compulsion to control is an idea of responsibility. Total control is a type of moral necessity.

T.– You desire absolute control. Is it a moral problem? An issue of responsibility?

In other cases, there is a link between control and self-esteem, a link that reinforces these two beliefs with each other.

T. - What is the relationship between control and personal value?
T. - If you renounced your absolute control, would you fear losing your personal value?
T.– When you believe that you control everything, how do you judge yourself? And how do you feel?

Control can be linked to a vague ideation of perfection, of being special and different.

T. – Is there a relationship between control and your fear of making mistakes?
T. – Is there a relationship between control and your ideal of perfection?

The goal of having everything under control is not really a concrete goal, but a mental obsession. The patient fears the internal feelings linked with the demise of his or her ideation of absolute control.

This intervention is aimed towards the exploration and assessment of the emotions related to the desire for and the renouncement of absolute control. It is important that the patient learn what he or she actually feels in relationship with his or her ideas about absolute control.

> T.– For you, the renouncement of absolute control is a negative emotional state. However, what does it mean to tolerate a negative emotional state? Are you sure that you would be unable to tolerate this situation?

In addition, the therapist should encourage the patient to explore the pros and cons of the belief that absolute control is necessary.

> T. - What are the pros of always thinking in terms of absolute control?
> T. - What are the cons of always thinking in terms of absolute control?
> T. – How does this attempt to keep everything in control damage your life, your projects, and/or your goals?

The therapist must encourage the patient to imagine a different cognitive and emotional state of mind.

> T. - Can we try to imagine the benefit of not being mentally focused on this obsession with control?

The final segment of the treatment deals with the active and behavioural exposure to situations of non absolute control. The patient should dismiss the dichotomous opposition between absolute control and total lack of control. An active renouncement of control should mean a decreased but manageable degree of control. The therapist leads the patient to recognize that it is possible to implement and tolerate a partial renouncement to control everything without losing an acceptable degree of control over our lives.

During the session, the therapist and the patient jointly plan a behavioral program to actively renounce control.

The therapist assesses the reframing of the belief of insufficient control using items 10, 11, and 12 in Table 2 (see Table 2 at the end of section 3.5).

4. Conclusion

The present paper has outlined the basic elements of a psychotherapeutic cognitive treatment for ED, focused on biased beliefs in the domain of worry and control. Further research should evaluate the efficacy of this therapeutic protocol and its capacity to equal and perhaps increase the proven efficacy of other psychotherapeutic treatments for ED.

Table 2. Assessment of the phases of control-focused treatment of ED

		Strongly agree	Agree	Neutral	Disagree	Strongly disagree
Assessment of the patient's belief of control at the beginning of treatment						
1	The patient believes that he or she must strictly control eating, fat, and/or weight	☐	☐	☐	☐	☐
2	The patient believes that if he or she manages to control eating, fat, and/or weight he or she will have a feeling of general control	☐	☐	☐	☐	☐
3	The patient believes that control is an important aspect of life, and worries about it	☐	☐	☐	☐	☐
Assessment of the patient's reframing of the belief of insufficient control						
4	The patient criticizes the idea that his/her sense of control depends on eating, weight, and fat	☐	☐	☐	☐	☐
5	The patient accepts the idea that it is possible to tolerate a situation of insufficient control	☐	☐	☐	☐	☐
6	The patient agrees that he or she can accept negative emotions linked to a situation of decreased control	☐	☐	☐	☐	☐
7	The patient accepts the idea that it is possible to find remedies to cope with a situation of insufficient control	☐	☐	☐	☐	☐
8	The patient accepts the idea that there are situations of partial control in which we do not feel fear or anxiety.	☐	☐	☐	☐	☐
9	The patient recognizes that he or she actually has a acceptable degree of control.	☐	☐	☐	☐	☐
Assessment of the patient's reframing of the belief of compulsory control						
10	The patient criticizes the idea that absolute control is necessary	☐	☐	☐	☐	☐
11	The patient explores the ideas underlying his/her desire for absolute control (for example: responsibility, self-esteem, and so on)	☐	☐	☐	☐	☐
12	The patient plans a program to actively renounce control	☐	☐	☐	☐	☐

REFERENCES

Borkovec, T. D. (1993). The nature, functions, and origins of worry. In G. Davey & F. Tallis (Eds.), Worrying: Perspectives on theory, assessment and treatment. Chichester, England: Wiley, pp. 5-33

Borkovec, T. D., & Roemer L. (1995). Perceived functions of worry among generalized anxiety disorder subjects: distraction from more emotionally distressing topics? *Journal of Behavioral Health Service & Research, 26*, 25-30.

Bruch, H. (1973). *Eating Disorders: Obesity, Anorexia Nervosa and The Person Within*. New York: Basic Books.

Button, E. J. (1985). Eating disorders: A quest for control? In E. J. Button (Ed.), *Personal Construct Theory and Mental Health*. London: Croom Helm, pp. 153-168.

Davey, G. C. L., Startup, H. M., MacDonald, C. B., Jenkins, D., & Patterson, K. (2005). The use of "as many as can" versus "feel like continuing" stop rules during worrying. *Cognitive Therapy and Research, 29*, 155-169.

Davey, G. C. L., Tallis, F., & Capuzzo, N. (1996). Beliefs about the consequences of worrying. *Cognitive Therapy and Research, 20*, 499-520.

Fairburn, C. G., & Harrison, P. J. (2003). Eating disorders. *The Lancet, 361*, 407-416.

Fairburn, C. G., Cooper, Z., Shafran, R. (2003). Cognitive behavior therapy for eating disorders: a "transdiagnostic" theory and treatment. *Behavior Research and Therapy, 41*, 509-528.

Lehay, R. L. & Holland, S. J. (2000). *Treatment Plans and Interventions for Depression and Anxiety Disorders*. New York: The Guilford Press.

Lehay, R. L. (2002). Pessimism and the evolution of negativity. *Journal of Cognitive Psychotherapy, 16*, 295-316.

Moulding, R., & Kyrios, M. (2006). Anxiety disorders and control related beliefs: the exemplar of Obsessive–Compulsive Disorder (OCD). *Clinical Psychology Review, 26*, 573-583.

Sassaroli, S., & Ruggiero, G. M. (2002). I costrutti dell'ansia: obbligo di controllo, perfezionismo patologico, pensiero catastrofico, autovalutazione negativa e intolleranza dell'incertezza [The constructs of anxiety: Compulsion to control, pathological perfectionism, catastrophic thought, negative self-evaluation, and intolerance of uncertainty]. *Psicoterapia Cognitiva e Comportamentale, 8*, 45-60.

Sassaroli, S., Bertelli, S., Decoppi, M., Crosina, M., Milos, G., & Ruggiero, G.M. (2005). Worry and eating disorders: A psychopathological association. *Eating Behaviors, 6*, 301-307.

Sassaroli, S., Gallucci, M., & Ruggiero, G. M. (2007). Low perception of control as a cognitive factor of eating disorders. Its independent effects on measures of eating disorders and its interactive effects with perfectionism and self-esteem. *Journal of Behavior Therapy and Experimental Psychiatry, 39*, 467-488.

Segal, Z., Williams, M., & Teasdale, J. (2001). *Mindfulness-Based Cognitive Therapy for Depression*. New York: Guilford Press.

Slade, P. (1982). Toward a functional analysis of anorexia nervosa and bulimia nervosa. *British Journal of Clinical Psychology, 21*, 167-179.

Startup, H. M. & Davey, G. C. L. (2001). Mood as input and catastrophic worrying. *Journal of Abnormal Psychology, 110*, 83-96.

Vasey, M. W. & Borkovec, T. D. (1992). A catastrophizing assessment of worrisome thoughts. *Cognitive Therapy and Research, 16*, 1-16.

Wells, A. (1999). A cognitive model of generalized anxiety disorder. *Behavior Modification, 23*, 526-555.

In: Cognitive Therapy of Eating Disorders…
Editors: S. Sassaroli and G.M. Ruggiero
ISBN: 978-1-60876-617-8

Chapter 4

PATHOGENESIS OF BINGE EATING DISORDERS: LOSS OF CONTROL, IMPULSIVITY AND INTOLERANCE OF EMOTIONS

Piergiuseppe Vinai[1,2], Silvia Cardetti[1,2], Gabriela Carpegna[1,2], Noemi Ferrato[1,2], Paola Vallauri[1,2], Patrizia Todisco[3], and Elena Tugnoli[1]

[1] "Studi Cognitivi" Cognitive Psychotherapy School, Milano, Italy,
[2] GNOSIS, No-profit Research Group
[3] Eating Disorders Unit Spedali Civili Brescia

ABSTRACT

The chapter deals with clinical definition, nosography and pathogenesis of the binge eating disorder. Among pathogenetic hypotheses, the restraint theory, and the affect-driven models -a domain which includes the trade-off theory, the escape from self-awareness model, the masking theory, the blocking model, and the narrow emotional window model- are discussed. In conclusion, the binge eating disorder is conceptualized as a psychological disorders linked to feelings of emotional dyscontrol.

DEFINITION

Binge Eating Disorder (BED) was firstly described by A.Stunkard in 1959, as an eating disorder characterized by recurrent episodes of binge eating without compensatory weight-control behaviours, but fifty years later its diagnostic criteria are not yet completely defined. BED has been included in the DSM-IV B appendix (A.P.A., 1994) as a research category: this collocation was due to need for further researches in support of BED as a diagnostic construct. Recent studies (Grilo et al, 2009) support the hypothesis that BED is a stable condition (Pope, 2006) with a distinct psychopathology differing from other eating disorders.

Table 1. Diagnostic criteria for BED (APA 1994)

Recurrent episodes of binge eating associated with 3 or more of the following: *eating much more rapidly than normal* *eating until feeling uncomfortably full,* *eating large amount of food when not feeling hungry,* *eating alone because of being embarrassed by how much one is eating* *or feeling disgusted with oneself, depressed or very guilty after overeating.* *Marked distress regarding binge eating is present.* *The binge eating occurs, on average, at least 2/week, for 6 months.* *It is not associated with the regular use of inappropriate compensatory behaviors.*

The pathology is quite common among obese individuals, up to 30% of people who try to lose weight may suffer from BED. Approximately 2% of all adults in the United States suffer from BED. (Striegel-Moore, 2003) Concerning the prevalence of BED in Italy, rates have been shown to vary from 0,32 % (Faravelli et al., 2006) to 18.1% (Biondi & Spinosa, 2000) among obese people.

Despite the proliferation of studies (French, 1997; Moyer et al,. 1997; Fairburn, 1998; Hodges et al., 1998; Jackson et al., 2000; Womble et al., 2001; Striegel-Moore et al., 2002; Bulik et al., 2003) no specific risk factors have been identified until today, however genetic, neuroendocrine, familiar, social and psychological factors seem to be involved in pathogenesis of BED.

Past researches on risk factors for BED (Wolf & Crowther 1983; Greenberg & Harvey, 1987; Filstead, Parrella, & Ebbitt, 1988) were not based on APA 2000 diagnostic criteria or they didn't differentiate bulimic and BED patients, so it's quite impossible to compare those results with recent ones. Fairburn et al (1998) were the first to perform a retrospective study on risk factors for BED. Comparing 52 BED patients with 102 bulimic subjects they found among first ones a greater tendency to childhood obesity; on the other hand, patients affected by BN were during childhood more perfectionist and have a lower self esteem. After that study many others investigated risk factors for BED (French, 1997; Moyer, DiPietro, Berkowitz, & Stunkard, 1997; Fairburn, 1998; Hodges, Cochrane, & Brewerton, 1998; Jackson, Grilo, & Masheb, 2000; Womble et al., 2001; Striegel-Moore, Dohm, Pike, Wilfle, & Fairburn, 2002; Bulik, Sullivan, & Kendler, 2003), founding that in its pathogenesis are involved genetic (Bulik, Sullivan, & Kendler 2003), neuroendocrine, familiar, social and psychological factors. Among the last ones intolerance of negative emotions, seem to play a preminent role in onset and maintenaice of BED.

BED patients' families were characterized by high levels of criticism regarding body weight and shape, low interpersonal contact and high expectancies. Moreover the mothers were more anxious and worrying than those of control subjects (Fairburn et al., 1998). Negative self evaluation, sense of inefficacy (Didie & Fitzgibbon 2005), low self esteem, such as impulsivity (Galanti et al., 2007), difficulties in dealing with intense emotions (Whiteside et al., 2007) and over-evaluation of shape and weight (Mond et al., 2006) promote the onset of the pathology, even if the mechanism of their influence on BED is not yet completely clear. The diagnosis of a personality disorder during youth increases the risk for BED in adulthood (Johnson et al., 2006) and there are high perceived level of stress precede the onset of the pathology (Striegel-Moore et al., 2007). An Italian study (Fassino et al., 2002) reported that obese BED patients have lower scores on the Self-Directedness subscale of the Temperament and Character Inventory (TCI) compared with other obese subjects. This scoring seem to be a strong predictor for onset of BED. These results were confirmed by other authors (Hodges, Cochrane, & Brewerton 1998; French et al. 1997) that also report a low cohesion in these families. More recently, Grilo and Masheb (2001) assessing a sample of 145 BED through the Childhood Trauma Questionnaire found that 83% of the sample reports a childhood mistreat.

Despite these evidences, prospective studies didn't find a causal role of families in development of BED. Psychosocial factors seem to be more important in its pathogenesis. Physical abuses and to be bullyed by pears are specific risk factors (Striegel-Moore et al., 2002) and dissatisfaction for own shape and weight (Womble et al., 2001) explain about the 70% of the variance of symptoms.

Nosographic Hypothesis

Several nosographic models of BED have been proposed by authors, since the first classification by Stunkard (1959); nevertheless there is not yet a unanimous classification of this eating disorder. Brody (1994) don't considered BED an eating disorder but only one of the way of eating of obese subjects such as over eat during the meals. Stunkard and Allison (2003) affirmed that it emerges when obesity and depression coexist in a patient, but data from international literature affirm that not all BED patients are affected by depression. (Grilo 2001; Stice 2001), while is more frequent in BED subjects the co existence of obesity disinhibition and impulsivity (De Zwann et al., 1994, Galanti et al., 2007). Devlin et al. (2003) suggest that binge eating is a typical way of eating of obese subjects having problems with their own body image but this hypothesis was subsequently disconfirmed; Didie & Fitzgibbon (2005) reported that psychological distress among BED patients is related to their eating behaviour and not to their weight. Moreover binge episodes seem more related to impulsivity and disinhibition than to caloric restrictions (Galanti et al. 2007; Stein et al. 2007). Stein et al. (2007) think that binge episodes are more related to negative emotions than to hunger or diet, but coexistence of food deprivation and negative emotions seem to increase the possibility of a binge episode.

Fairburn et al (2000) found a spontaneous remission of symptoms in subject affected by BED; the inconstancy of symptoms and the needless of a specific treatment have conduct some researchers to sustain that BED was an Eating Disorder Not Otherwise Specified

(EDNOS), considering binging only a symptom often present also in other eating disorders. Nevertheless a cluster analysis (Mizes & Sloan, 1998) found in patients affected by BED a different evolution of BMI, different bulimic behaviours and different ideas on ideal weight and body dissatisfaction. In our clinical experiences these results are confirmed: binge eaters worry less than subjects affected by bulimia nervosa and, most important, they experiment an unpleasant perception of loss of control on their own eating, differently from obese subjects not affected by BED.

Until a few years ago Fairburn et al. (2000) supposed that was not a specific eating disorder because it was not stable and had frequently spontaneous remissions, but the same authors changed their opinions on BED considering it more stable that it was supposed.

However, data regarding recovery rates of BED are controversial, Fichter and Quadflieg (2007) reported the recovery rates at 2, 6, and 12 years to be 65, 78, and 67%, respectively. Pope et al. (2006). reported an average duration of BED of 14.4 years in their family study. Probably BED differs from other eating disorders in terms of a greater tendency toward recovery and fluctuation, although this may be embedded in a chronic pattern of remission and relapse (Wonderlich,et al 2009).

Hay & Fairburn (1998) consider bulimia nervosa purging, bulimia nervosa non-purging & BED forms of increasing severity of the same pathology. Against this hypothesis is the evidence that bulimic patients, either purging or not, have common characteristics such as intolerance of uncertainty, control over eating, over-evaluation of body shape and weight. These factors don't play a preeminent role in BED. These patients are not so pervasively worrying on body shape and weight, so for they weight increasing is only a side effect of binging that they tolerate such as they cannot modify their state. In fact they don't reduce food intake when do not binge. Moreover bulimic patients after binge episodes constantly and immediately try to eliminate the excessive food intake (Masheb & Grilo 2000) through purging behaviour and physic exercise. BED patients rarely purge or diet. There are other characteristics differencing BED from bulimic patients. The core cognitive construct of people affected by bulimia is the weight control and their attention is focused on body shape. Bulimic subjects seem to be characterized by uncertainty intolerance e compulsion to control, binge eaters, instead, are dissatisfied of their weight, but they do not pay much attention on it, or they are unhopeful about weight loss: in effect, they often get on diet, but with scarce motivation and results. Moreover these attempts are not directed to loose the weight gained with the last binge, like bulimic subjects do (Masheb & Grilo 2000) and binges do not often follow food restriction as in bulimia nervosa. In our opinion, binge eaters think more to handling of emotion than weight control. Among BED distribution among genders is similar (Yanowsky, 1993), binge episodes precede dieting (Santonastaso et al., 1999), age of onset is lower, average BMI is higher (Raymond et al., 1995) and BED patients introduce during binge episodes less food than bulimic patients do Guss et al. (1994).

In our opinion BED is a peculiar pathology, because these patients don't think and don't feed themselves (yet not during binge episodes) as obese and bulimic patients do. In particular it is different the way of thinking about food: binge eaters consider it an allied in fighting negative emotions, that bring with it guilty and overweight. Subjects affected by bulimia nervosa consider food an enemy and work hardly to control it, even if sometimes they are defeated and indulge in binging.

Even the motivation that induces a binge eater to ask for a psychotherapy is different: he often looks for a weight reduction with the unrealistic hope of maintaining binges. When a binge has occurred, bulimic subject try immediately to repair with compensatory behaviours, while binge eater is more passive and seized by guilt, discomfort and resignation. However they distinguish from people affected by mood disorder for impulsivity and loss of control, more typical of border personality disorder. Patients affected by BED partially respond to therapy of bulimia nervosa or therapy for depression.

Our hypothesis is confirmed by several researches: among obese patients the level of psychopathology (Cacheline et al. 1999; Wilson et al. 1993) and body dissatisfaction (Telch et al. 1988) is related to the tendency to compulsive eating and not with BMI. Moreover even though BED patients are more frequently involved in diets than other obese subjects, there is no relationship between dieting and binge episodes' frequency (Wilfley et al., 2000). Impulsivity (Galanti et al. 2007) and difficulty in regulation of emotions seem to be the driving factors of binge episodes, more than dietary restriction and iper evaluation of weight and body shape (Whiteside et al. 2007). Even after binge episodes there is a great difference between bulimic and BED patients. The firsts immediately try to remediate either purging or dieting the seconds accept passively the effects of binge episodes. All these considerations induces us think that BED is a proper eating disorder with own specific onset and maintaining mechanism.

PATHOGENESIS

Pathogenetic mechanisms of BED have not been cleared yet. Two main categories of theoretical models try to explain onset and maintenance of binge episodes (Stein et al. 2007): the Restraint Theory (Howard & Porzelius 1999) and the Affect-driven Models.

Restraint Theory

Patients pathologically focused on shape and weight restrain their food intake until deprivation of food induces binge episodes (Howard & Porzelius 1999). The dichotomic thinking "if you don't control everything, you don't control anything" induces a negative mood and a lower self esteem contributing to maintain the pathology. The attempt to compensate binge eating induces further episodes of loss of control on eating.

This mechanism is at the basis of pathogenesis of Bulimia Nervosa but its relevance in BED is not clear. Dietary restriction is not frequent among BED patients and they have more a chaotic than a restrictive diet (Wilfley et al. 2000; Galanti et al. 2007; Whiteside et al. 2007).

Affect-Driven Models

According with others (Stein et al. 2007), we (Vinai & Todisco, 2007, 2008) think that emotive dysregulation plays a preeminent role in onset and maintenance of BED. Many theoretical models tried to explain the relationship between emotion and food intake; below we recall some of them.

The **trade-off theory** hypothesize that binge-eating is maintained by a trade-off' in which a highly aversive emotional state (i.e. depression) is exchanged for a less aversive state such as sense of guilty for overeating. Kenardy, Arnow, & Agras (1996) found that binge-eaters had significantly greater distress and lower tolerance of negative mood compared to controls, furthermore the emotions reported before binges were more aversive than those reported below.

The **escape from self-awareness model** (Heatherton & Baumeister 1991) proposes that binge eating is an attempt to escape from self-awareness. Binge eaters suffer from high standards and expectations and an acute sensitivity to the external demands. When they fall, develop an emotional distress due to an unflattering view of self and concern on others' perception of themselves. They attempt to escape from this unpleasant state narrowing attention to food and avoiding broadly meaningful thought, obeying to the rule: "What I don't see, it doesn't exist". Moreover, during binging, there is a sort of stop to the time, the patient doesn't think to past feelings and future consequences of his behaviour. This fact could allow patient to repeat binge episode even if, as soon as he finished to eat, he feels bad every time. This process disengages normal inhibitions against eating (Heatherton & Baumeister, 1991)

The **masking theory** (Polivy & Herman 1999) hypothesizes that patients avoid dealing with the actual source of their negative affect by engaging in binge eating, in this way the loss of control on food intake can be misused to mask the real causes of emotional distress.

The **blocking model** hypothesize that bulimic behaviour is induced by the attempt to block the emotions when they are perceived too strong from the subject (Root, Fallon 1989).

Patients refer frequently to feel intolerable negative emotions before binge episodes: food stops them inducing a sort of emotional anaesthesia, the only way they think to have to control emotions. On the other hand, as morphine induce a dependence, binge episodes tend to maintain themselves: if a patient doesn't experience other possibilities to front negative affects he becomes more and more unable to deal with them involving himself in endless spiral made of food excess and negative emotions.

The narrow emotional window model (Vinai & Todisco, 2007) summarize the mechanism of onset and maintenance of BED in the following scheme: a personality characterized by impulsivity, perfectionism, low self esteem, drive for control, when deals with interpersonal problems if has a narrow emotional window risks to binge to sustain anxiety due to perception of unsustainable emotions. The sense of guilt and the shame due to weight gain maintains high levels of anxiety that contribute to sustain binge eating. In effect several researches revealed high levels of anxiety in patients affected by BED, since childhood (Tanofsky-Kraffs et al, 2008; Czaje et al, 2009). Children presenting Loss of Control (LOC) eating shown to experience more anxiety and eating related distress than others, and report more frequently emotional eating.

The dysfunctional belief sustaining this behaviour is the conviction that several emotions are not tolerable, this induces binge eaters think that the only way to front them is avoid their perception, a sort of emotional anaesthesia (i.e. alexithymia), instead of learning to deal with them, so the most of the time they don't recognize emotions. In effect several studies put in evidence the presence of alexithymia among patients dealing with BED (Pinaquy, et al, 2003, Carano et al. 2006). Recently Carano et al. (2006) found that difficulty in identifying and describing feelings were significantly associated with more severe BED, as well as with the presence of lower self-esteem and higher body dissatisfaction. Basing on these results, the authors hypothesize that alexithymia could play an indirect role in onset and maintenance of BED.

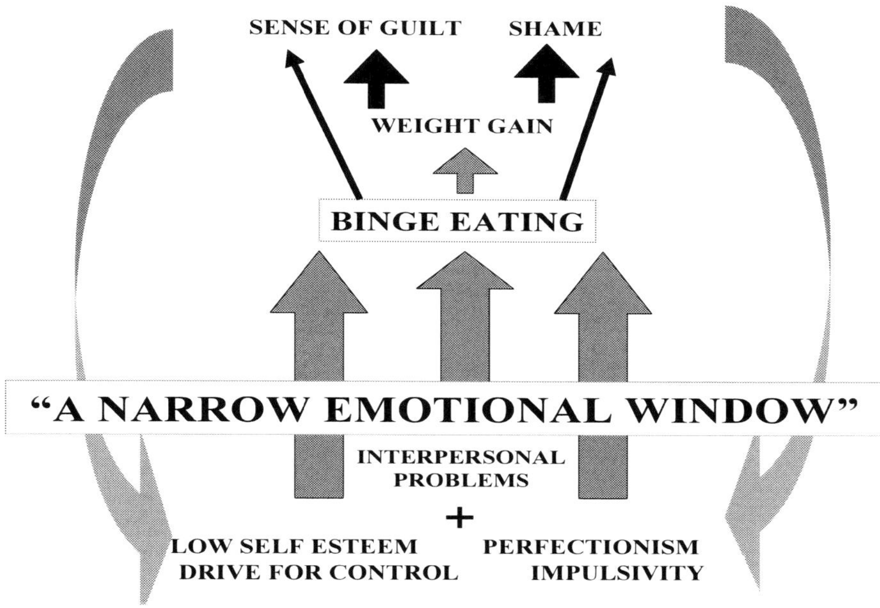

Figure 1. The narrow emotional window model.

So, binge eaters only felt those emotions reaching a so much higher intensity that it's impossible not to feel them. This behaviour induces suddenly intense anxiety and, given the conviction of being unable to front it, the patient feels himself powerless (Vinai & Todisco, 2007). Bingeing is the results the failure of the attempt to control anxiety due to emotional arousal.. Summarizing one of the crucial factors sustaining BED is the coexistence of alexithymia and intolerance of emotions in subjects that fear emotions, probably due to their incapability of recognize and deal with them.

The role of anxiety it's confirmed by several studies. Stice et al (2000) researching on 631 patients found a relationship between negative emotions such as anxiety, boredom, anger and binge episodes. In a recent research (Czaja, 2009) on children it was found that children presenting LOC eating used significant more maladaptive strategies for the regulation of anxiety than for the regulation of other emotion (sadness, anger).

Frequently patients are unable to distinguish physical sensations related to anxiety from hunger and overeat trying to reduce its unpleasant sensations and the sense of weakness and loose of control related to this emotion. Masheb & Grilo (2006) found that frequently BED patients overeat when are affected by dysphoric emotions such as anxiety, the most frequent, mood, loneliness tiredness and anger: The authors found no relationship between BMI and binge episodes, while they seem related to disinhibition, worry on food and overvaluation of shape and weight.

These patients don't tolerate intense emotions so are frequently debated between the unpleasant sensation of absence of emotions and the fear of a too strong emotion.

Binge eating is the only answer to fear of emotions thought intolerable: loneliness, sense of lack of value, conviction to be unable to front difficulties, sense of guilt. Given his low elf esteem and intolerance to anxiety, the patient doesn't think that in the future he will overcome the emotional difficulty, so his distress has to be solved immediately. So food is seen as the easier instrument to reduce anxiety. Patients frequently describe this feeling as something similar to the craving described by patients drugs addicted, inducing them to binge in a state similar to a trance. Also in a prospective study (Tanoffsky-Kraff et al., 2008) children experiencing LOC eating reported a sense of "numbing" that made difficult for them recall the amount of eaten food.

Anxiety due to weight management is a problem adding to fear of increasing emotions. In effect, psychological characteristics of these patients, like unrealistic expectations regarding weight loss and dichotomous thinking don't help them to loose weight, so they have frequently histories of drop outs from diets that reinforce emotional distress linked to weight reduction. These failures confirm their conviction to be unable to loose weight and achieve primary goals related to weight loss: attractiveness, social desirability, interpersonal relationships, self esteem, work possibilities and healt.

Summarizing, people affected by binge eating feel themselves ineffective in deal with emotions, so much frightening to loose control and induce binging. At the same time, self judgement on the chosen solution (food) bring patient to a negative self evaluation that reinforce low self esteem and increase fear of deal with negative affects.

REFERENCES

APA, American Psychiatric Association (1994). *Diagnostic and Statistical Manual of Mental Disorders (DSM-IV), 4th edn.* Washington DC: American Psychiatric Press.

Biondi, M., & Spinosa, E. (2000). Obesity and Binge Eating: prevalence, significance, therapeutic possibilities in a selected population of obese adolescents. *Minerva Pediatrica, 52*, 521.

Bulik, C. M., Sullivan, P. F., & Kendler, K.S. (1998). Heritability of binge-eating and broadly defined bulimia nervosa. *Biological Psychiatry, 44*, 1210-8.

Bulik, C. M., Sullivan, P. F., & Kendler, K. S. (2003). Genetic and environmental contributions to obesity and binge eating. *International Journal of Eating Disorders, 33*, 293-8.

Cachelin, F. M., Striegel-Moore, R. H., Elder, K. A., Pike, K. M., Wilfley, D. E., & Fairburn, C. G. (1999). Natural course of a community sample of women with binge eating disorder. *International Journal of Eating Disorders, 25*, 45-54.

Carano, A., De Berardis, D., Gambi, F., Di Paolo, C., Campanella, D., Pelusi, L., Sepede, G., Mancini, E., La Rovere, R., Salini, G., Cotellessa, C., Salerno, R. M., Ferro, F. M. (2006). Alexithymia and body image in adult outpatients with binge eating disorder. *International Journal of Eating Disorders, 39*, 332-40.

Czaja, J. M. A., Rief, W., & Hilbert, A. (2009). Emotion regulation in binge eating Children, *International Journal of Eating Disorder, 42*, 356-362.

De Zwaan, M., Mitchell, J. E., Seim, H. C., Specker, S. M., Pyle, R. L., Raymond, N. C., & Crosby, R. B. (1994). Eating related and general psychopathology in obese females with binge eating disorder. *International Journal of Eating Disorders, 15*, 43-52.

Devlin, M. J., Goldfein, J. A., & Dobrow, I. (2003). What is this thing called BED? Current status of binge eating disorder nosology. *International Journal of Eating Disorders,* 34 (Suppl 1), 2-18.

Didie, E. R., & Fitzgibbon, M. (2005). Binge eating *Eating Behaviors, 6,* 35-41.

Fairburn, C. G., Cooper, Z., Doll, H. A., Norman, P., & O'Connor, M. (2000). The natural course of bulimia nervosa and binge eating disorder in young women. *Archives of General Psychiatry, 57*, 659-65.

Fairburn, C. G., Doll, H. A., Welch, S. L., Hay, P. J., Davies, B. A., & O'Connor, M. E. (1998). Risk factors for binge eating disorder. *Archives of General Psychiatry, 55*, 425–432.

Faravelli, C., Ravaldi, C., Truglia, E., Zucchi, T., Cosci, F., & Ricca, V. (2006). Clinical epidemiology of eating disorders: results from the Sesto Fiorentino study. *Psychotherapy and Psychosomatics, 75*, 376-83

Fassino, S., Leombruni, P., Pierò, A., Daga, G.A., Amianto, F., Rovera, G., & Rovera, G. G. (2002). Temperament and character in obese *Comprehensive Psychiatry*, *43,* :431-7.

Fichter, M. M., Quadflieg, N. Long-term stability of eating disorder diagnoses. *International Journal of Eating Disorders* 2007;40:S61–S66

Filstead,, W. J., Parrella, D. P., & Ebbitt, J. (1988) High-risk situations for engaging in substance abuse and binge-eating behaviors. *Journal of Studies on Alcohol and Drugs, 49*, 136-41.

French, S. A., Story, M., Neumark-Sztainer, D., Downes, B., Resnick, M., & Blum, R. (1997). Ethnic differences in psychosocial and health behavior correlates of dieting, purging, and binge eating in a population-based sample of adolescent females. *International Journal of Eating Disorder, 22*, 315-22

Galanti, K., Gluck, M. E., & Geliebter, A. (2007). Test meal intake in obese *International Journal of Eating Disorder,40*, 727-32

Greenberg, B. R., & Harvey, P. D. (1987). Affective lability versus depression as determinants of bing eating. *Addictive Behaviors, 12*, 357-61.

Grilo, C. M., Masheb, R. M., Wilson, G.T. (2001). Subtyping binge eating disorder. *Journal of Consulting and Clinical Psychology, 69,* 1066-72.

Grilo, C. M., & Masheb, R. M. (2001). Childhood psychological, physical, and sexual maltreatment in outpatient with binge eating disorder: frequency and association with gender, obesity, and eating-related psychopathology. *Obesity Research*, 9, 320-325.

Grilo, C. M., White, M. A., & Masheb, R. M. (2009). DSM-IV psychiatric disorder comorbidity and its correlates in binge eating disorder. *International Journal of Eating Disorders, 42*, 228–234

Guss, J. L., Kissilef, H. R., Walsh, B. T., & Devlin, M. J. (1994). Binge eating behaviour in patients with eating disorders. *Obesity Research, 2*, 355-363.

Hay ,P., Fairburn, C. (1998). The validity of the DSM-IV scheme for classifying bulimic eating disorders. *International Journal of Eating Disorders, 23*, 7-15.

Heatherton, T.F., Baumeister, R.F. (1991). Binge Eating as escape from self-awareness. *Psychological Bulletin, 110*, 86-108

Hodges, E. L., Cochrane, C. E., & Brewerton, T. D. (1998). Family characteristics of binge-eating disorder patients. *International Journal of Eating Disorders, 23,* 145-51.

Howard, C. E., & Porzelius, L. K. (1999). The role of dieting *Clinical Psychology Review, 19*, 25-44.

Jackson, T. D., Grilo, C. M., & Masheb, R. M. (2000). Teasing history, onset of obesity, current eating disorder psychopathology, body dissatisfaction, and psychological functioning in binge eating disorder. *Obesity Research, 8*, 451-8.

Johnson, J. G., Cohen, P., Kasen, S., & Brook, J. S. (2006). Personality disorder *International Journal of Eating Disorders, 39*, 184-92.

Kenardy, J., Arnow, B., & Agras, W. S. (1996). The aversiveness of specific emotional states associated with binge-eating in obese subjects. *Australian and New Zealand Journal of Psychiatry, 30*, 839–844.

Masheb, R. M., & Grilo, C. M. (2000). On the relation of attempting to lose weight, restraint, and binge eating in outpatients with binge eating disorder. *Obesity Research, 8*, 638-45

Masheb, R. M., & Grilo, C.M. (2006). Emotional overeating *International Journal of Eating Disorder, 39*, 141-6

Mizes, J. S., & Sloan, D. M. (1998). An empirical analysis of eating disorder, not otherwise specified: preliminary support for a distinct subgroup. *International Journal Eating Disorder, 23*, 233-42.

Mond, J. M., Hay, P. J., Rodgers, B., & Owen, C. (2006). Recurrent binge eating *Behaviour Research and Therapy, 45*, 929-38.

Moyer, D. M., Di Pietro, L., Berkowitz, R. I., & Stunkard, A. J. (1997). Childhood sexual abuse and precursors of binge eating in an adolescent female population. *International Journal of Eating Disorder, 21*, 23-30.

Pinaquy, S., Chabrol, H., & Simon, C. (2003). Emotional eating, alexithymia, and binge-eating disorder in obese women. *Obesity Research, 11*, 195.

Polivy, J., & Herman, C. P. (1999). Distress and eating *International Journal of Eating Disorder, 26*, 153-64.

Pope, H. G., Lalonde, J. K., Pindyck, L. J., Walsh, B. T., Bulik, C. M., & Crow, S. J. (2006). Binge eating disorder: A stable syndrome. *American Journal of Psychiatry,163*, 2181–2183.

Raymond, N. C., Mussel, M. P., Mitchell, J. E., De Zwan. M., & Crosby, R. D. (1995). An age-matched comparison of subjectswith binge eating disorder and bulimia nervosa. *International Journal of Eating Disorders, 18*, 135-143.

Santonastaso, P. (1999). A preventive intervention program in adolescent schoolgirls: a longitudinal study. *Psychotherapy and Psychosomatic, 68*, 46-50.

Stein, R. I., Kenardy, J., Wiseman, C. V., Dounchis, J. Z,, Arnow, B. A., & Wilfley, D. E. (2007). What's driving the binge in binge eating *International Journal Eating Disorder, 40*, 195-203.

Stice, E., Agras, W. S., Telch, C. F., Halmi, K. A., Mitchell, J. E., & Wilson, T. (2001). Subtyping binge eating-disordered women along dieting and negative affect dimensions. *International Journal of Eating Disorders, 30*, 11-27.

Striegel-Moore, R. H., Dohm, F. A., Pike, K. M., Wilfley, D. E., & Fairburn, C. G. (2002). Abuse, bullying, and discrimination as risk factors for binge eating disorder. *American Journal of Psychiatry, 159*, 1902-7.

Striegel-Moore, R. H., & Franko, D. L. (2003). Epidemiology of binge eating disorder. *International Journal of Eating Disorder, 34*, (suppl. 1) 19-29

Stunkard, A.J., & Allison, K.C. (2003). Binge Eating Disorder: Disorder or Marker? *Internation Journal of Eating Disorder, 34*, 107-116.

Tanofsky-Kraff, M., Marcus, D. M., Yanosky, S. Z., & Yanosky, J. A., (2008). Loss of control eating disorder in children age 12 years and younger: Proposed research criteria, *Eating Behaviors, 9*, 360-365.

Telch, C. F., Agras, W. S., & Rossiter E. M. (1988). Binge eating increases with increasing adiposity. *International Journal of Eating Disorders; 7*, 115-119.

Vinai, P., & Todisco P. (2007). *Quando le Emozioni Diventano Cibo*. Milano: Libreria Cortina.

Todisco P, & Vinai P (2008). *La Fame Infinita*. Torino: Centro scientifico editore.

Whiteside, U., Chen, E., Neighbors, C., Hunter, D., Lo, T., & Larimer, M. (2007). Difficulties regulating emotions *Eating Behaviour, 8*, 162-9.

Wilfley, D.E. (2000). Comorbid psychopathology in binge eating disorder: relation to eating disorder severity at baseline and following treatment. *Journal of Consulting and Clinical Psychology ,68*, 641-9.

Wilson, G. T., Nonas, C. A., & Rosenblum, G. D. (1993). Assessment of binge eating in obese patients. *International Journal of Eating Disorder, 8*, 173-179.

Wolf, E. M., & Crowther, J. H. (1983). Personality and eating habit variables as predictors of severity of binge eating and weight. *Addictive Behaviour, 8*, 335-44

Womble, L. G., Williamson, D. A., Martin, C. K., Zucker, N. L., Thaw, J. M., Netemeyer, R., Lovejoy, J. C., & Greenway, F. L. (2001). Psychosocial variables associated with binge eating in obese males and females. *International Journal of Eating Disorder, 30*, 217-21.

Wonderlich, S. A., Gordon, K. H., Mitchell, J. E., Crosby, R.D., Engel, S. G. The validity and clinical utility of binge eating disorder.*International Journal of Eating Disorder* 2009 Dec;42(8):687-705.,

Yanovski, S. Z. (1993). Binge eating disorder. Current knowledge and future directions. *Obesity Research, 1*, 306-324.

In: Cognitive Therapy of Eating Disorders...
Editors: S. Sassaroli and G.M. Ruggiero
ISBN: 978-1-60876-617-8

Chapter 5

PARENTAL CRITICISM, RESPONSIBILITY AND HUMILIATION IN EATING DISORDERS

Marina Apparigliato[2], Francesca Fiore[1], Giovanni Maria Ruggiero[1], Clarice Mezzaluna[2], Carmelo Lamela[3], and Sandra Sassaroli[2]

[1]Psicoterapia Cognitiva e Ricerca, Post-graduate Cognitive Psychotherapy School, Milano, Italy

[2]Studi Cognitivi, Post-graduate Cognitive Psychotherapy School , Milano, San Benedetto del Tronto, Italy

[3]Scuola Cognitiva Firenze, Post-graduate Cognitive Psychotherapy School, Firenze, Italy

ABSTRACT

Th is chapter explores the developmental ground of the cognitive beliefs of control and perfectionism: criticism in the relationship with parents of individuals with eating disorders. Eating disorders would be related to a process in which perceived criticism is the initial factor and perfectionism and control are intervening factors. In addition, the link between perceived criticism and two possible correlates like sense of responsibility and humiliation is explored.

INTRODUCTION

Parental criticism is a relational style, particularly detrimental and source of important distresses for children. We define parental criticism as a repetitive and pervading recourse to blaming by one or both parents towards their children. Many studies gave evidence of the psychopathological implications of a relational style based on reproach. As a matter of fact, criticism has been connected with different psychological disorders during the years of growth (Asarnow et al., 1994; Hibbs et al., 1991; Schwartz et al., 1990; Stubbe et al., 1993) and during the adult age, such as the tendency to relapses in depressed and schizophrenic patients (Butzlaff & Hooley, 1998) and worse treatment results as to the obsessive-compulsive disorder (Chambless & Steketee, 1999) and the post traumatic stress disorder (Tarrier, Sommerfield, & Pilgrim 2000).

Among the clinicians who regularly attend to patients with eating disorders, the connection between this disorder and parental criticism is well-known. Numerous authors (Bruch, 1973; Guidano & Liotti, 1983; Reda, 1986; Lorenzini & Sassaroli, 2000) pointed out how often one can find parents with both high expectations and reproaching and blaming behaviour towards any attempt of the construction of an autonomous identity in the history of these patients. According to Hilde Bruch (1973) the anorexia nervosa is connected with an identity and an autonomy disorder due to the fact that the parents have always imposed their will to the daughter without considering her wishes. The daughter's answer to this intrusive and blaming attitude is often an extreme compliance which makes her a girl that truly satisfies her parents, but who, whenever facing the intricacy of the problems linked with her adolescence, feels disorientated, empty and impotent.

The experimental data we hold, concerning the criticism of the parents of patients with eating disorders, refer to the positive correlation between the presence of this variable in the parents and the clinical course and clinical progress of the daughters as well as the increased tendency to drop-outs and relapses of these patients. Van Furth, Strien, Martina, Son, Hendrikx, and Engeland (1996) pointed out that maternal criticism is the best predictor of the clinical course of the daughter when compared with other indexes such as emotional over-involvement, hostility, diagnosis, duration of disorder, weight, age, body-mass index. Le Grange (1999) revealed an important correlation between parental criticism and the drop-out or the therapeutic failures in adolescents with an anorexia nervosa diagnosis.

The intricate links between parental criticism and eating disorders, pointed out by clinicians and subject of therapeutic intervention, require a wider experimental analysis which justifies the numerous clinical reports on the subject.

A Cognitive Analysis of Criticism

An exhaustive cognitive analysis permits to define the blaming person as a subject that pursues the aim to modify and to control the behaviour, the attitudes and the convictions of others by practicing reproaches, being convinced to know what is good or bad for the others.

Blaming is a behaviour that can be commonly observed in the education ambit. As a matter of fact, the lessons a child receives include a series of rules which will help him/her to distinguish what is right from what is wrong. Unfortunately, the blaming person exercises intense, pervading and extended reproaches which result to be detrimental for whom is subjected to them. Furthermore, although the use of reproaches as an instrument meant to help the child to learn the rules is comprehensive, we must keep in mind that the moral development does not consist in the mere acquisition of a series of rules, but that it is rather fostered by encouraging the development of the emotional capacities, (as emotions are determinant for decisions, also for moral decisions) or by encouraging the development of the empathic capacity and of the meta-cognitive abilities which are necessary to understand the mind of the other person and the consequences our actions can have on him/her.

The blaming parent constantly reproaches his/her child by judging his/her behaviour, attitudes or decisions as not correct, even if these are the result of personal preferences. He/She therefore makes normative esteems even in fields in which it would be convenient to encourage the child's expression of his/her own preferences and an autonomous construction of his/her identity.

We hold the opinion that this takes place due to the fact that the blaming parent tends to consider his/her intents as standards that are universally valid or anyhow valid for the person subjected to the critic. This operation implies the intents of the other person is not taken into consideration or, anyway, in case this should occur, not to renounce the own point of view and thus to commit meta-cognitive errors (Fonagy et al., 1991; Fonagy & Target, 2000; Liotti, 1992; Perris & Mc Gorry, 2000; Semerari, 1999).

Nearly always, the blaming person has the aim to change the other person, by making sure that he/her follows his/her directives. This desire to modify the behaviour of the other person by means of reproaches presumes the belief that the other person has the possibility to behave in a different way and, most of all, that it is possible to induce him/her to change by either communicating that he/her commits an error or by disapproving him/her. When this happens, which is quite frequent in the case of future anorexics who become extremely condescending, this implies an extremely high price for the criticized subject in terms of self-esteem, confidence in the own possibilities and as far as the exploration of the own resources is concerned.

In other cases the criticized subject does not comply with the blaming parent's requests, thus increasing the recourse of the parent to reproach, despite the failure of the own educational method, he/her will reintroduce it with major insistence, convinced that this will lead the subject to understand and change, or believing that sooner or later his/her turn will come and that it is important not to miss that occasion.

The Consequences of Criticism

Growing up in an environment filled with criticism can undermine many aspects of people's lives. As with other types of abuse, consistent parental criticism is not recognized by the person who is subjected to it, but limits self-esteem. Children do not have the intellectual capacity to question the veracity of their parent's criticism. Rather, they internalize their parent's beliefs that they are not good enough, that they can never do anything right.

The validation data of the Perceived Criticism Inventory, an instrument we created in order to esteem the quantity of criticism received, as well as some qualitative aspects of the reproach (Apparigliato et al., 2007) confirms the frequent clinical observation, according to which particularly the more criticised subjects are those who are less conscious of the criticism received and the more prone to retain it a valid method of education. Using this instrument, we made an explorative research, meant to outline an experimental study, from which emerges a close relationship between parental criticism and low self-esteem as well as a close association between the content of the received reproaches and the degree of consent with these statements.

Another important point which emerged regards the link between parental criticism and pathological perfectionism in children. This association is cited in international literature and was subject to numerous experimental examinations. Frost, Lahart, and Rosenblate (1991) observed that mothers and fathers of perfectionists are perceived by their own children as more critic, more blaming and less permissive. Other authors pointed out that highly controlling mothers tend to have children with perfectionist concerns (Kenney-Benson & Pomerantz, 2005). The research about perfectionism has established that this construct is multidimensional in that it consists of personal aspects (self-oriented perfectionism) and social aspects (other-oriented perfectionism and socially prescribed perfectionism) and also adaptive (high standards) and maladaptive (concern over mistakes) components (Frost et al., 1990; Hamachek, 1978; Hewitt & Flett, 1990). Neurotic perfectionists experienced their parents as less encouraging, more demanding and more critical than did normal perfectionists (Rice, Ashby, & Preusser, 1996) So whenever parental expectations tend to associate more adaptive aspects of perfectionism, then criticism seems to be a key element for the increase of maladaptive aspects (Rice, Lopez, & Vergara, 2005) such as intolerance towards error which is experienced as irreparable and catastrophic (Hamachek, 1978; Frost et al., 1990; Sassaroli & Ruggiero, 2002). Normal perfectionists are motivated by needs for achievement, whereas neurotic perfectionists are motivated by fears of failure and of criticism. Flett, Hewitt, and Singer (1995) examined the association between dimensions of perfectionism and parental authority styles and found that socially prescribed perfectionism is associated with reports of exposure to an authoritarian parenting style characterized by restriction, punishment and overcontrol. Even if this association was only present for the men in this study. On the contrary, Tozzi et al. (2004) suggest features of perfectionism may be genetically determined. They examine the structure of perfectionism using classical twin design models. The results suggest that perfectionism, is partially heritable. However, not all facets of perfectionism appear to be equally heritable. Additive genetic factors appear to contribute more strongly to high standards.

Our data, still of an exploratory value, confirm the connection between parental criticism and perfectionism. In particular, the dimensions of criticism which appear chiefly correlated with the pathological aspects of perfectionism as well as with low levels of self-esteem regard incapacity contents and a modality using forms of psychological violence. These aspects are more predictive of perfectionism than the quantity of received criticism.

A large body of research assumes that both perfectionism and low self-esteem are common antecedents of eating disorders (Fairburn & Harrison, 2003; Halmi et al, 2000; Hewitt, Flett, & Ediger, 1995; Vitousek & Hollon, 1990) and even maladaptive eating attitudes in non-clinical individuals (Button et al., 1996; Sassaroli & Ruggiero, 2005).

Another result of parental criticism which is frequent in clinical observation is the development of a certain personal disorientation and an insufficient construction of the own identity. Resorting to the normative criteria inherent in criticism, does in fact not encourage the exploration of the own preferences or, in case this is done, does not facilitate an attitude of self-confidence and confidence in the own opinions. The criticised subject tends to develop a dependence on the interpersonal contest. One of the most common consequences of growing up in a critical environment is, in fact, the endless quest for external validation. Criticism teaches children that confirmation of their worthiness or unworthiness exists outside themselves. Other people's words are invested with the power to validate or invalidate their sense of self. It is also typical to find these characteristics in patients with eating disorders.

Parental Criticism and Control in ED

For Sassaroli, Gallucci, and Ruggiero (2008) the construct of control, conceptualized as anxious perception of low control over external threats and emotional reactions, is applicable also to ED. In fact, the need for ED subjects to feel in control of their lives, which gets displaced by controlling eating, weight, and body shape, implies a pervading perception of insufficient control.

Individuals with eating disorders pursue a sense of control by continuously monitoring the food, the weight and the shape of their bodies. These forms of control over the food seem to lead to a major sense of control over the own life which would otherwise be lived in an extremely anxious manner, in a scarcely explored, vague and dangerous world. The control they are really pursuing is a kind of absolute control and, as such, impossible, which, far from being a solution for their anxious fears, is a central construct of the anxiety itself, as well as a fundamental element of preservation. Anorexic subjects manage this control capacity better than the bulimic subjects who experience the catastrophic fears of the damage, typical for anxious subjects, even more.

We conjecture that the control, which comprises both the perception of its insufficiency and the intent to pursue it at any cost, by means of compulsive behaviour, can be connected with parental criticism.

Individuals with eating disorders, already perfectionists by nature, tend to perform well in strongly reproaching and blaming as well as intrusive environments, incrementing their perfectionism especially in its pathologic fear-of-error dimension (Frost et al., 1991; Rice et al., 2005). In the very moment in which - often during the adolescent age or anyway after an increase of the world's complexity, typical when approaching the adult age, - they do not succeed in reaching their standard of performance control, they find themselves devoid of a new modality to approach realty. The absolute control reveals itself as being unrealistic, but irremissible and is therefore pursued in a more restricted and manageable ambit (Sassaroli, Gallucci, & Ruggiero, 2008).

A critic environment does not only foster perfectionism, but it justifies the perception of an insufficient control. The blaming parent continuously substitutes his/her child by deciding what is right and what is wrong for him/her, even in ambits of no normative nature. In this way he/she does not allow the child to explore; not only his/her own preferences, but neither his/her own modalities of approaching the world and of coping with it. The very moment in which this occurs, the error is pointed out, as that kind of behaviour/attitude results to be wrong, as it does not comply with the parent's modality. The result is a sense of personal incapacity. This incapacity can be principally centred on a practical-cognitive level (Bandura, 1988) or on an emotive level with the consequent development of beliefs of emotional fragility and the conviction not to be able to support negative emotions (Bandura, 1990; Mineka & Thomas, 1999).

The meta-cognitive deficit we conjecture for the blaming person could justify other characteristics in the criticized subject connected with the low perception of control. The capacity of the adult to construct a place of thoughts, intentions, desires and emotions for the child and to imagine the child as having autonomous emotions and beliefs is the keystone to transmit the security of affection (Fonagy et al., 1991) and is an important element which promotes the development of a good emotional competence. A parent not capable of thinking about the child's mental experience does not facilitate the formation of the sense of the self within the child (Fonagy et al., 1995) and prejudices his/her reflective function. The reflective function, which appears when the child during his/her growth starts to develop a "theory of the mind", is linked with the development of the adaptive abilities regarding the regulation of emotions. This does, as a matter of fact, permit the child to his/her own mental operation and that of others, and the capacity to mentally portray an emotion is a fundamental condition to avoid that the emotion becomes irrepressible (Fonagy et al., 1991; Fonagy & Target, 1997). A sense of emotional self-efficacy fosters a sense of control of reality which, on the contrary, is rendered insufficient by a scarce sense of self-efficacy.

The Relationship between Maladaptive Perfectionism and Criticism

The association between perceived criticism and maladaptive perfectionism is a well established finding, as previously suggested by Brewin, Firth-Cozens, Furnham, & McManus (1992), Vieth & Trull (1999), Kawamura, Frost, & Harmatz (2001), Huprich (2003), and Irons, Gilbert, Baldwin, Baccus, & Palmer (2006). All these scholars have explored and confirmed models in which relations with parents dominated by conflict and criticism and maladaptive perfectionism were connected in disorders other than ED.

However, it is not clear how these two factors would interact with each other in ED. In this section of the chapter we aimed at addressing the question whether we should consider perceived criticism as a predisposing factor for the development of maladaptive perfectionism or vice-versa, that means that perfectionism would be a sort of temperamental feature which enhances the proneness to perceive sufferance generated from criticism of others.

Generally, perceived criticism is considered as a developmental factor for ED, distant in time. In fact, Kawamura, Frost, & Harmatz (2001) in their empirical research defined perceived criticism as related to harsh parenting styles. This suggests that perceived criticism could be a early relational experience. In addition, the lack of a large body of empirical research focused on the role of perceived criticism in ED did not encourage the hypothesis of a proximal and direct effect of this variable on the development of symptoms of ED.

However, criticism reported in present time could be influenced not only by past events, but also by a present personal vulnerability to any criticism, even if tolerable. In fact, empirical results regarding the question of the real behavior of parents as remembered by individuals are still controversial. For example, Brewin, Andrews, and Furnham (1996) found that self-criticism is related to perceived parental criticism, but not to parents' own reports of criticism. On the other hand, other research supports the association between open verbal abuse during childhood perpetrated by parents and negative self-schemata and either depression or anxiety symptoms in adults (Rose & Abramson, 1992; Sachs-Ericsson, Verona, Joiner, & Preacher, 2006). In conclusion, the results of these studies do not consent any firm conclusions regarding the temporal relation between criticism and perfectionism.

In an empirical research carried out by our research team, we aimed at exploring the issue of the relationship between criticism and perfectionism by comparing two models. The first model assumed that criticism is a relational factor which brings to develop a perfectionistic personality. The second model assumed that temperamental perfectionism could be related with a higher vulnerability to perceive and interpret as episodes of criticism any relational past event. Thus, in this second model perceived criticism is conceptualized as a sort of side-effect of perfectionism.

The results showed that perceived criticism would precede maladaptive perfectionism in the path that leads to drive for thinness in individuals affected by ED. Thus, restrictive dieting and eating overcontrol in ED could be related with a causal process in which perceived criticism is the relational factor which facilitates the intergenerational transmission of perfectionism and, in turn, the developmental root of the rising of ED. This is in agreement with Kawamura, Frost, and Harmatz (2001) and Soenens, Elliot, Goossens, Vansteenkiste, Luyten, and Duriez (2005). The finding that perceived criticism precedes perfectionism partially supports the hypothesis that perceived criticism is not only a perception but a concrete early relational experience. From a cognitive viewpoint, this suggests that criticized individuals may learn to develop a perfectionistic attitude which helps the patient to cope with the emotional sufferance generated by criticism.

However, the results were the opposite with respect to the bulimic symptomatology, in which maladaptive perfectionism preceded perceived criticism. The clinical interpretation of this finding could be that, in the case of bulimic symptomatology, perfectionism should play a more distal role than criticism in the causal process. Thus, where concerning bulimia, it seems more plausible that perfectionism is a temperamental attitude which precedes and possibly increases the vulnerability of individuals to criticism. This suggests that the perception of criticism in bulimia would be more a condition of subjective vulnerability and intolerance to interpersonal conflict than a factual experience of being criticized. This is in agreement with the finding of Brewin, Andrews and Furnham (1996), who found that self-criticism is related to perceived parental criticism, but not to parents' own reports of criticism. However, in our opinion this result does not totally exclude criticism as a really stressful life event in bulimia.

Criticism, Humiliation and Responsibility in Eating Disorders

Another viewpoint from which the role played by parental criticism in the psychopathology of ED could be analyzed is the exploration of two possible emotional consequences of a blaming relationships with either parents or other significant ones: feelings of humiliation and a sense of inflated responsibility.

Concerning the presence of feelings of humiliation in ED, to our knowledge there are no studies clearly devoted to this topic. However, there are some studies about shame in individuals with ED (Frank, 1991; Burney & Irwin, 2000; Gee & Troop, 2003; Swan & Andrews, 2003). Although shame is not exactly humiliation (Silver, Conte, Miceli, & Poggi, 1986; Miller, 1993; Gilbert, 1998), it is frequently associated with it and its role played in ED suggests that also humiliation might be present in the list of the psychological factors of ED.

A possible rationale of the presence of sense of humiliation in ED is that a sense of humiliation is a plausible inner consequence of perceived criticism (Klein, 1988). In fact, both humiliation and fear of criticism from others are interpersonal states. Winner (1988) and Dews and Winner (1997) have shown that children are particularly sensitive to criticism and tend to react to criticism developing feelings of humiliation. In fact, 5- to 6-year-olds children are not able to distinguish literal from ironic criticism and do not find funny ironic teasing (Keltner, Capps, Kring, Young, & Heerey, 2001), while explicit awareness of meaning and purpose of irony, coupled with appreciation of its playful, humorous side, consolidates sometime between ages 11 and 13 years (Demorest, Meyer, Phelps, Gardner, & Winner, 1984). In adults also there is a clear connection between perceveid criticism and sensitivity to social put-down and relational humiliation (Gilbert & Miles, 2000). In addition, humiliation may involve also a depressive perception of loss of social control (Silver, Conte, Miceli, & Poggi,1986; Farmer & McGuffin, 2003). This finding echoes back to the theory of ED which implies the cognitive belief of lack of control. In fact, according to Miller (1988), "humiliation involves being put into a lowly, debased, and powerless position by someone who has, at that moment, greater power than oneself" (p. 46). Given that human agency, sense of power, and sense of control are all related with each other (Bandura, 1990), plausibly a loss of power implies a loss of control.

Our analysis confirmed that humiliation and criticism are linked with each other and are present in the psychopathological process of ED. However, we have not described the specific action of humiliation in the process. Humiliation may be conceptualized as either an emotional state implied by criticism but unable to exert a specific and independent role or a active factor able to interact with criticism, moderating or mediating the effect of a perception of criticism. In addition, humiliation may be related also with cognitive and relational factors other than criticism. We are at the beginning of our reflection on this factor. At the present moment, we can only stress that humiliation belongs to the emotional palette of eating disorders and that it deserves further research.

The theoretical link between inflated responsibility and ED lies on the concept that ED have much in common with the obssessive-compulsive spectrum (Halmi et al., 2000; Thornton & Russell, 1997). As widely known, inflated responsibility is commonly considered the core belief of obsessionality (Salkovskis, 1985). Salkovskis defined responsibility as the belief that one has power which is pivotal to bring about or prevent negative outcomes. Inflated responsibility is "an inflated belief in the probability of being the cause of serious harm to others or self, or failing to avert harm where this may has been possible" (Salkovskis 1985, p. 575). Some research has investigated the role of cognitive variables linked to inflated responsibility in ED. Rachman and Shafran (1999) have hypothesized that individuals with ED may consider overeating immoral. This may depend on a thought-action fusion process. According to this process, individuals with ED would tend to consider unwanted thoughts about overeating as morally equivalent to actually eating forbidden foods. In conclusion, a portion of individuals with ED may judge thinking about eating and increasing in fatness as morally unacceptable. This belief is clearly connected to a cognition of inflated responsibility and may be present at least in a portion of ED individuals. However, Fassino, Piero, Daga, Leombruni, Mortara, and Rovera (2002) used the Temperament and Character Inventory (TCI, Cloninger, Przybeck, Svrakic, & Wetzel, 1994) and found that individuals with ED have a lower sense of responsibility than controls. Yet, we must notice that in the TCI the scale of responsibility is considered a sub-dimension of the larger domain of self-directedness, which is the ability of directing one's own life according to personal goals and values. Thus, low sense of responsibility should be interpreted as a low sense of self-directedness, and the tendency to consider the other as dominant and influencing the subjects behavior. Actually the Cloninger's definition of Responsibility is very far from the Inflated

Responsibility of the cognitive tradition. Thus, the TCI may be able to measure the tendency of ED subjects to involve in behaviors of avoidance and feelings of anxiety.

A research from Sassaroli and Ruggiero (2009) has shown that a population of individuals with ED population can show higher average scores than the control group on responsibility, but also that this responsibility would have a smaller predictive contribution than perfectionism and low self-esteem. The study suggests that the sense of responsibility is significantly high in individuals with ED and may play a psychopatological role in the cognitive model of ED but also that this contribution is not comparable to that of perfectionism and low self-esteem. Actually, results from hierarchical linear regression and from interaction analysis carried out in the same above mentioned study suggested that the effect of responsibility is totally adsorbed by that of pathological perfectionism. To our opinion, this result suggests that in ED responsibility is a sort of restricted subdomain of pathological perfectionism than absent. Therefore, ED individuals would tend to judge thinking about eating and increasing in fatness as morally unacceptable (Rachman & Shafran, 1999) but there is no part of such judgment that does not belong to the ampler cognitive realm of perfectionism.

In other words, the study confirms that pathological perfectionism remains the core belief of ED. The hierarchical regression suggests that in perfectionism is present a cognitive component linked to responsibility and morality, but such component does not play any role independent from perfectionism.

References

Apparigliato, M., Ruggiero, G. M., & Sassaroli, S. (2007). Il Perceived Criticism Inventory (PCI): un nuovo strumento di valutazione del criticismo genitoriale [The Perceived Criticism Inventory (PCI): a new instrument for evaluating parental criticism]. *Psicoterapia Cognitiva e Comportamentale, 13*, 275-300.

Asarnow, J. R., Tompson, M., Hamilton, E. B., Goldstein, M. J., & Guthrie, D. (1994). Family-expressed emotion, childhood-onset depression, and childhood-onset schizophrenia spectrum disorders: is expressed emotion a nonspecific correlate of child psychopathology or a specific risk factor for depression? *Journal of Abnormal Child Psychology, 22*, 129-46.

Bandura, A. (1988). Perceived self-efficacy: Exercise of control through self-belief. *Educational Psychologist, 28*, 117-148.

Bandura, A. (1990). Perceived self-efficacy in the exercise of personal agency. *Journal of Applied Sport Psychology, 2*, 128-163.

Brewin, C. R., Andrews, B., & Furnham, A. (1996). Self-critical attitudes and parental criticism in young women. *British Journal of Medical Psychology, 69*, 69-78.

Bruch, H. (1973). *Eating Disorders: Obesity, Anorexia Nervosa and the Person Within*. New York: Basic Books.

Burney, J., & Irwin, H. J. (2000). Shame and guilt in women with eating disorder symptomatology. *Journal of Clinical Psychology, 56*, 51–61.

Button, E. J., Sonuga-Barke, E. J., Davies, J., & Thompson, M. (1996). A prospective study of self-esteem in the prediction of eating problems in adolescent schoolgirls: questionnaire findings. *British Journal of Clinical Psychology, 35*, 193-203.

Butzlaff, R. L., & Hooley, J. M. (1998). Expressed emotion and psychiatric relapse: a meta-analysis. *Archives of General Psychiatry, 55*, 547-552.

Chambless, D. L., & Steketee, G. (1999). Expressed emotion and behavior therapy outcome: a prospective study with obsessive compulsive and agoraphobic outpatients. *Journal of Consulting and Clinical Psychology, 67*, 658-665.

Cloninger, C. R., Przybeck, T. R., Svrakic, D. M., & Wetzel, R. D. (1994). *Temperament and Character Inventory (TCI): A Guide to Its Development and Use*. St. Louis: Center for Psychobiology of Personality Department of Psychiatry, Washington University

Demorest, A., Meyer, C., Phelps, E., Gardner, H., & Winner, E. (1984). Words speak louder than actions: Understanding deliberately false remarks. *Child Development, 55*, 1527-1534.

Dews, S., & Winner, E. (1997). Attributing meaning to deliberately false utterances: The case of irony. In C. Mandell & A. McCabe (Eds.). *The Problem of Meaning: Behavioral and Cognitive Perspectives*. New York: Elsevier Science, pp. 377- 414.

Fairburn, C. G., & Harrison, P. J. (2003). Eating disorders. *The Lancet, 361*, 407-416.

Farmer, A. E., & McGuffin, P. (2003). Humiliation, loss and other types of life events and difficulties: a comparison of depressed subjects, healthy controls and their siblings. *Psychological Medicine, 33*, 1169-1175.

Fassino, S., Piero, A., Daga, G., Leombruni, P., Mortara, P., & Rovera, G. (2002). Attentional biases and frontal functioning in anorexia nervosa. International Journal of *Eating Disorders, 31*, 274-283.

Flett, G. L, Hewitt, P. L., & Singer, A. (1995). Perfectionism and parental authority styles. *Individual Psychology, 51* , 50-60.

Fonagy, P, Steele, M., Steele, H., Moran, G.S., & Higgit, A.C. (1991), The capacity for understanding mental states: the reflective self parent and child and its significance for securety of attachment. *Journal of Infant Mental Health, 12*, 201-218.

Fonagy, P., & Target, M. (1996). Playing with reality I: Theory of mind and the normal development of psychic reality. *International Journal of Psychoanalysis, 77*, 217-233.

Fonagy, P., & Target, M. (1997), Attachment and reflective function: their role in self-organization. *Developmental Psychopathology, 9*, 679-700.

Fonagy, P., Steele, M., Steele, H., Leigh, T., Kennedy, R., Matton, G., & Target, M. (1995)., Attachment, The reflective self, and borderline states: the predictive specificity of the adult attachment interview and pathological emotional development. In S. Goldberg, R. Muir, & J. Kerr (Eds.). *Attachment Theory: Social, Developmental, and Clinical Perspectives*. Analytic Press, Hillsdale, New York, pp. 233-278.

Frank, E. S. (1991). Shame and guilt in eating disorders. *American Journal of Orthopsychiatry, 61*, 303–306.

Frost, R. O., Lahart, C., & Rosenblate, R. (1991). The development of perfectionism: a study of daughters and their parents. *Cognitive Therapy and Research, 15*, 469-489.

Frost, R. O., Marten, P., Lahart, C., & Rosenblate, R. (1990). The dimensions of perfectionism. *Cognitive Therapy and Research, 14*, 449-468.

Gee, A. & Troop, N. A. (2003). Shame, depressive symptoms and eating, weight and shape concerns in a non-clinical sample. *Eating and Weight Disorders, 8*, 72-75.

Gilbert, P. & Miles, J. (2000). *Body Shame: Conceptualisation, Research and Treatment.* London, New York: Psychology Press.

Gilbert, P. (1998). What is shame? Some core issues and controversies. In P. Gilbert & B. Andrews (Eds.), *Shame: Interpersonal Behavior, Psychopathology and Culture*. New York: Oxford University Press, pp 3-36.

Guidano, V. F., & Liotti, G. (1983). *Cognitive Processes and Emotional Disorders*. New York, The Guilford Press.

Halmi, K. A., Sunday, S. R., Strober, M., Kaplan, A., Woodside, D. B., & Fichter, M. (2000). Perfectionism in anorexia nervosa: Variation by clinical subtype, obsessionality, and pathological eating behavior. *American Journal of Psychiatry, 157*, 1799–1805.

Hamachek, D. E. (1978). Psychodynamics of normal and neurotic perfectionism. *Psychology, 15*, 27-33.

Hewitt , P. L., & Flett, G. L. (1990). Dimensions of perfectionism in unipolar depression. *Journal of Abnormal Psychology, 100*, 98-10

Hewitt, P. L., Flett, G. L., & Ediger, E. (1995). Perfectionism traits and perfectionistic self-presentation in eating disorder attitudes, characteristics, and symptoms. *International Journal of Eating Disorders, 18*, 317-326.

Hibbs, E. D., Hamburger, S. D., Lenane, M., Rapoport, J. L., Kruesi, M. J., Keyson, C. S., & Goldstein, M. J. (1991). Determinants of expressed emotion in families of disturbed and normal children. *Journal of Child Psychology and Psychiatry, 32*, 757-770.

Huprich, S. K. (2003). Depressive personality and its relationship to depressed mood, interpersonal loss, negative parental perceptions, and perfectionism. *Journal of Nervous & Mental Disease, 191*, 73-79.

Irons, C., Gilbert, P., Baldwin, M. W., Baccus, J. R., & Palmer, M. (2006). Parental recall, attachment relating and self-attacking/self-reassurance: their relationship with depression. *British Journal of Medical Psychology, 45*, 297-308.

Kawamura, K. Y., Frost, R. O., & Harmatz, M. G. (2001). The relationship of perceived parenting styles to perfectionism. *Personality and Individual Differences, 32*, 317-327.

Keltner, D,. Capps, L., Kring, A. M., Young, R. C. & Heerey, E. A. (2001). Just teasing: A conceptual analysis and empirical review. *Psychological Bulletin, 2*, 229-248.

Kenney-Benson, G. A., & Pomerantz, E. (2005). The role of mother's use of control in children's perfectionism: Implications for the development of children's depressive symptoms. *Journal of Personality, 73*, 23-46

Klein, D. C. (1991). The humiliation dynamic: An overview. *Journal of Primary Prevention, 12*, 93-121.

Le Grange, D. (1999). Family therapy for adolescent anorexia nervosa. *Journal of Clinical Psychology, 55*, 727-739.

Liotti, G. (1992). Egocentrism and the Cognitive Psychotherapy of Personality Disorders. *Journal of Cognitive Psychotherapy: an International Quarterly, 6*, 43-58.

Lorenzini, R., & Sassaroli, S. (2000). *La Mente Prigioniera [The Imprisoned Mind].* Milano: Raffaello Cortina.

Miller, W.I. (1993). *Humiliation: And Other Essays on Honor, Social Discomfort, and Violence*. Ithaca: Cornell University Press.

Mineka, S., & Thomas, C. (1999). Mechanisms of change in exposure therapy for anxiety disorders. In T. Dalgleish & M. Power (Eds.), *Handbook of Cognition and Emotion.* Chichester, UK: John Wiley and Sons, Ltd. pp. 613-636.

Perris, C., & Mc Gorry, P. D. (1998). *Cognitive Psychotherapy of Psychiatric and Personality Disorders*. Chichester, UK: John Wiley and Sons, Ltd.

Rachman, S., & Shafran, R. (1999). Cognitive distortions: thought-action fusion. *Clinical Psychology & Psychotherapy, 6*, 80-85.

Reda, M. (1986). *Sistemi Cognitivi Complessi e Psicoterapia [Complex Cognitive Systems and Psychotherapy]*. Roma: Nuova Italia Scientifica.

Rice, K. G., Ashby, J. S., & Preusser, K. J. (1996). Perfectionism, relationships with parents and self-esteem. *Individual Psychology, 52*, 246-260.

Rice, K. G., Lopez, F. G., & Vergara, D. (2005). Parental/social influences on perfectionism and adult attachment orientations. *Journal of Social and Clinical Psychology, 24*, 580-605.

Rose, D.T., Abramson, L.Y., 1992. Developmental predictors of depressive cognitive styles: developmental perspectives on depression. In D. Cicchetti & S.L. Toth (Eds.), *Developmental Perspectives on Depression*. Rochester symposium on developmental psychopathology, vol. 4, pp. 323-349.

Sachs-Ericsson, N., Verona, E., Joiner, T., & Preacher, K. J. (2006). Parental verbal abuse and the mediating role of self-criticism in adult internalizing disorders. *Journal of Affective Disorders, 93*, 71-78.

Salkovskis, P. M. (1985). Obsessional-compulsive problems: a cognitive-behavioural analysis. *Behaviour Research and Therapy, 23*, 571-583.

Sassaroli, S., & Ruggiero, G. M. (2002). I costrutti dell'ansia: obbligo di controllo, perfezionismo patologico, pensiero catastrofico, autovalutazione negativa e intolleranza dell'incertezza [The constructs of anxiety: compulsion to control, pathological perfectionism, catastrophic thought, negative self-evaluation, and intolerance of uncertainty]. *Psicoterapia Cognitiva e Comportamentale, 8*, 45-60.

Sassaroli, S., & Ruggiero G. M. (2008). The control and worry-centered treatment of eating disorders. International Journal of Child and Adolescent Health, 2, 229-242.

Sassaroli, S., & Ruggiero, G. M. (2005). The role of stress in the association between low self-esteem, perfectionism, and worry, and eating disorders. *International Journal of Eating Disorders, 37*, 135-141.

Sassaroli, S., & Ruggiero, G. M. (2009). Autostima, metarimuginio, perfezionismo, responsabilità e rimuginio nei disturbi alimentari [Self-esteem, meta-worry, perfectionism, responsibility and worry in eating disorders]. *Ricerca in Psicoterapia/Research in Psychotherapy, 12*, 21-36, available http://www.spr-italia.it/pdf/spr_volume_12.pdf

Sassaroli, S., Gallucci, M., & Ruggiero, G.M. (2008). Low perception of control as a cognitive factor of eating disorders. Its independent effects on measures of eating disorders and its interactive effects with perfectionism and self-esteem. *Journal of Behavior Therapy and Experimental Psychiatry, 39*, 467-488

Schwartz, C. E., Dorer, D. J., Beardslee, W. R., Lavori, P. W. & Keller, M. B. (1990). Maternal expressed emotion and paternal affective disorder: risk for childhood depressive disorder, substance abuse or conduct disorder. *Journal of Psychiatry Research, 24*, 231-250.

Semerari, A. (Ed.) (1999). *Psicoterapia Cognitiva del Paziente Grave [Cognitive Psychotherapy for Severe Patient]*. Milano: Raffaello Cortina.

Silver, M., Conte, R., Miceli, M., & Poggi, I. (1986). Humiliation: Feeling, social control, and the construction of identity. *Journal for the Theory of Social Behaviour, 16*, 269-283.

Soenens, B., Elliot, A. J., Goossens, L., Vansteenkiste, M., Luyten, P., & Duriez, B. (2005). The intergenerational transmission of perfectionism: Parents' psychological control as intervening variable. *Journal of Family Psychology, 19*, 358-366.

Stubbe, D. E., Zahner, G. E. P., Goldstein, M. J., & Leckman, J. F. (1993). Diagnostic specificity of a brief measure of expressed emotion: a community study of children. *Journal of Child Psychology and Psychiatry, 34*, 139-154.

Swan, S., & Andrews, B. (2003). The relationship between shame, eating disorders and disclosure in treatment. *British Journal of Clinical Psychology, 42*, 367-78.

Tarrier, N., Sommerfield, C. & Pilgrim H. (1999). Relatives' expressed emotion and PTSD treatment outcome. *Psychological Medicine, 29*, 801-811.

Thornton, C. & Russell, J. (1997). Obsessive–compulsive comorbidity in the dieting disorders. *International Journal of Eating Disorders, 21*, 83–87.

Tozzi, F., Aggen, S. H., Neale, B. M., Anderson, C. B., Mazzeo, S. E., Neale, M. C., et al. (2004). The structure of perfectionism: A twin study. *Behavior Genetics, 34*, 483-496.

Van Furth, E. F., Van Strien, D. C., Martina, L. M. L., Van Son, M. J. M., Hendrickx, J. J. P., & Van Engeland, H. (1996). Expressed emotion and the prediction of outcome in adolescent eating disorders. T*he International Journal of Eating Disorders, 1*, 19-31.

Vieth, A. Z., & Trull, T. J. (1999). Family patterns of perfectionism: an examination of college students and their parents. *Journal of Personality Assessment, 72*, 49-67.

Vitousek, K. B., & Hollon, K. B. (1990). The investigation of schematic content and processing in eating disorders. *Cognitive Therapy and Research, 14*, 191-214.

Winner, E. (1988). *The Point of Words: Children's Understanding of Metaphor And Irony.* Cambridge, MA: Harvard University Press.

In: Cognitive Therapy of Eating Disorders...
Editors: S. Sassaroli and G.M. Ruggiero
ISBN: 978-1-60876-617-8

Chapter 6

WEAK CENTRAL COHERENCE IN ANOREXIA NERVOSA

***Eva Kemps*[1]*, Carolina Lopez*[2] *and Kate Tchanturia*[2]**
[1]School of Psychology, Flinders University, Adelaide, Australia
[2]Division of Psychological Medicine, Eating Disorders Research Unit, Institute of Psychiatry, King's College London, UK

ABSTRACT

This chapter reports emerging evidence suggesting that some individuals with anorexia nervosa, like those with autism spectrum disorders, display "weak central coherence", a cognitive style characterized by a tendency to focus on detail at the expense of seeing the overall gestalt. This excessive attention to detail can seriously compromise these patients' psychological well-being and overall quality of life. It can also shape some of the symptoms and personality features that maintain the illness. This chapter addresses the history, concept and measurement of central coherence, and presents converging evidence from neuropsychological and clinical sources in relation to coherence problems in anorexia. Importantly, the chapter also describes how such evidence can be usefully translated into clinical practice and how weak central coherence and central beliefs concerning control may interact with each other.

INTRODUCTION

Recent models of the aetiology of eating disorders emphasise the neuro-developmental origin of anorexia nervosa (AN) (Connan, Campbell, Katzman, Lightman & Treasure, 2003; Southgate, Tchanturia & Treasure, 2005). It is argued that neuro-cognitive abnormalities play a causal and perpetuating role in AN symptomatology (Lena, Fiocco & Leyenaar, 2004). Evidence from neuropsychological research shows that individuals with AN display impaired functioning across a range of cognitive domains, including executive functioning, visual-spatial ability, attention, learning and memory (Lauer, 2002). These cognitive deficits are not indicative of low intelligence (Blanz, Detzner, Lay, Rose & Schmidt, 1997), and are at least partially independent of nutritional status (Kingston, Szmukler, Andrewes, Tress & Desmond, 1996). Instead, deficits in some cognitive areas have been linked to aspects of personality in AN, such as obsessive and compulsive traits (Tchanturia et al., 2004). Sub-optimal cognitive task performance in AN has also been attributed to neuroanatomical abnormalities, particularly of the fronto-temporal cortical circuits (Uher, Treasure & Campbell, 2002).

Emerging evidence points to another cognitive anomaly in the neuropsychological profile of AN, known as "weak central coherence" or a detail-focused information processing style. This chapter reviews the literature to date. In particular, it addresses the history, concept and measurement of central coherence, and presents converging evidence from neuropsychological and clinical sources for coherence problems in AN. Importantly, the chapter also describes how such evidence can be usefully translated into clinical practice, in order to improve the treatment and outcome of AN.

Concept of Central Coherence

The term "central coherence" originated in the autism spectrum disorders (ASD) literature. It was introduced by Frith (1989) to describe the natural tendency to integrate information into a global and meaningful "whole". Weak central coherence then refers to a bias toward local or analytical processing, that is, focusing on details at the cost of seeing the bigger picture or overall gestalt. This style of information processing is characteristic of children and adults with ASD. Indeed, a recent review of more than 50 empirical studies of the weak coherence account yielded robust findings of local bias in ASD; however, findings regarding weak global processing were mixed (Happé & Frith, 2006). This led the authors to conclude that the cognitive style of people with ASD is characterised by a superiority in detail-focused processing, accompanied by a bias against, rather than a deficit in, global processing.

There are clear similarities in the clinical profiles of ASD and AN. Most notably, the behaviour and personality of individuals with AN are also characterised by a preoccupation with detail (Brecelj Anderluh, Tchanturia, Rabe-Hesketh & Treasure, 2003). Furthermore, there is an over-representation of ASD in AN. Reported prevalence rates of a co-morbid diagnosis of ASD in AN individuals range from 20 to 33% (Rastam, Gillberg & Wentz, 2003; Wentz et al., 2005) compared to 0.6% in the general population (Charman, 2002). These commonalities between ASD and AN provided the impetus for investigations of the weak coherence account in AN.

Measurement of Central Coherence

Over the past 20 years, the ASD literature has developed, adopted and modified a range of cognitive tasks to measure central coherence. Tasks of central coherence can broadly be classified based on whether they require predominantly local or global processing. The Block Design subtest of the Wechsler intelligence scales and the Embedded Figures Test (Witkin, Oltman, Raskin & Karp, 1971) are exemplars of tasks that require a local or analytical approach, and have been widely used in ASD research (Happé & Frith, 2006). The Block

Design subtest requires participants to arrange red-and-white blocks to re-create patterned configurations, while the Embedded Figures Test requires participants to locate and trace simple geometric shapes that are embedded within more complex figures. Performance on both tasks benefits from a disregard for the configuration as a whole in favour of its constituent parts.

The Homograph Reading Task (Frith & Snowling, 1983) and the Sentence Completion Task (Happé, Briskman & Frith, 2001) were developed more recently, and favour a global processing strategy. In the Homograph Reading Task, participants are asked to read aloud sentences containing homographs (e.g., "bow"). The context of the sentence determines the correct pronunciation and meaning of the homograph (e.g., "He took a *bow* when everyone clapped" versus "He took the *bow* from his music case"). In the Sentence Completion Task, participants are presented with sentence stems and asked to complete the sentences. The sentence stems are designed to cue local associations that are nonsensical in the context of the whole sentence. For example, in response to the sentence stem "The sea tastes of salt and ...", "pepper" would be a local completion, whereas "water" would be a globally coherent completion. Successful performance on the Homograph Reading and Sentence Completion tasks requires that the words are interpreted according to the context of the sentence rather than processed in isolation.

Other measures of central coherence that have been used specifically in AN samples are the Object Assembly subtest of the Wechsler intelligence scales, the Matching Familiar Figures Test (Kagan, 1966) and the Rey-Osterrieth Complex Figure Test (Osterrieth, 1944). The Object Assembly subtest requires participants to assemble puzzle pieces to form familiar objects. Successful completion is contingent upon attendance to the resulting object as a whole in preference to the individual puzzle pieces. In the Matching Familiar Figures Test, participants are presented with a target picture and asked to select from a set of highly similar pictures the one that is identical to the target picture. Performance on this task benefits from a detail-oriented search with little regard for the overall appearance of the pictures. The Rey-Osterrieth Complex Figure Test presents participants with a complex figure. Participants are first asked to copy the figure (Copy trial), and then to reconstruct it from memory (Recall trial). A focus on the major organisational features of the figure is indicative of a coherent drawing style (Booth, 2006).

Common to all tasks of central coherence is an emphasis on response speed and accuracy. Weak central coherence is evident from peaks of performance on tasks of local processing and/or sub-standard performance on tasks of global processing.

Weak Central Coherence in AN

Evidence for weak central coherence in AN comes from two sources: neuropsychological studies and clinical observations.

Neuropsychological Studies

In the past decade, there has been a surge in neuropsychological studies of central coherence in AN. These have demonstrated consistent findings of weak global processing in AN. For example, Gillberg, Gillberg, Rastam and Johansson (1996) found that adolescents with AN performed more poorly on the Object Assembly subtest than age-, gender- and education-matched controls. The authors noted that the AN patients tended to become obsessed with details when solving the puzzles. When participants were re-tested 3 years later, the AN sample again showed poorer performance on this task (Gillberg, Rastam, Wentz & Gillberg, 2007). Several other studies have also reported lower performance scores on the Object Assembly subtest in AN patients relative to healthy controls (Mathias & Kent, 1998; Thompson, 1993; Tokley & Kemps, 2007).

Further evidence for weak global processing in AN comes from studies that compared AN women and non-eating disordered controls on the Rey-Osterrieth Complex Figure Test. For example, Sherman et al. (2006) found that AN patients displayed a piece-meal drawing style when copying the figure, and were less accurate than controls in their recall of the figure. Moreover, poor coherence on the Copy trial contributed to the patients' lower recall scores on the Recall trial. Lopez et al. (2008) replicated these findings, and, in addition, showed that AN patients took longer than healthy controls to produce appropriate (i.e., global) completions on the Sentence Completion Task.

Consistent with the weak coherence account, there is also evidence for a bias toward local processing in AN, although findings are less clear-cut. For instance, a number of studies have shown that patients with AN demonstrate a greater aptitude for disembedding the hidden geometric shapes of the Embedded Figures Test than do non-eating disordered control participants (Lopez et al., 2008; Sours, 1969; Tokley & Kemps, 2007). However, others have reported a trough on this task in AN individuals (e.g., Basseches & Karp, 1984; McLaughlin, Karp & Herzog, 1985). In support of a local bias in AN, Southgate, Tchanturia and Treasure (2008) found that, relative to healthy controls, AN women showed greater efficiency on the Matching Familiar Figures Test, as demonstrated by faster response times and superior accuracy in identifying the target pictures. Yet, unlike individuals with ASD (Happé, 1994; Shah & Frith, 1993), those with AN, do not show enhanced performance on the Block Design subtest (Gillberg et al., 1996, 2007; Mathias & Kent, 1998; Thompson, 1993). Indeed, some studies have demonstrated poorer performance on this task in AN patients (Kingston et al., 1996).

Nevertheless, AN individuals have been reported to show enhanced performance on several other tasks. In particular, Strupp, Weingartner, Kaye and Gwirtsman, (1986) found that AN patients performed better than healthy controls on tasks that require effortful processing (i.e., intentional learning), but did more poorly on tasks that assessed automatic processing (i.e., incidental learning). They attributed this pattern of cognitive performance to a narrowing of the focus of attention on the details of the tasks with little appreciation of the larger context. Furthermore, Pieters and colleagues (2003, 2004, 2005) showed that individuals with AN were faster than control participants on detail orientated drawing and copying tasks. Although these studies were not specifically designed to address the central coherence hypothesis, they do support a detail-focused processing style in AN.

Thus, the neuropsychological research to date provides support for the weak coherence account of AN. The evidence suggests that individuals with AN, like those with ASD, show a superiority in local or detail-focused processing, coupled with a weakness in global or context-driven processing. Nevertheless, there are some inconsistent and even negative results. Diversity of AN samples (e.g., variations in duration and severity of illness) and methodological differences (e.g., variations in task administration) across studies could account for these mixed results. Additionally, measures of central coherence were designed or modified for assessing people with ASD, and hence, may not be sufficiently sensitive to detect coherence problems in individuals with higher intelligence quotients and greater verbal proficiency, such as those with AN.

Mechanisms Underlying Weak Central Coherence in AN

To date, only a handful of studies has examined potential mechanisms underlying weak central coherence in AN. These have focused exclusively on possible links between coherence problems and obsessive compulsive personality traits in AN. Specifically, Tokley and Kemps (2007) showed that obsessive compulsive personality traits contributed to poor performance on the Object Assembly subtest in women with AN. Similarly, Lopez et al. (2008) reported an association between obsessive compulsive traits and poor coherence on the Rey-Osterrieth Complex Figure Test. In contrast, Southgate et al. (2008) found that obsessive compulsive features did not correlate with performance on the Matching Familiar Figures Test. Differences in measures of obsessive compulsive symptomatology across studies could explain these conflicting findings. Further support for the contribution of obsessive compulsive traits to coherence problems in AN comes from reports of comparable deficits in global processing in AN and obsessive compulsive disorder (OCD) (Sherman et al., 2006). Specifically, OCD patients have been shown to also use a detail-oriented drawing style to copy the Rey-Osterrieth Complex figure, which similarly accounted for their subsequent deficits in figure recall (Savage et al., 1999, 2000).

Additionally, the aforementioned studies found that depression and anxiety, although elevated in AN individuals, were not related to indices of weak central coherence. This is consistent with numerous other investigations that have failed to find a relationship between cognitive performance and depression or anxiety in patients with AN (Green, Elliman, Wakeling & Rogers, 1996; Kingston et al., 1996; Mathias & Kent, 1998).

Clinical Observations

Clinical observations provide converging evidence for the weak coherence account of AN. It is well documented that AN patients exhibit an extreme attention to detail in their eating behaviours. Individuals with AN are so focused on details about food and weight (e.g., engage in calorie counting), they fail to see the bigger picture of nutritional health. This difficulty to see the bigger picture may also account for their disregard of the long-term consequences of unhealthy weight control methods, such as purging and the use of laxatives and diuretics. Moreover, AN individuals are not aware that their lives have essentially been reduced to a preoccupation with food. This preoccupation is evident from studies that have shown attentional biases toward food, weight and body shape words in AN patients on the modified Stroop task (e.g., Ben-Tovim, Walker, Fok & Yap, 1989) and the dot probe task (e.g., Rieger et al., 1998). Additionally, a recent survey found that AN individuals experience substantially more preoccupying thoughts about food, weight and body shape than do dieting and non-dieting controls (Kemps, Tiggemann, Wade, Ben-Tovim & Breyer, 2006). Importantly, the excessive focus on detail in AN is not restricted to food and eating behaviours, but extends to other aspects of life, including academic pursuits, work and family life.

It has further been suggested that a detail-oriented processing style may contribute to the body image disturbance in AN. Individuals with AN typically perceive themselves as fat, even though they are clearly underweight (DSM-IV-TR, American Psychiatric Association, 2000). Proponents of the weak coherence account attribute this distortion of body image to an excessive focus on the size of individual body parts, particularly the hips and thighs, at the expense of perceiving the emaciated state of the body as a whole (Gillberg et al., 1996; Sherman et al., 2006).

The detail-focused cognitive style of AN patients may help them to achieve a sense of control. Individuals with AN have a distorted perception of low control over external events and internal emotional states, and an associated obsessive and compulsive desire for control (Sassaroli, Gallucci & Ruggiero, 2009). Their quest for control is seemingly achieved through extreme dietary restriction (Button, 1985). Indeed, by narrowing their focus on issues surrounding food, eating, weight and body shape, AN individuals perceive their lives to be more manageable and controllable. Thus, weak central coherence may serve as a mechanism that helps to reduce the anxiety associated with dealing with the bigger, global context. Furthermore, the tendency to get bogged down by details may trigger obsessive-compulsive personality traits, such as perfectionism, which are thought to contribute to the maintenance of AN (Schmidt & Treasure, 2006).

Implications for Treatment and Outcome of AN

Neuropsychological evidence for weak central coherence in AN not only advances our theoretical understanding of the cognitive vulnerabilities inherent in this disorder, but, importantly, it also provides a target for therapeutic intervention. Indeed, a recent treatment model for eating disorders (Treasure, Tchanturia & Schmidt, 2005) has outlined a treatment approach that specifically addresses cognitive limitations in AN. In particular, the model proposes that current knowledge regarding neuropsychological processing can be translated into treatment in the form of cognitive remediation.

The basic premise of Cognitive Remediation Therapy (CRT) is that practice in a cognitive skill will improve performance of that skill, and instil confidence in using it in everyday life. The hallmark of this approach is that it engages the patient in stimulating and positive mental activities without the burden or complexity of confronting issues or emotions that relate to their eating disorder. CRT has been shown to be successful in improving executive functioning in patients with schizophrenia (Wykes & Reeder, 2005). Emerging evidence from case reports indicates that it is also an effective tool for increasing cognitive flexibility in individuals with AN (Davies & Tchanturia, 2005; Tchanturia, Whitney & Treasure, 2006; Tchanturia, Davies & Campbell, 2007).

Recent pilot work suggests that CRT also holds promise as an intervention to counteract the overly detailed focus in AN. Indeed, the second and third authors have successfully trialled a CRT module tailored to moderate the bias toward local processing in AN (see Baldock & Tchanturia, 2007; Pretorius & Tchanturia, 2007). Specifically, over the course of 10 face-to-face sessions, AN patients develop a more holistic pattern of analysis through targeted exercise on a range of cognitive tasks. In one such task, the geometric figures task, patients are asked to describe a geometric figure for another to draw. Patients gradually learn to dampen the tendency to identify details, which make it difficult for the person drawing to produce an accurate representation of the figure, and instead to begin with global features of the figure. Other tasks designed to enhance global processing involve coming up with a catchy title for a short article, summarising a text in bullet points or giving directions using a map for which a context-driven strategy is more effective than detailed instructions. Importantly, patients also learn to implement the newly acquired strategies in real life situations. Qualitative feedback from patients indicates that the cognitive skills learned in CRT do indeed generalise to improve their everyday lives (Whitney, Easter & Tchanturia, in press).

Lopez, Roberts, Tchanturia and Treasure (2008) have recently piloted a shortened 3-session intervention called neuropsychological feedback. Unlike CRT, it encourages learning by reflecting on information processing strategies rather than intensive practice of cognitive skills, and is particularly suitable for outpatient settings and less severe cases. Following an initial neuropsychological assessment, an individualised feedback module is formulated in which patients reflect on the origin of their detail-oriented information processing bias and its adverse impact on their quality of life, and consider strategies to transcend this bias with regard to food, weight and body image, as well as other areas of life. CRT and neuropsychological feedback offer potential scope as pre-treatments or add-ons to traditional psychotherapies, such as Cognitive Behaviour Therapy.

Conclusion

There is a growing body of evidence for the weak coherence account in AN. Neuropsychological data show that people with AN display a bias favouring detail-focused processing over processing of configurational information. This cognitive style is at least partially attributable to obsessive compulsive personality traits, and is reflected in the psychopathology of AN. CRT and neuropsychological feedback may prove beneficial to counteract the tendency to focus on detail and develop more holistic information processing strategies.

Nevertheless, many questions remain to be answered. In particular, it has yet to be determined whether weak coherence represents a trait vulnerability or an effect of illness state. This issue could be addressed via cross-sectional comparisons of underweight and weight restored AN individuals, or by investigating the effect of weight gain on coherence in a longitudinal context. An initial exploration by Lopez, Tchanturia, Stahl and Treasure (2008) found that long-term recovered AN women continued to show weak central coherence, indicative of a trait characteristic. On a related matter, examination of central coherence in first-degree relatives of AN individuals could ascertain whether coherence problems, like set-shifting difficulties (Holliday, Tchanturia, Landau, Collier & Treasure, 2005), are part of the endophenotype in AN. Weak central coherence has been found to be familial in ASD (Briskman, Happé & Frith, 2001; Happé et al., 2001). The ASD literature further suggests that weak coherence may be linked to reduced brain connectivity (Happé & Frith, 2006). Brain imaging studies might usefully establish whether disturbed neural connectivity could also account for weak central coherence in AN.

REFERENCES

American Psychiatric Association. (2000). *Diagnostic and Statistical Manual of Mental Disorders (DSM-IV-TR) (4th ed. Text Revision)*. Washington, DC: APA.

Baldock, E., & Tchanturia, K. (2007). Translating laboratory research into practice: Foundations, functions and future of cognitive remediation therapy for anorexia nervosa. *Therapy, 4*, 285-292.

Basseches, H. I., & Karp, S. (1984). Field dependence in young anorectic and obese women. *Psychotherapy and Psychosomatics, 41*, 33-37.

Ben-Tovim, D. I., Walker, M. K., Fok, D., & Yap, E. (1989). An adaptation of the Stroop test for measuring shape and food concerns in eating disorders: A quantitative measure of psychopathology. *International Journal of Eating Disorders, 8*, 681-687.

Blanz, B., Schmidt, M. H., Gipel, C., & Lay, B. (1997). Kann die Behandlung im häuslichen Milieu die stationäre Behandlung von Kindern und Jugendlichen mit psychiatrischen Störungen ersetzen? [Can the treatment in the domestic milieu replace the inpatient treatment of children and youth with psychiatric disorders?] In A. Marneros & P. Brieger (Eds.). *Psychiatrie als Therapiefach [Psychiatry as a specialization of psychotherapy]*. Roderer: Regensburg, pp. 255-259.

Booth, R. (2006). *Local-global processing and cognitive style in autism spectrum disorders and typical development.* London: King's College London, Institute of Psychiatry.

Brecelj-Anderluh, M., Tchanturia, K., Rabe-Hesketh, S., & Treasure, J. (2003). Childhood obsessive-compulsive personality traits in adult women with eating disorders: Defining a broader eating disorder phenotype. *American Journal of Psychiatry, 160*, 242-247.

Briskman, J., Happé, F., & Frith, U. (2001). Exploring the cognitive phenotype of autism: Weak "central coherence" in parents and siblings with autism: II. Real-life skills and preferences. *Journal of Child Psychology and Psychiatry, 42*, 309-316.

Button, E. (1985). Eating disorders: A quest for control? In E. Button (Eds), *Personal Construct Theory and Mental Health,* pp. 153-168. London: Croom Helm.

Charman, T. (2002). The prevalence of autism spectrum disorders: Recent evidence and future challenges. *European Child & Adolescent Psychiatry, 11*, 249-256.

Connan, F., Campbell, I. C., Katzman, M., Lightman, S. L., & Treasure, J. (2003). A neurodevelopmental model for anorexia nervosa. *Physiology & Behavior, 79*, 13-24.

Davies, H., & Tchanturia, K. (2005). Cognitive remediation therapy as an intervention for acute anorexia nervosa: A case report. *European Eating Disorders Review, 13*, 311-316.

Frith, U. (1989). *Autism: Explaining the Enigma.* Oxford: Blackwell.

Frith, U., & Snowling, M. (1983). Reading for meaning and reading for sound in autistic and dyslexic children. *Journal of Developmental Psychology, 1*, 329-342.

Gillberg, I. C., Gillberg, C., Råstam, M., & Johansson, M. (1996). The cognitive profile of anorexia nervosa: A comparative study including a community-based sample. *Comprehensive Psychiatry, 37*, 23-30.

Gillberg, I. C., Rastam, M., Wentz, E., & Gillberg, C. (2007). Cognitive and executive functions in anorexia nervosa ten years after onset of eating disorder. *Journal of Clinical and Experimental Neuropsychology, 29*, 170-178.

Green, M. W., Elliman, N. A., Wakeling, A., & Rogers, P. J. (1996). Cognitive functioning, weight change and therapy in anorexia nervosa. *Journal of Psychiatric Research, 30*, 401-410.

Happé, F., & Frith, U. (2006). The weak coherence account: Detail focused cognitive style in Autism Spectrum Disorders. *Journal of Autism and Developmental Disorders, 36*, 5-25.

Happé, F., Briskman, J., & Frith, U. (2001). Exploring the cognitive phenotype of autism: Weak "central coherence" in parents and siblings of children with autism: I. Experimental tests. *Journal of Child Psychology and Psychiatry, 42*, 299-307.

Happé, F. G. E. (1994). Wechsler IQ profile and theory of mind in autism : A research note. *Journal of Child Psychology and Psychiatry, 37*, 873-877.

Holliday, J., Tchanturia, K., Landau, S., Collier, D., & Treasure, J. (2005). Is impaired set-shifting an endophenotype of anorexia nervosa. *American Journal of Psychiatry, 162*, 2269-2275.

Kagan, J. (1966). Reflection-Impulsivity: The generality and dynamics of conceptual time. *Journal of Abnormal Psychology, 1*, 17-24.

Kemps, E., Tiggemann, M., Wade, T., Ben-Tovim, D., & Breyer, R. (2006). Selective working memory deficits in anorexia nervosa. *European Eating Disorders Review, 14*, 97-103.

Kingston, K., Szmukler, G., Andrewes, D., Tress, B., & Desmond, P. (1996). Neuropsychological and structural brain changes in anorexia nervosa before and after refeeding. *Psychological Medicine, 26*, 15-28.

Lauer, C. (2002), Enrolments in higher education: do economic incentives matter? *Education & Training, 44*, 179-185.

Lena, S. M., Fiocco, A. J., & Leyenaar, J. K. (2004). The role of cognitive deficits in the development of eating disorders. *Neuropsychology Review, 14*, 99-113.

Lopez, C., Roberts, M., Tchanturia, K., & Treasure, J. (2008). Using neuropsychological feedback therapeutically in treatment for anorexia nervosa: Two illustrative case reports. *European Eating Disorders Review, 41*, 340-347.

Lopez, C., Roberts, M. E., Tchanturia, K., & Treasure, J. (2008). Using neuropsychological feedback therapeutically in treatment for anorexia nervosa: two illustrative case reports. *European Eating Disorders Review, 16*, 411-420.

Lopez, C., Tchanturia, K., Stahl, D., Booth, R., Holliday, J., & Treasure, J. (2008). An examination of central coherence in women with anorexia nervosa. *International Journal of Eating Disorders, 41*, 143-152.

Lopez, C., Tchanturia, K., Stahl, D., & Treasure, J. (2008). Central coherence in women with bulimia nervosa. *International Journal of Eating Disorders, 41,* 340-347.

Mathias, J. L., & Kent, P. S. (1998). Neuropsychological consequences of extreme weight loss and dietary restriction in patients with anorexia nervosa. *Journal of Clinical and Experimental Neuropsychology, 20*, 548-564.

McLaughlin, E. F., Karp, S. A., & Herzog, D. B. (1985). Sense of ineffectiveness in women with eating disorders: A clinical study of anorexia nervosa and bulimia. *International Journal of Eating Disorders, 4*, 511-523.

Osterrieth, P. (1944). Le test de copie d'une figure complex: Contribution à l'étude de la perception et de la memoire [Test of copying a complex figure: A contribution to the study of perception and memory]. *Archives de Psychologie, 30*, 286-350.

Pieters, G., Hulstijn, W., Vandereyken, W., Maas, Y., Probst, M., Peuskens, J. et al. (2005). Fast psychomotor functioning in anorexia nervosa: effect of weight restoration. *Journal of Clinical and Experimental Neuropsychology, 27*, 931-942.

Pieters, G., Maas, Y., Hulstijn, W., Vandereyken, W., Probst, M., Peuskens, J. et al. (2004). Differentiation of cognitive and motor aspects in a digit symbol substitution test in anorexia nervosa patients, before and after weight restoration. *Psychopathology, 37*, 227-232.

Pieters, G., Sabbe, B., Hulstijn, W., Probst, M., Vandereyken, W., & Peuskens, J. (2003). Fast psychomotor functioning in underweight anorexia nervosa patients. *Journal of Psychiatric Research, 37*, 501-508.

Pretorius, N., & Tchanturia, K. (2007). Anorexia nervosa: How people think and how we address it in psychological treatment. *Therapy, 4*, 501-508.

Rastam, M., Gillberg, C., & Wentz, E. (2003). Outcome of teenage-onset anorexia nervosa in a Swedish community-based sample. *European Child & Adolescent Psychiatry, 12*, 78-90.

Rieger, E., Schotte, D. E., Touyz, S. W., Beumont, P. J. V., Griffiths, R., & Russell, J. (1998). Attentional biases in eating disorders: A visual probe detection procedure. *International Journal of Eating Disorders, 23*, 199-205.

Sassaroli, S., Gallucci, M., & Ruggiero, G. M. (2008). Low perception of control as a cognitive factor of eating disorders. Its independent effects on measures of eating disorders and its interactive effects with perfectionism and self-esteem. *Journal of Behavior Therapy and Experimental Psychiatry, 39*, 467-488

Savage, C. R., Baer, L., Keuthen, N., Brown, H. D., Rauch, S. L., & Jenike, M. A. (1999). Organizational strategies mediate nonverbal memory impairment in obsessive-compulsive disorder. *Biological Psychiatry, 45*, 905-916.

Savage, C. R., Deckersbach, T., Rauch, S. L., Baer, L., Reid, T., & Jenike, M. A. (2000). Strategic processing and episodic memory impairment in obsessive compulsive disorder. *Neuropsychology, 14*, 141-151.

Schmidt, U., & Treasure, J. (2006). Anorexia nervosa: valued and visible. A cognitive-interpersonal maintenance model and its implications for research and practice. *British Journal of Clinical Psychology, 45*, 343-366.

Shah, A., & Frith, U. (1993). Why do autistic individuals show superior performance on the Block Design task? *Journal of Child Psychology and Psychiatry, 34,* 1351-1364.

Sherman, B. J., Savage, C. R., Eddy, K. T., Blais, M. A., Deckersbach, T., Jackson, S. C., Franko, D. L., Rauch, S. L., & Herzog, D. B. (2006). Strategic memory in adults with anorexia nervosa: Are there similarities to obsessive compulsive spectrum disorders? *International Journal of Eating Disorders, 39*, 468-476.

Sours, J. A. (1969). The anorexia nervosa syndrome: Phenomenologic and psychodynamic components. *Psychiatry Quarterly, 43*, 240-256.

Southgate, L., Tchanturia, K., & Treasure, J. (2005). Building a model of the aetiology of eating disorders by translating experimental neuroscience into clinical practice. *Journal of Mental Health, 14*, 553-566.

Southgate, L. Tchanturia, K., & Treasure, J. (2008). Information processing bias in anorexia nervosa. *Psychiatry Research, 160*, 221-227.

Strupp, B. J., Weingartner, H., Kaye, W., & Gwirtsman, H. (1986). Cognitive processing in anorexia nervosa: A disturbance in automatic information processing. *Neuropsychobiology, 15*, 89-94.

Tchanturia, K., Davies, H., & Campbell, I.C. (2007). Cognitive remediation therapy for patients with anorexia nervosa: Preliminary findings. *Annals of General Psychiatry, 6*, 14

Tchanturia, K., Happé, F., Godley, J., Treasure, J., Bara-Carril, N., & Schmidt, U. (2004). 'Theory of mind' in anorexia nervosa. *European Eating Disorders Review, 12,* 361 - 366.

Tchanturia, K., Morris, R.G., Brecelj Anderluh, M., Collier, D.A., Nikolaou, V., & Treasure, J. (2004). Set shifting in anorexia nervosa: An examination before and after weight gain, in full recovery and relationship to childhood and adult OCPD traits. *Journal of Psychiatric Research, 38*, 545-552.

Tchanturia, K., Whitney, J., & Treasure, J. (2006). Can cognitive exercises help treat anorexia nervosa? A case report. *Eating and Weight Disorders, 11*, E112-E117.

Thompson, S. B. N. (1993). Implications of neuropsychological test results of women in a new phase of anorexia nervosa. *European Eating Disorders Review, 1*, 152-165.

Tokley, M., & Kemps, E. (2007). Preoccupation with detail contributes to poor abstraction in women with anorexia nervosa. *Journal of Clinical and Experimental Neuropsychology, 29*, 734-741.

Treasure, J., Tchanturia, K., & Schmidt, U. (2005). Developing a model of the treatment for eating disorder: using neuroscience research to examine the how rather than the what of change. *Counselling and Psychotherapy Research, 5,* 187-190.

Uher, R., Treasure, J., & Campbell, I. C. (2002). Neuroanatomical bases of eating disorders. In H. D'haenen, J.A. den Boer, & P. Willner (Eds.), *Biological Psychiatry*. Swansey, UK: Wiley & Sons, pp. 1173-1179.

Wentz, E., Lacey, H., Waller, G., Rastam, M., Turk, J., & Gillberg, C. (2005). Childhood onset neuropsychiatric disorders in adult eating disorder patients. European *Child & Adolescent Psychiatry*, 14, 431-437.

Whitney, J., Easter, A., & Tchanturia, K. (in press). Services users' feedback on cognitive training in the treatment of anorexia nervosa. *International Journal of Eating Disorders.*

Witkin, H. A., Oltman, P., Raskin, E., & Karp, S. A. (1971). *A Manual for the Embedded Figures Test*. Palo Alto, CA: Consulting Psychologists Press, Inc.

Wykes, T., & Reeder, C. (2005). *Cognitive Remediation Therapy for Schizophrenia: Theory and Practice.* London: Routledge.

In: Cognitive Therapy of Eating Disorders...
Editors: S. Sassaroli and G.M. Ruggiero

ISBN: 978-1-60876-617-8

Chapter 7

IMPULSIVITY IN EATING DISORDERS

***J. Hubert Lacey*[1] *and Kate Webb*[2]**
[1]Professor of Psychiatry, Clinical Director, St George's Eating Disorders Service, London
[2]Specialist Registrar, Honorary Research Assistant, St George's Eating Disorders Service, London
Academic Department of Psychiatry, Level 6 Hunter Wing
St George's University of London
Tooting London SW17 0RE

ABSTRACT

This chapter will discuss impulsivity most commonly associated with bulimia nervosa but also in anorexia nervosa. The complex inter-relationship between personality disorders and impulsivity in eating disorders, cognitive correlates and therapeutic issues related to impulsivity in eating disorders will also be explored. There is a subgroup of patients with eating disorders who exhibit impulsive behaviour alongside their eating disorder, originally described and named in the literature by Lacey and Evans (1986). The changing role of women in society may well be in part responsible for the changing symptomatology and presentation of eating disorders over the years. The results of studies looking at the relationship between impulsive behaviour and eating disorders are mixed, probably due to the heterogeneous nature of the methodologies used, including variations of the definition of impulsivity. However, there is no doubt that patients with eating disorders who also exhibit non food related impulsive behaviours, have a poorer outcome than those who do not and that this in turn has significant clinical and service provision implications. This chapter will discuss impulsivity most commonly associated with bulimia nervosa but also in anorexia nervosa.

IMPULSIVITY

Impulsivity has not been clearly defined in the literature although most definitions refer to the speed, undesirability and loss of cognitive control that characterise the behaviour or response (Coles, 1997). The variation in the definition of the term impulsivity, has been troublesome when interpreting the results of research looking at the relationship between eating disorders and impulsive behaviour.

ICD-10 Classification of Mental and Behavioural Disorders (ICD-10) and the Diagnostic and Statistical Manual of Mental Disorders, fourth edition (DSM-IV), have sections categorising Habit and Impulse Disorders and Impulse Control Disorders not elsewhere classified respectively, as well as using the term impulsive in the criteria for many other disorders. They define this behaviour as the propensity to act repeatedly with no rational motivation, a lack of control and in a way that is harmful to self and / or others. The increasing tension and arousal that occurs is discussed, as well as the relief that follows the action. They also suggest that the behaviours may or may not be planned or consciously resisted. However, although this description is consistent with the clinical notion of impulsivity, it remains non-specific compared to the dictionary or psychometric definition.

The Shorter Oxford English Dictionary (2002) definition of impulse is more specific: 'sudden or involuntary inclination to act, without premeditation' and impulsive: 'apt to be moved by sudden impulse or emotion, prompted by sudden impulse'.

Impulsivity has also been conceptualised psychometrically. Eysenck, Pearson, Easting and Allsop (1985), described impulsivity as a dimensional personality trait which leads to behaving without stopping to think, acting on the spur of the moment and without thinking about possible complications. They also described 'venturesomeness' as a second impulsivity dimension, as being aware of the risks of certain behaviours but finding enjoyment in carrying them out. Barratt proposed a unidimensional model of impulsivity that has since been revised to a tridimensional model that differentiates among 'motor impulsiveness', cognitive impulsiveness' and 'nonplanning impulsiveness' dimensions (Parker & Bagby, 1997). Dickman (1990), described two impulsivity dimensions, 'dysfunctional impulsivity', a tendency to behave with little consideration for the problems involved and 'functional impulsivity', a tendency to behave without consideration when the action is beneficial. A study by Dawe, Gullo & Loxton (2004), suggests a two factor model for impulsivity, 'reward sensitivity' and 'rash impulsiveness', after looking at evidence from factor analytic studies describing measures of impulsivity taken from many different personality theorists.

The Relationship between Impulsivity and Eating Disorders

Studies looking at impulsivity and eating disorders have often used different measurement scales, measuring different components of impulsivity based on various theoretical constructs and this has confused the picture concerning the relationship between the two.

Bulimia Nervosa

It is clear that some patients with bulimia nervosa present with co-morbid self-damaging and other behaviours that display dyscontrol and that these patients have been found not to respond well to conventional outpatient cognitive behavioural therapy. Although it is known that these patients present a treatment problem and make disproportionate demands on eating disorders services, diagnostic classification is difficult and contentious and this is reflected in the literature. The definition of impulsivity and how this relates to eating disorders and personality pathology, have been highly variable. Rates of multi-impulsivity amongst patients with bulimia nervosa correspondingly vary in the literature from around 3-80% depending on the criteria used and the nature of the sample.

The first author coined the term 'multi-impulsive bulimia' to distinguish a subgroup of patients with bulimia nervosa who may require more intensive and modified additions to their treatment plan (Lacey & Evans, 1986). The diagnostic criteria for 'multi-impulsive bulimia' proposed by the first author, is bulimia nervosa with one or more of the following behaviours: gross alcohol abuse, 'street drug' abuse, multiple overdoses, repeated self damage, sexual disinhibition or shoplifting. These behaviours are associated with a sense of being out of control, are interchangeable and impulsive and suppression of these behaviours leads to the emergence of underlying depression and intense anger.

Since then, this diagnostic construct has sparked much debate in the literature and has led to discussions concerning the definition of impulsivity, whether the behaviours described are impulsive in nature, how many behaviours are necessary for diagnosis, for how long should they be present and as to whether there should be a separate subgroup 'multi-impulsive bulimia' at all.

Arguments Against

According to DSM-IV and ICD-10, some behaviours would be classified under impulse control disorders and habit and impulse disorders respectively. Others such as alcohol and substance misuse, sexual and eating disordered behaviours are classified elsewhere but often thought of as impulsive in the clinical sense of the term. However, some authors have suggested that these behaviours should not be described as impulsive. Fahy and Eisler (1993) and Newton, Freeman and Munro (1993), found that patients with the so called 'multi-impulsive bulimia' do not score more highly than patients with more straightforward bulimia nervosa on psychometric impulsivity rating scales, although the majority of 'multi-impulsive bulimic' patients in their studies only had one other impulsive behaviour in addition to their eating disordered behaviours. Patients with bulimia nervosa have been found to have higher global impulsivity scores using Barrett's Impulsivity Scale (BIS, Patton, 1995), than the non clinical population and patients with anorexia nervosa - restrictive subtype (Rosval et al, 2006). In the same study, patients with binge-purge symptoms scored more highly on certain elements of impulsivity such as the behavioural/ motor components and patients with bulimia nervosa also scored more highly on non planning (to act recklessly) components of impulsivity, perhaps making them more prone than the non clinical population or patients with other eating disorders, to non food related self-damaging behaviours. Binge eating itself may be seen as impulsive but patients sometimes use bingeing as a behaviour to regulate emotion and also as a physiological and psychological consequence of dietary restraint.

It has also been found that patients with bulimia nervosa have raised levels of obsessionality and that their difficulty in responding to situations in a flexible manner may well be an important aetiological factor in the development of binge-purge symptoms (Fahy, 1991). The associated behaviours in 'multi-impulsive bulimia' have been described as having a strong similarity to obsessive compulsive disorder and may well be compulsive rather than impulsive in nature. These patients often describe a feeling of intolerable tension and anxiety that is relieved by use of the behaviour but often spend many hours trying to resist carrying out the act (Newton et al, 1993). Impulsive and compulsive personality traits in bulimia nervosa have also been studied and it has been found that many patients have high scores for both, suggesting that they are not mutually exclusive traits as some unidimensional models of impulsivity-compulsivity have proposed (Engel et al, 2005).

Myers et al (2006), when using LCA (latent class analysis), found that patients with 'multi-impulsive bulimia', had a significantly higher risk of having a life time history of an anxiety disorder, particularly post traumatic stress disorder and to a lesser extent obsessive compulsive disorder. They suggested that the multi-impulsivity in bulimia nervosa may be a method of dealing with 'trauma related affect' and the behaviours may therefore be seen more in terms of regulating anxiety. Multi-impulsivity is associated with higher rates of childhood trauma, particularly physical, sexual and emotional abuse (Corstorphine, Waller, Lawson & Ganis, 2007; Waller, 1991). Affective disturbance has also been implicated by Sohlberg, Norring, Holmgren and Rosmark (1989), as a trigger for these behaviours, as it has been proposed that they serve to regulate negative affect. Patients who exhibit these self damaging behaviours have been found to have high scores on the Beck's Depression Inventory (BDI, Steer,1999), but the relationship between impulsivity and depression is not clear. Fahy and Eisler (1993) proposed that the presence of impulsivity may influence the expression of the eating disorder in both anorexia or bulimia nervosa but they did not feel that there was enough evidence to suggest that the behaviours described by Lacey and Evans (1986), for the diagnosis of 'multi-impulsive bulimia', arise from an underlying impulse control disorder. They also proposed that these behaviours serve to regulate affect, rather than a failure to consider the adverse consequences or risks of the behaviour concerned.

Ainsworth, Waller and Kennedy (2002), described the concept of 'threat processing' in patients with bulimia nervosa. They suggest that in using a cognitive-behavioural model to treat bulimia nervosa, the focus of therapy tends to be on food, weight and shape problems and that this may be too superficial an approach. They discussed the idea that bulimic symptoms and perhaps other impulsive behaviours may serve the function of an 'escape from awareness' through dissociation or cognitive or schema avoidance. They also consider why some patients with bulimia nervosa may develop multiple impulsive behaviours and suggest that each behaviour may serve a different function, or that one particular behaviour no longer seems fit for purpose and is substituted for another.

Welch & Fairburn (1996) proposed that behaviours set out in the criteria for 'multi-impulsive bulimia' (Lacey & Evans, 1986) are not all related in the same way to bulimia nervosa and that behaviours such as alcohol misuse and repeated overdoses are more related to general psychopathology or affect regulation. They also suggested that substance misuse may not be impulsive in nature, e.g. amphetamine misuse for appetite control. They therefore argued that there is no place for a specific category of 'multi-impulsive bulimia'. They did however, find that self harm, particularly cutting was more common in the bulimic population than the general psychiatric population. Favaro and Santonastaso (2002), confirmed this and found a specific link between self injurious behaviour and eating disorders. They went further to divide self injurious behaviour into compulsive (e.g. nail biting, hair pulling and self induced vomiting) and impulsive (e.g. suicide attempts, cutting, burning, laxatives/ diuretic misuse and alcohol/ substance misuse) and found that both types had a significant clinical impact on anorexia and bulimia nervosa. Fahy and Eisler (1993), found there to be no difference in outcome for patients with high scores on the impulsivity measure that they used and there were only short term differences when they used the number of impulsive behaviours in addition to eating disordered behaviours as the criteria. They agreed that there was not enough evidence for a separate subgroup, 'multi-impulsive bulimia'. However, they tended to use patients at the milder end of the spectrum and only had a small number of patients who displayed three or more non food related impulsive behaviours.

Arguments for

Cluster analytic studies looking at personality pathology in patients with eating disorders, suggest that there are three clusters of personality traits. These have been consistent in their findings and Westen and Harnden-Fischer (2001), found a high functioniong / perfectionistic cluster where patients with bulimia were overrepresented; a constricted / overcontrolled cluster where 78.3% of the patients either had a lifetime diagnosis of anorexia nervosa - restrictive or binge-purge subtype and a dysregulated/ undercontrolled cluster where 100% of the patients had a lifetime diagnosis of bulimia nervosa or anorexia nervosa - binge-purge subtype. The dysregulated/ undercontrolled cluster appears to be highly specific to patients with binge-purge symptoms although it should not be assumed that all patients with binge purge symptoms, have personality traits that fit into this group. This is consistent with the nature of bingeing and purging which may or may not be planned but is usually associated with a sense of being out of control. There is sometimes an assumption, never convincingly shown, that a specific personality subtype is linked to a specific eating disorder diagnosis. These theories become confused when there is overlap between anorectic and bulimic psychopathology and when a single patient traverses through various eating disorder diagnoses over the course of their life, although it may be argued that their psychopathology remains the same despite a change in weight and eating disordered behaviours. Westen and Harnden-Fischer (2001) suggest that it would be more helpful to classify patients with eating disorders, not only by their eating behaviours but also by personality which may have significant aetiological, therapeutic and prognostic implications.

Fichter, Quadflieg and Rief (1994), discussed the possibility of a new axis one disorder, 'multi-impulsive disorder' or an axis two disorder, 'multi-impulsive personality disorder'. In their study, patients with 'multi-impulsive bulimia', defined as bulimia nervosa with at least three non food related impulsive behaviours, did not show higher eating disorder pathology. However, they did show more general psychopathology than patients with bulimia nervosa but no significant increase in psychiatric co-morbidity. They argued that to define a new disorder, would help in the development of suitable treatments for this group of patients, where focusing only on their eating disorder will clearly miss aspects of their behaviour that need to be dealt with to ensure recovery. A recent study (Myers et al, 2006), used LCA (latent class analysis) to identify latent groups within their patient sample. Using this technique, they found evidence to support a subgroup 'multi-impulsive bulimia', using the criteria of bulimia nervosa with three or more non food related impulsive behaviours (Fichter et al, 1994). These include self report of suicide attempt, self report of self harming, one or more episodes of stealing (other than food), self report of severe or very severe abuse of alcohol, promiscuity (five or more sexual partners in the past two years or ten or more since puberty) and self report of severe or very severe drug abuse.

Fichter et al. (1994), found that patients with 'multi-impulsive bulimia' tended to have more broken relationships, lower levels of education, higher levels of psychosocial stressors and a lower maximum level of adaptive functioning prior to admission (DSM III – axis IV).

They proposed that the impulsivity in these patients may be related to a tendency to react emotionally which may present itself in aggression and hostility as well as anxiety and depression. Lacey (1993), also described these patients as being older, having lower employment levels and less likely to be in a stable relationship. They were more likely to have a partner or family with a history of alcohol misuse.

It has also been suggested that 'multi-impulsive bulimia' is perhaps a variant of borderline personality disorder. The nature of the co-existence of personality pathology and eating disorders remains unclear and the criteria for the diagnosis of an eating disorder does not take axis two pathology into account. Various models for the relationship have been proposed (Sansone & Levitt, 2004). These include a chance co-existence; common aetiology; a spectrum model, suggesting that the eating disorder is actually a sub-clinical form of borderline personality disorder; that either disorder predisposes the patient to the other; that one is a complication of the other or that they exacerbate each other. The personality pathology in 'multi-impulsive' patients may be at the milder end of the spectrum, making it difficult to give a firm diagnosis of a personality disorder. It may also be that if a patient starves, in the case of anorexia nervosa, they are predisposed to developing personality pathology which improves during weight gain, therefore not strictly a personality disorder. Perhaps, as clinicians, we should pay more attention to multi-axial classification which is currently incorporated into DSM-IV and think about personality pathology in a more dimensional manner. Symptoms that do not meet the criteria for a personality disorder diagnosis, may still have an adverse effect on the predisposing, precipitating and maintaining factors for axis one disorders, complicating treatment and recovery

Despite the arguments in the literature, there seems little doubt that patients with bulimia nervosa who also exhibit at least three non food related self damaging or maladaptive behaviours (Fichter et al, 1994), have a more severe disorder and a poorer prognosis. The term impulsive, when used to describe these behaviours associated with eating disorders, although clinically relevant, may be a misnomer if defined by the dictionary or psychometrically. However, this should not take us away from the fact that treatment for these patients needs careful consideration. For treatments to develop, some form of categorisation in ICD-10 and DSM-IV would be helpful for consistent research in this area. The first author proposed that 'multi-impulsive bulimia' should either be a subcategory of bulimia nervosa in axis one or 'multi-impulsive personality disorder' in axis two (Lacey & Evans, 1986).

Anorexia Nervosa

Multi-impulsivity also occurs in patients with anorexia nervosa. Cluster analytic studies (Westen & Harnden-Fischer, 2001), suggest that we should not assume that one cluster of personality traits is related to a particular eating disorder, particularly in an individual patient who may exhibit diagnostic instability over a lifetime. This study showed that all patients with a lifetime diagnosis of pure anorexia nervosa - restrictive subtype belonged to the constrictive / over controlled cluster or the high functioning / perfectionistic cluster. Patients with anorexia nervosa - binge-purge subtype, belonged to all three clusters including the under controlled / dysregulated cluster, suggesting that they may be more likely than the restrictive patients to develop a 'multi-impulsive eating disorder'.

Rosval et al (2006), used the BIS to study impulsivity in patients with bulimia nervosa and anorexia nervosa - restrictive and binge-purge subtype. They found that patients with all eating disorders showed impairments compared with the non clinical population in the attentional (planning) component of impulsivity. When they looked at the motoric or behavioural component of impulsivity, all binge eaters, including patients with anorexia nervosa - binge-purge subtype showed significantly more impairment than the restrictive and non-clinical groups. Interestingly, the scores for the non-planning (to act recklessly) component of impulsivity were lower for both anorectic subtypes compared to the non-clinical group. These results suggest that all patients with eating disorders have a propensity for impulsive thinking. They also show that bingeing and purging is also linked to behavioural impulsivity but for patients with anorexia - binge-purge subtype, this may be tempered by cautiousness.

Anorexia nervosa - restrictive subtype, is usually associated with a high level of control, discipline, perfectionism and risk avoidance and a low level of sensation seeking. It has been shown that following restorative weight gain, patients with anorexia nervosa have abnormally high serotonergic activity which correlates with impulse control. This suggests that there may be an underlying biological factor, predisposing patients who are likely to develop anorexia nervosa to highly controlled personalities. However, there are patients with anorexia nervosa - restrictive subtype who exhibit behaviour such as self harm, unplanned suicide attempts, violence, substance misuse, kleptomania, stealing and anger outbursts (Fessler, 2002). Strober, Freeman and Morrell (1999), found that approximately 30% of patients with restrictive anorexia nervosa will develop binge eating at some point during the course of their disorder.

There have been various hypotheses as to why these patients exhibit self damaging, impulsive behaviours. Different personality factors may lead to the development of the same symptoms, therefore impulsive behaviour may originate from a variety of sources, not only core personality factors. Underweight anorectic patients have also been found to have a deficit in serotonergic functioning which has been implicated in impulsive behaviour in other disorders including bulimia nervosa (Bruce et al, 2005). The 'logic of scarcity' theory, discussed by Fessler (2001), is based on the idea that the body adapts itself to a change in resource availability; e.g. amenorrhoea occurs when starving, as reproduction is prolonged and requires high amounts of energy to sustain. It was suggested that the same logic may apply to behavioural and emotional responses; e.g. if the future seems bright, there is no point in taking risks to destroy it. However, if you may starve to death, seeking opportunities to gain large rewards seems beneficial, even if there may be significant personal costs involved. Binge eating is a good way of maximising intake if food is scarce or at risk of being removed and the capacity for anger and aggression may stop a competitor taking food or drink. Patients with anorexia nervosa - restrictive subtype, may focus these impulsive urges into non food related, more mal-adaptive behaviours because of their specific anorectic psychopathology.

Perception of Control in Eating Disorders

Sassaroli, Gallucci & Ruggiero (2008), studied low perception of control as a cognitive factor of eating disorders. They looked at the main and interactive effects of concern over mistakes (perfectionism measure), self esteem and perception of control on three measures of eating disorders – drive for thinness, bulimia and body dissatisfaction. The authors found that a low perception of control, over food, weight and shape and general feelings and events, was also an important cognitive factor of eating disorders and that there was an interaction between all three cognitive factors studied. There was a subgroup of people with high levels of self esteem and perception of control, with high levels of drive for thinness. This suggests that people with restrictive anorexia nervosa may develop an illusion of high self esteem and high perception of control when they attempt to regain a sense of control by using eating disordered behaviours and 'constricting' their lifestyle to lessen the threat of unpredictable emotions and external events. The effects were not as clear cut for patients with bulimia nervosa. This study does not look at the impulsivity as a cognitive factor. It would seem likely that impulsivity and a low perception of control would not co-exist in the same patient but it may be that these multi-impulsive behaviours are also a way of seeking increased control, albeit in a maladaptive way as with eating disordered behaviours.

PROGNOSIS

There have been relatively few outcome studies for patients with multi-impulsive eating disorders. Sohlberg et al. (1989) found that impulsive behaviours such as alcohol or substance misuse, recent suicide attempt, bingeing or stealing, were the strongest predictor of a poor prognosis for patients with both anorexia and bulimia nervosa over a four to six year follow up.

Fichter, Quadflieg and Rief (1994) followed the course of patients with 'multi-impulsive bulimia', using the criteria of three or more non-food related behaviours and patients with bulimia nervosa, during treatment and over a two year follow up period following discharge. They found that at discharge from inpatient treatment, both groups showed considerable improvements in terms of eating disorder symptoms and general psychopathology but that the multi-impulsive patients were still more anxious, depressed, demoralised, angry and hostile and these differences remained at two year follow up. At this stage, bulimic symptoms were still marked in the multi-impulsive bulimic group and significantly more severe than the bulimic patients, despite there being no differences at the start of treatment. The multi-impulsive group also had more psychiatric inpatient days before and after treatment, despite a higher treatment drop out rate, as well as attending their GP surgery more in the two year follow up.

St George's Eating Disorders Service offers a specialised inpatient programme for patients with multi-impulsive eating disorders, bulimia nervosa or anorexia nervosa. The programme is based on the principle of relinquishing all impulsive behaviours and by using the various psychotherapeutic treatments on offer, to learn to verbalise their distress and manage the difficult emotions that arise. The long term outcome of this programme was evaluated by Corfe and Lacey, who contacted patients who had undergone a minimum of two weeks treatment as an inpatient. Total impulsive behaviours had significantly reduced at ten year follow up: 57% reported no impulsive behaviours and 20% were free of both eating disordered and other impulsive behaviours.

CLINICAL IMPLICATIONS OF IMPULSIVITY IN EATING DISORDERS

Although cognitive behavioural therapy in an outpatient setting is currently the gold standard treatment for bulimia nervosa (NICE), approximately 50% of patients continue to binge and vomit following treatment (Agras, Walsh & Fairburn et al. 2000) and patients with multi-impulsive eating disorders have a poorer outcome.

Dialectical Behaviour Therapy (DBT) for Bulimia Nervosa

DBT was developed by Linehan, to treat borderline personality disorder. The treatment is based on the hypothesis that the aetiological basis for the development of this disorder is bio-social; an individual who is 'emotionally vulnerable' who also grows up in an 'invalidating environment' (Linehan, 1993). The treatment is largely based on cognitive behavioural therapy techniques but also incorporates thinking from psychodynamic psychotherapy and certain aspects of Zen Buddhism, although the application of such meditation techniques is psychological and not religious. The relationship between the patient and therapist is important and the treatment has four components. These include weekly individual therapy, weekly group skills training (core mindfulness, interpersonal effectiveness, emotion modulation and distress tolerance skills) and telephone contact with the individual therapist between sessions. The team treating patients also have a weekly consultation group (Palmer et al, 2003; Kiehn & Swales, 1995).

DBT has been successfully adapted for the treatment of eating disorders, particularly those who exhibit multiple 'self-damaging' and 'self-defeating' behaviours (Palmer et al, 2003) and who appear not to respond to standard treatment approaches. DBT for eating disorders is based on an affect regulation model of eating disorders and aims to help patients replace their eating disordered behaviours with other affect regulating skills. It is usually carried out on an outpatient basis but has also been adapted for use in day and inpatients. Palmer et al (2003), measured eating disordered behaviours, self harm episodes and hospital inpatient days before, during and after dialectical behaviour therapy for seven patients who had a diagnosed eating disorder (including two with anorexia nervosa) and borderline personality disorder. They found a reduction in the number of inpatient days and self harm events and that by eighteen months after treatment, no patients had a full syndrome eating disorder. Safer, Telch & Agras (2001), randomly assigned 31 women with bulimia nervosa to a waiting list group and a DBT group and showed significant reductions in binge/purge behaviour with the DBT group compared to the waiting list group. These finding are encouraging but more research is needed with larger group sizes to look at the use of DBT in the treatment of eating disorders.

Inpatient Eclectic Treatment Programme for 'Multi-Impulsive' Eating Disorders

Patients with bulimia nervosa or anorexia nervosa, with three or more impulsive behaviours, do not respond well to outpatient treatment. Because of the interchangeable nature of their symptoms, if treated in outpatients, one type of behaviour may be given up only to be substituted for another. In order to fully recover, a patient must give up all behaviours simultaneously and this may only be possible in the containing environment of an inpatient ward that allows for intensive treatment. This treatment is given at St George's Eating Disorders Service, London on the inpatient unit for a patient group defined as having 'multi-impulsive bulimia nervosa or anorexia nervosa' (Lacey & Read, 1993).

The inpatient unit is an eighteen bedded unit with additional day patients. The patients are referred from community mental health teams and come from a wide area of the United Kingdom. Patients are assessed in outpatients and then prepared for admission prior to coming in to hospital. Occasionally emergency treatment, either on a medical ward, or on the St George's Eating Disorders Service intensive care programme, is necessary prior to assessment for the full recovery programme. On admission, patients go into a two week mutual assessment phase where they will be seen by a staff member from each professional background on the multi-disciplinary team including nursing, dietetics, occupational therapy, psychiatry, clinical psychology, family therapy and psychotherapy. At the end of the assessment phase, the team decides with the patient, whether the inpatient programme is appropriate for them and whether or not the patient feels able to commit themselves completely to recovery from their eating disorder. If so, they will be seen in a multi-disciplinary ward round to go through their aims and objectives for their admission. The aims should include behavioural control as well as changes at psychological, psychodynamic and social levels. The patient also agrees a verbal contract that includes no bingeing or vomiting, no restriction of diet, no violence to self, others or hospital property, no alcohol or illicit substances, no new sexual relationships whilst in treatment and to engage with the staff and work within the spirit of the programme.

The programme has several components:

1. Individual work with a **nurse (key worker),** who will meet with the patient regularly throughout their admission and help them with their aims and objectives of their inpatient stay. The keyworker will help guide the patient through each phase of treatment and will be involved in helping the patient with their prescribed diet which is reviewed regularly by the ward **dietician.**
2. The patient will also be allocated to an **individual psychotherapist**. As the patient starts to manage their eating disorder and other impulsive behaviours, underlying emotional and interpersonal problems will usually begin to emerge. Individual psychotherapy will often be psychodynamic in nature and will look at these issues in depth. The patient is then encouraged to explore new ways of dealing with these underlying feelings and emotions that have perhaps been hidden through the use of impulsive behaviours over a long period of time. Some patients will find it harder to move from the behavioural orientated treatment and may need more emphasis on this area at the beginning of treatment before moving into psychodynamic psychotherapy. Some patients benefit from a cognitive behavioural therapy or schema focussed approach to their treatment.
3. **Psychotherapy groups** are also attended twice weekly by the patients and are psychodynamically orientated.
4. **Psychodrama** is attended weekly by patients. This style of group therapy was pioneered by Moreno (1998), based on the hypothesis that acting in itself can be

cathartic and that by enacting life experiences and personal problems, deep emotion and conflict may be experienced at a conscious level, in the safe environment of the group. This is often a painful and difficult experience, particularly for patients who usually talk in a detached manner in other forms of psychotherapy. However, it can have a profound effect on improving awareness and motivation to recover. Role reversal may also help to improve interpersonal skills by improving empathy and compassion for the other.

5. **Family therapy** is offered subject to assessment, with parents and/or sexual partner and is thought to be an integral part of treatment. Information sessions for families are offered at the beginning of treatment regardless of whether the patient and their family have agreed to formal family therapy. These give an opportunity for families to find out more about eating disorders in general and to explore appropriate ways of responding to and helping the patient.
6. **Carers groups** are run on a regular basis and offer an opportunity for carers of family members or friends with eating disorders, to discuss their difficulties with others in a similar situation, in a safe and confidential setting.
7. **Occupational therapy groups** make up a large proportion of the programme and include creative therapies and reality orientated groups.

Creative Groups

Projective Art

Projective art may be a helpful aid to expression of feelings and emotion as it allows patients to express themselves non-verbally. They can then discuss the meaning of their work as a group which helps them to allow others to speak rather than dominating the space in the group themselves and allows them to express feelings in a contained manner with set time boundaries.

Craft

This group is generally low key but can be helpful for 'multi-impulsive' patients to learn to tolerate imperfection in the work that they do and to be able to wait for results rather than seek instant gratification. They may be tempted to 'binge' on the resources available in the art room and are encouraged to plan the session carefully and set their own boundaries around the items they use. Exposure to using sharp instruments in an adaptive manner, may also be beneficial to them.

Reality Orientated Groups

Menu Planning and Meal Cookery

The focus of this group for patients with 'multi-impulsive eating disorders' is on the reduction of the maladaptive, out of control nature of their eating disordered behaviours. The patients are taught to adhere to planned menus and to eat self prepared meals. This is clearly a difficult process for these patients who find it hard to work in a structured way and may feel that they are being over controlled. Enabling them to tolerate and contain the inevitable distress caused by eating normally is important. They are helped to be able to cope emotionally with normal eating and eating in the presence of others, including family and friends.

Lifestyle Redesign and Independent Living Skills

This group helps to enable patients to discover adaptive and meaningful work/ leisure and self care activities. This is often challenging due to problems in coping without the maladaptive behaviours that serve to regulate the difficult emotions that usually emerge as the behaviours cease. This group also serves to help patients budget, limit their spending and cope with debt which may have become out of control.

Communication and Assertion Skills

Patients with a multi-impulsive element to their eating disorder sometimes communicate in an aggressive way and may dominate others. This group helps them to communicate with others in an assertive but sensitive way that will help them to be heard but avoid alienation. Learning to manage relationships and abstain from risky sexual activity or abusive relationships is also dealt with in this group.

Stress Management Skills

Cognitive behavioural therapy principles are used to teach patients skills to help them manage anxiety, anger and mood with particular focus on learning to tolerate frustration, delayed gratification and dissatisfaction. They are also taught strategies to help them de-escalate, manage and tolerate intense emotional distress.

A transference relationship with the unit often develops reflecting the patients' internal dynamics, particularly once symptoms are under control and intense emotions start to emerge. The unit becomes a containing, empathic environment with firm behavioural boundaries. Problems of staff splitting, power struggles with the patient and inconsistent responses to behaviours on the ward, are dealt with by having multi-disciplinary team ward rounds twice a week where all decisions about a patient's care are made.

The patient will gradually work through the programme taking more and more responsibility for meals and monitoring their behaviour as time goes on. If the verbal contract is broken and the patient is destructive to themselves or others on the ward, a period of 'time-out' may be given. This involves the patient going home for a week to reflect on their treatment and to consider whether they feel ready to put their emotions into the treatment on offer, rather than behaviours. Usually the patient returns ready to recommit to the programme. After 8 weeks as an inpatient (this may be longer for patients with 'multi-impulsive anorexia nervosa', depending on the amount of weight to gain), the patient will gradually 'step-down' to the day patient phase for approximately 15 weeks and then to outpatient follow up. They will continue for ten sessions with the individual psychotherapist they have seen in the inpatient and day patient phase and attend a transition group when they move to outpatients, to help with the inevitable difficult process of detachment from the ward environment.

Pharmacotherapy

The use of psychotropic medications in the treatment of eating disorders and associated impulsive behaviours is a complex subject and a detailed discussion is beyond the scope of this chapter. A serotonin deficit has been associated with impulsive behaviours and Fluoxetine, a selective serotonin reuptake inhibitor (SSRI), has been licensed for the treatment of bulimia nervosa. SSRIs may also be used to help improve symptoms of borderline personality disorder such as aggression, lability of mood, 'rejection sensitivity', inappropriate anger, promiscuity, substance misuse and rash spending (Fagin, 2004), suggesting they may be helpful in treating symptoms for patients with a 'multi-impulsive eating disorder'. Mood stabilisers and anticonvulsants may also be a useful adjunct. The effect of psychotropic medication is likely to be modest and more research is needed in this area. Medication is usually used to target specific symptoms rather than the core disorder (Sansone & Sansone, 2004) and should be used alongside psychological therapies. Care needs to be taken with dosage and physical monitoring when using medications in patients with eating disorders.

Conclusion

Multi-impulsive eating disorders, both anorexia nervosa and bulimia nervosa present a significant clinical challenge. Impulsivity in eating disorders has been more extensively researched and despite debates in the literature about the nature of the associated behaviours it is clear that these patients make disproportionate demands on mental health services and need to be taken into consideration during service planning and development. The term 'multi-impulsive' when naming an eating disorder, is not completely satisfactory but we would argue that on symptomatic, diagnostic and treatment grounds, it is better than other options. Patients with 'multi-impulsive bulimia' could also be described as having borderline personality disorder but patients with borderline personality disorder do not usually demonstrate bulimic behaviour and other personality types can be recognised in many patients with 'multi-impulsive bulimia'. The real advantage to the term 'multi-impulsive bulimia' is that it emphasises the range of behaviours. It also implies that the behaviours are driven by a common psychopathology which can be addressed therapeutically either from a cognitive-behavioural or dynamic approach. We are firmly of the opinion that to address one behaviour alone, merely pushes the patient to deal with his/her emotions by the use of other behaviours. The implication of the multi-impulsive diagnosis is that all behaviours need to be addressed contemporaneously. This leads to an emotional release which can then be addressed psychotherapeutically.

References

Agras, W. S., Walsh, B. T., & Fairburn, C. G. (2000). A multi-centre comparison of cognitive–behavioural therapy and interpersonal psychotherapy for bulimia nervosa. *Archives of General Psychiatry, 57*, 459 -466

Ainsworth, C., Waller, G., & Kennedy, F. (2002). Threat processing in women with bulimia. *Clinical Psychology Review, 22*, 1155-1178.

Bruce, K. R., Steiger, H., Joober, R., Kin, N. M. K. N. Y., Israel, M., & Young, S.N. (2005). Association of the promoter polymorphism – 1438G/A of the 5-HT2A receptor gene with behavioural impulsiveness and serotonin function in women with bulimia nervosa. *American Journal of Medical Genetics, Part B (Neuropsychiatric Genetics), 137B*, 40-44.

Dawe, S., Gullo, M. J., & Loxton, N. J. (2004). Reward drive and rash impulsiveness as dimensions of impulsivity: implications for substance misuse. *Addictive Behaviour, 29*, 1389-1405.

Corstorphine, E., Waller, G., Lawson, R., & Ganis, C. (2007). Trauma and multi-impulsivity in the eating disorders. *Eating Behaviours, 8,* 23-30.

Dickman, S. J. (1990). Functional and dysfunctional impulsivity: personality and cognitive correlates. *Journal of Personality and Social Psychology, 58*, 95-102.

Eisler, I. (1993). Family models of eating disorders. In: Szmukler G. Dare C. Treasure J. (Eds.). *Handbook of eating disorders: theory, treatment and research*. England: John Wiley & Sons Ltd. pp. 155-176.

Engel, S. G., Corneliussen, S. J., Wonderlich, S. A., Crosby, R. D., le Grange, D., Crow, S., Klein, K., Bardone-Cone, A., Peterson, C., Joiner, T., Mitchell, J.E., & Steiger, H. (2005). Impulsivity and compulsivity in bulimia nervosa. *International Journal of Eating Disorders, 38,* 244-251.

Eysenck, S. B. J., Pearson, P.R., Easting, G., & Allsopp, J.F. (1985). Age norms for impulsiveness, venturesomeness and empathy in adults. *Personality and Individual Differences, 6,* 613-619.

Fagin, L. (2004). Management of personality disorders in acute inpatient settings. Part 1: Borderline personality disorders. *Advances in Psychiatric Treatment, 10*, 93-99.

Fahy, T. A. (1991). Obsessional Symptoms in eating disorders. *Behavior Research and Therapy, 29*, 113-117.

Fahy, T., & Eisler, I. (1993). Impulsivity and eating disorders. *British Journal of Psychiatry, 162*, 193-197.

Favaro, A., & Santonastaso, P. (2002). The spectrum of self-injurious behaviour in eating disorders. *Eating Disorders, 10*, 215-225.

Fessler, D. M. T. (2002). Pseudoparadoxical impulsivity in restrictive anorexia nervosa: a consequence of the logic of scarcity. *International Journal of Eating Disorders, 31*, 376-388.

Fichter, M. M., Quadflieg, N., & Rief, W. (1994). Course of multi-impulsive bulimia. *Psychological Medicine, 24*, 591-604.

Lacey, J. H., & Evans, C.D.H. (1986). The impulsivist: a multi-impulsive personality disorder. *British Journal of Addiction, 81*, 641-649.

Lacey, J. H., & Read, T.R.C. (1993). Multi-impulsive bulimia: description of an inpatient eclectic treatment programme and a pilot follow-up study of its efficacy. *Eating Disorders Review, 1*, 22-31.

Linehan, M. M. (1993). *Cognitive-behavioural Treatment of Borderline Personality Disorders*. Guilford, New York.

Moreno, J. K. (1998). Long-term psychodynamic psychotherapy for eating disorders: A descriptive case report. *Journal for Specialist in Group Work. 23*, 269-284.

Myers, T. C., Wonderlich, S.A., Crosby, R., Mitchell, J.E., Steffen, K.J., Smyth, J., & Miltenberger, R. (2006). Is multi-impulsive bulimia a distinct type of bulimia nervosa: psychopathology and EMA findings. *International Journal of Eating Disorders, 39*, 655-661.

Newton, J. R., Freeman, C. P., & Munro, J. (1993). Impulsivity and dyscontrol in bulimia nervosa: is impulsivity an independent phenomenon or a marker of severity? *Acta Psychiatrica Scandinavica, 87*, 389-394.

Palmer, R. L., Birchall, H., Damani, S., Gatward, N., McGrain, L., & Parker, L. (2003). A dialectical behavior therapy program for people with an eating disorder and borderline personality disorder-description and outcome. *International Journal of Eating Disorders, 33*, 281-6.

Kiehn, B., & Swales, M. (1995). An overview of dialectical behavior therapy in the treatment of borderline personality disorder. *Psychiatry On-line*: http://www.cmhc.com/articles/dbt1.htr

Parker, J. D. A., & Bagby, R.M. (1997). Impulsivity in adults: A critical review of measurement approaches. In C.C. Webster & M.A. Jackson (Eds.). *Impulsivity, Theory, Assessment and Treatment*. New York & London: The Guilford Press, pp. 180-194.

Rosval, L., Steiger, H., Bruce, K., Israel, M., Richardson, J., & Aubut, M. (2006). Impulsivity in women with eating disorders: problem of response inhibition, planning or attention. *International Journal of Eating Disorders, 39*, 590-593.

Safer, D. L., Telch, C. F., & Agras, W. S. (2001). Dialectical behaviour therapy for bulimia nervosa. *American Journal of Psychiatry, 158*, 632-634.

Sansone, R. A., & Levitt, J. L. (2004). Borderline personality and eating disorders. *Eating Disorders, 13*, 71-83.

Sassaroli, S., Gallucci, M., & Ruggiero, G. M. (2008). Low perception of control as a cognitive factor of eating disorders. Its independent effects on measures of eating disorders and its interactive effects with perfectionism and self-esteem. *Journal of Behavior Therapy and Experimental Psychiatry, 39*, 467-488.

Trumble, W. R., & Stevenson, A. (2002). *Shorter Oxford English Dictionary*. Oxford: Oxford University Press.

Patton, J. H., Stanford, M. S. & Barratt, E. S. (1995). Factor structure of the Barratt impulsiveness scale. *Journal of Clinical Psychology, 51*, 768-774.

Steer, R. A., Ball, R., Ranieri, W. F., & Beck, A. T. (1999). Dimensions of the Beck Depression Inventory. *Journal of clinical psychology, 55*,: 117–28.

Sohlberg, S., Norring, C., Holmgren, S., & Rosmark, B. (1989). Impulsivity and long-term prognosis of psychiatric patients with anorexia nervosa/ bulimia nervosa. *Journal of Nervous and Mental Disease, 177*, 249-258.

Strober, M., Freeman, R., & Morrell, W. (1999). Atypical cases of anorexia nervosa: Separation from typical cases in and outcome in a long-term prospective study. *International Journal of Eating Disorders, 25*, 135-142.

Waller, G. (1991). Sexual abuse as a factor in the eating disorders. *British Journal of Psychiatry, 159*, 664-671.

Fairburn, C. G., Welch, S. L., Norman, P. A., O'Connor, B. A., & Doll, H. A. (1996). Bias and bulimia nervosa: How typical are clinic cases? *American Journal of Psychiatry, 153*, 386-391.

Westen, D., & Harnden-Fischer, J. (2001). Personality profiles in eating disorders: rethinking the distinction between axis I and axis II. *American Journal of Psychiatry, 158*, 547-562.

In: Cognitive Therapy of Eating Disorders...
Editors: S. Sassaroli and G.M. Ruggiero

ISBN: 978-1-60876-617-8

Chapter 8

Group Cognitive Behavioral Therapy in Hospitalized Adolescent Females with Eating Disorders

Daniel Stein[1*], Eynat Zubery[2] and Yael Latzer[3]

[1]The Pediatric Psychosomatic Department, Safra Children's Hospital, The Chaim Sheba Medical Center, Tel Hashomer, affiliated with the Sackler Faculty of Medicine, Tel Aviv University, Tel Aviv, Israel

[2]Eating Disorders Unit, Davidson Clinic, Shalvata Mental Health Center, Clalit Health Services, affiliated with the Sackler Faculty of Medicine, Tel Aviv University, Israel

[3]Eating Disorders Clinic, Psychiatric Division, Rambam Medical Center, Haifa, and the Faculty of Social Welfare and Health studies, Haifa University, Israel

Abstract

The aim of the present chapter is to describe a group intervention model based on cognitive behavioral therapy (CBT) principles that has been carried out for the past several years in an adolescent eating disorders (ED) inpatient department in Israel. In this chapter we will relate to the difficulties inherent in the application of CBT to this population, describe our model, highlight our findings with several vignettes, and discuss the implications of our findings in the overall management of ED patients.

Introduction

Eating disorders (EDs) are among the psychiatric disorders considered specifically difficult to treat, necessitating multi-professional interventions in patients with significant

* Correspondence to: Daniel Stein, M.D.
Pediatric Psychosomatic Department, Safra Children's Hospital,
The Chaim Sheba Medical Center, Tel Hashomer, 52621, Israel
Phone: 972-03-5302690, Fax: 972-3-5305129
E-mail: dstein@netvision.net.il

physiological and psychiatric complications, who are often reluctant to be treated. CBT, along with interpersonal therapy (IPT), are the only psychotherapeutic interventions currently validated, in randomized controlled trials (RCTs), in adult outpatients with bulimia nervosa (BN) and binge eating disorder (BED) (Fassino et al, 2004). Several case-series and RCT's have recently demonstrated the efficacy of CBT also in adolescent outpatients with BED (Schapman-Williams et al, 2006) and BN (Lock, 2005; Wilson & Sysko, 2006; Schmidt & Treasure, 2006; Schmidt et al., 2007).

In anorexia nervosa (AN), there is still a lack of empirical evidence to favor any psychotherapeutic intervention over another (Fairburn, 2005; Herpertz-Dahlmann & Salbach-Andrae, 2009), with the exception of family therapy for adolescents with relatively short term AN (Lock et al, 2005). The improvement with any psychotherapeutic intervention – psychodynamic psychotherapy, CBT, or family therapy in adult AN patients is still only modest (Dare et al., 2001).

The evidence base for CBT in AN is scare and of limited value. One RCT has found that previously hospitalized adult AN patients have shown significantly less relapse with individual CBT in comparison to standardized nutritional counseling (Pike et al, 2001). Another controlled pilot study in adult AN patients (Treasure et al, 1995) has shown similar increase in weight and improvement in nutritional status that persisted at one year follow-up, with cognitive analytical and educational behavioral strategies. Still a third study has shown more favorable results in adult AN outpatients treated with a combination of supportive therapy and nutritional counseling in comparison to either IPT, and CBT (McIntosh et al, 2005). In adolescents, a small randomized study comparing CBT with behavioral family therapy (Ball & Mitchell, 2004) has found no significant outcome differences between the two modalities. Sixty percent of the patients in both groups have maintained their weight within 10% of average weight and had regular menstrual cycles at post-treatment and at 6 months' follow-up, but most of the patients have not reached symptomatic recovery.

The lack of efficacy of CBT in AN patients, specifically among adolescents, is the result of the fear that these patients may have with regard to change in general (Schmidt & Treasure, 2006), and recovery in particular. Renunciation the of the ED might be interpreted by adolescent AN patients as leading to the loss of their entire identity, and as enforcing them to grow up and become independent in the face of pervasive feelings of ineffectiveness and incapacity (Goodsitt, 1997; Bachar et al, 1999; Stein et al, 2003). Other factors that interfere with CBT in AN include the need for weight gain and, if it is achieved, for its constant monitoring, and the little influence that CBT has on core features of AN such as perfectionism, ineffectiveness, mood intolerance, and interpersonal difficulties (Garner & Garfinkel, 1997; Fairburn, Shafran, & Cooper, 2003).

A group format has notable advantages in the treatment of ED adolescents by enabling the interplay of the seemingly contradictory processes of identification with ones peers and relying on their support, and promoting ones own self-identity amongst ones peers. From a different perspective, talking about problems from the perspective of different group members can assist with cognitive restructuring and decentering, getting away from excessive focus on specific details towards seeing the overall context (Schmidt, 2009). Groups for ED adolescents allow for the checking and alteration, through peer-based feedback, of such aspects as the participants' readiness for change, their overall interpersonal capabilities, the influence of the ED on self-identity (issues of uniqueness on the one hand and shame on the other), the regulation of affects and impulses, and the relationship with important adults (group facilitators). This is of considerable importance, since ED adolescents often show severe dysfunction in their regulatory and interpersonal capacities (Strober et al., 1997). The application of a CBT format generates a task oriented atmosphere, so that the group can focus on the most relevant ED-related treatment requirements, while still facilitating developmentally-related requirements.

Group CBT has been applied mostly in adult ambulatory BN and BED patients, showing usually (Mitchell et al., 1993; Oesterheld et al., 1987; Jacobi et al., 2002; Fossati et al., 2004; Openshaw et al., 2004; Quiroga et al., 2004; Nevonen & Bromberg, 2006), although not always (Thompson-Brenner et al, 2003), favorable changes that are maintained at 6-12 months follow up. In most CBT groups, Fairburn's three-stage individual CBT model (Fairburn et al, 1993), has been adapted to a group format. No, or moderate differences in favor of group CBT in the extent of and/or time required for improvement, have been found when comparing BN/BED patients treated with group or individual CBT (Chen et al, 2003), group CBT or group IPT (Wilfley et al, 2002; Nevonen & Bromberg, 2006), group CBT or psychodynamic group treatment (Quiroga et al, 2002), and group CBT or fluoxetine (Jacobi et al, 2002). Dropout from treatment is similar in individual and group CBT (Chen et al, 2003). Additionally, several open studies (Nye & Cash, 2006), and RCTs (Peterson et al, 2004), have used CBT group interventions that focus primarily on body image. These studies have usually shown reduction with group CBT in attitudinal disturbance, size overestimation, body image dysphoria and investment in appearance, and improvement in body and health/fitness related satisfaction, that persist at one and six months follow up.

By contrast, only a few open (Fernández-Aranda et al, 1998) and controlled (Channon et al, 1989; Crisp et al, 1991) studies have assessed the efficacy of group CBT in ambulatory adult AN patients, showing conflicting results. Thus, Fernández-Aranda et al (1998) and Crisp et al (1991) have shown a significant improvement in weight, ED symptoms, return of menstruation, and aspects of social and sexual adjustment that persisted at one year follow-up, whereas no symptomatic change was recorded by Channon et al (1989).

Reviewing the literature we found only one small open case series (Nichols & Gusella, 2003) in which 2 female adolescents with AN and 3 with BN participated in an 8 week group CBT format. Self-monitoring occurred on 50% of the days, being the highest during the first 3 weeks of treatment. Commitment to monitoring was related to the girls' self-reported readiness to change. AN girls self-monitored as frequently as those with BN.

A considerable minority of ED adolescents require inpatient intervention. Hospitalization is usually considered in the case of severe medical complications, very low weight or rapid weight loss, life endangering behaviors (e.g., refusal to drink), severe psychiatric morbidity (e.g., severe depression or acute suicidal risk), failure of previous ambulatory interventions, or familial psychopathology that does not enable outpatient treatment (Herpertz-Dahlmann & Salbach-Andrae, 2009).

Inpatient treatment of adolescent ED patients is challenging with regard to the conceptualization, planning, and choice of adequate treatment strategies. Unfortunately, there is a dearth of research in this field. In general, hospitalization is considered to be more detrimental for adolescents than for adults, as it likely interferes with the age appropriate developmental tasks of independence and self-reliance. Nevertheless, a different philosophy also exists, namely that early hospitalization of younger ED patients may be beneficial in reducing the risk for a chronic course and later multiple hospitalizations (Robin et al, 1998) as well as to avert potentially irreversible effects on physical growth and development. (Golden et al, 2003; Practice Guideline for the Treatment of Patients with EDs, 2006). If this is the case, the philosophy of an adolescent inpatient ED department should focus, in addition to incorporating an appropriately tailored multimodal ED-program (Anzai et al, 2003), also on supporting the ongoing developmental needs of the adolescent inpatient. The provision of a group CBT format might be specifically tailored for both aspects.

Description of the Adolescent Inpatient ED Department

The adolescent ED inpatient department, located at the Safra Children's Hospital, The Chaim Sheba Medical Center, Tel Hashomer, Israel, is a tertiary care facility that serves as a nationwide referral center. Patients are hospitalized in this department only if outpatient or other inpatient treatment has failed, according to accepted criteria for the hospitalization of adolescent AN and BN patients (Golden et al, 2003; Herpertz-Dahlmann & Salbach-Andrae, 2009). Twenty patients are hospitalized each time, and around 80 patients are hospitalized every year. Their ages vary from 10-18 years. Most inpatients are diagnosed with AN or BN, although patients with eating disorders not otherwise specified (ED-NOS) (APA, 1994) are also hospitalized when required. Patients are mostly diagnosed with at least one major comorbid psychiatric and/or personality disorder (APA, 1994). Mean duration of ED before hospitalization is 2.2±2.5 years, and mean duration of hospitalization in this department is 4.7±4.5 months.

The treatment protocol is multimodal and integrative. It includes, in line with other structured inpatient protocols (Agras, 1987; Anzai et al, 2003; Herpertz-Dahlmann & Salbach-Andrae, 2009), a behaviorally-oriented nutritional rehabilitation program, individual psychodynamically oriented psychotherapy, individual movement therapy, family therapy, and several group formats: psychodynamic group therapy, ED-related psychoeducational and CBT group interventions, and movement group therapy. The integrative approach embedded in the treatment policy of this department addresses symptomatic-oriented improvement alongside fostering the emotional development of this highly vulnerable group of adolescents.

Description of Our Group CBT Model

The group is open-ended, including, at each period of time, between 6-8 patients of all ED diagnoses considered eligible for participation. BN patients are included in this group within 4-6 weeks of their hospitalization, when they are less symptomatic both in the department and during their home visits. AN patients are referred to this group usually much later, when being within 2 kilograms of their required weight. Patients are not included in the group if they do not cooperate with their individual psychotherapy, are severely suicidal, or present with behavioral problems that might interfere with the intactness of the group.

Participation is voluntary, although patients are informed that they have to take part in this group to continue treatment in our post-hospitalization half-way out day program, as it includes a similar group format. In keeping with most other CBT groups, our intervention is based on the adaptation of Fairburn's three-stage individual CBT model (Fairburn et al, 1993) to a group format. Patients are taught how to fill out the daily self-monitoring, and later on, the dysfunctional thought records (DTR) by group coordinators who have expertise with CBT. Participants are requested to fill their self-monitoring each day, after every meal, unless they are in school (inpatients who are stabilized can learn in their school during hospitalization), or else are unable to fill their self-monitoring after each meal. In such case patients fill out their self-monitoring at the end of each day.

The group consists of twice weekly 90 minutes sessions. At the start of the first weekly session, the group coordinators review the self-monitoring of each participant. Thereafter one participant reads his or her self-monitoring of the past week. Participants are informed that with the exception of self-harm behaviors, the presence of maladaptive ED-related behaviors described in the self-monitoring format (e.g., purging, excessive exercise) will not change their planned weekly behavioral program. Participants are expected, nevertheless, to report about these behaviors, if they still exist, at the next weekly session that checks their ED-related status. If that is not done, patients are excluded from the group, but can return whenever they are ready to comply with the group's contract.

Patients are instructed that they have to inform in their self-mopitoring about all past week's ED-related and non-ED related behavioral events, but that they can "censor" emotional contents that they do not wish to share with others. This is, nevertheless, carried out with the premise that sharing their thoughts and emotions with their peers and group coordinators, rather than feeling shameful of them, is an important step towards recovery. Following the past week review, each group member relates to the contents of the self-monitoring, assisting the presenter to identify behaviors and cognitions that interfere with his or her well-being, and offering ways to cope with these issues. Participants are instructed to relate, in line with the content of the self monitoring, to issues that are relevant also for themselves. Following all participants, the group coordinators relate to contents of the self-monitoring, as well as to processes that occur in the group during the session. Thereafter, the presenter gives his or her feedback to the other participants. Group members and coordinators are instructed to give their feedback in a non-judgmental (factual and/or supportive) manner, and not to share the contents of the CBT group with people outside the group. Interactive discussions are encouraged and can happen at any time during or after the presentation, but the time frame is kept so that all participants have enough time to elicit their feedback reactions.

At the end of this session, the presenter chooses the topic from his or her past week self-monitoring that will be dealt with in the second weekly group CBT session. In this session, the group leader (DS), a highly experienced CBT therapist, assists the participant to go through the chosen topic with the DTR technique. Thereafter, participants and group coordinators give their feedback. In addition to the group format, patients can consult individually about their self-monitoring and DTRs with the group coordinators or their individual psychotherapists.

The group coordinators include the group leader, a child and adolescent psychiatrist, a clinical dietitian, a physical activity instructor, and a nurse. The coordinators assist the participants to identify maladaptive preoccupations and behaviors related to eating, body image, physical activity, overall functioning, self-evaluation, and any other chosen issue. All group coordinators have been trained to work with CBT in ED patients by the group leader.

PRESENTATION OF THE GROUP PROCESS

We present three vignettes, translated from Hebrew, each including a one-day self-monitoring, followed by the feedbacks of group members and coordinators. Patients gave the permission to present their self-monitoring.

1. ***A.S***, female, age 17, diagnosed with restricting type AN (AN-R) for the past three years. She has been recently released from the department after being hospitalized for 8 months, and continues treatment in our post-hospitalization half-way out day program. She maintains her target weight, but is still highly absorbed in her illness.

Breakfast: No

Morning snack: No

Lunch: Chicken, vegetable; at home, ate for 40 minutes; satiated; "spoke with a friend from the department when I woke up. She gave me motivation to continue to eat and keep my weight. I wish I could be in her position. Well may be it is not that great, but she, at least, can function. I cannot live anymore with doing nothing. I am pissed that I have to eat with assistance. But without help I wouldn't eat at all. And then what? I hate eating. I am fat, fat, fat….

Afternoon snack: No

Supper: Two slices of bread, cheese, egg, cucumber; at home, ate for 40 minutes; not hungry; "this is one of the most boring days I had. I am going to the mall to buy a present, and then meet with a friend from the department. At least one nice thing will happen today".

Night snack: No; "it's really a problem when I have my period. I am constipated, but still have to eat. A great problem for my stomach. It is so bloated. I sat with my friend on the roof of the mall and we talked for hours. I had such a great time. We talked about many things. I am beginning to think that maybe I was harassed when I was younger. Otherwise I cannot figure out why I am so fucked up with guys. I am afraid of them. I feel stressed out around them, cannot figure out why. We talked about her treatment and therapist, about illness, recovery, physical activity, and life in general. It was so good. Then we found out that we were locked on the roof of the mall. It was so funny. Luckily, they open the door in the end"

2. ***D.M,*** female, age 16, diagnosed with purging type AN (AN-P) for the past 1.5 years, hospitalized for 4 months. She has previously reached her target weight, but recently lost a few kilograms again. She is still highly preoccupied with occasional self-induced vomiting, and with ED-related obsessionality. This specific week, according to her own request, she gets only high calorie beverage for the 3 main meals and 3 snacks.

Breakfast: "Not hungry. I felt stuffed during and after the meal. I wanted so much to throw-up, but repeatedly told myself that it is not allowed. It irritates me that I feel so full, and that food is stuck in my throat. After being weighed, I called my Mom. I did not gain weight. I weigh the same. I am afraid that because of that they would not let me to go home for the weekend. Oh my god, what shall I do. I cannot deal with having to gain weight again. I thought that I would gain weight in today's checking, I really did. I don't know what happened. Mom said that she will pray that I will be able to go home for the weekend. She cannot understand why I am still so concerned with my weight after such a long hospitalization. And then Mom said that she cannot handle anymore the pressure that I put on her. When we ended the conversation I cried, and then made a necklace for my mother".

Morning snack: "Not hungry. Went to smoke a cigarette outside the department, before the weekly meeting with the staff. Went with the secretary. She is so sweet. I feel constantly under pressure. Please god, make that everything will be OK."

Lunch: Did not write.

Afternoon snack: "Not hungry. I am so tired. I cannot cope anymore. Mom said that she is going to release me from the hospital. This is not the support I need. I want to release myself, but I know that it is a mistake. I am alone. God, thank you for the little strength that you still give me. I cannot breathe. What will happen with me? Will I always be like that? I cannot imagine what will become of me in the future. Will it change when I will be skinny? I don't want anymore to be very skinny. Just a little. Again I want to throw-up, and again I know that I won't. Where is "DM" (her name) that was once so happy. Not "DM" that was so fat, although "DM" is still fat. I cannot imagine that when I will have less fat cells I will be happier. No, don't be so fucked up. Of course you will be happier when loosing weight again".

Supper: "Not hungry. Made a huge step. Mom was here, and I let her read things that I wrote, about why I feel so guilty. Mom asked why I felt like that. I reminded her how she told me that I disappoint everyone, and that I am stuck between all other family members, always having to be involved, to make others feel better. And during all the time that you (Mom) felt bad with yourself, I was always around you, feeling so anxious all the time that something bad will happen to you. And in the end, it was I who got hurt. Only now do I realize that what I have to do in this world in order to feel better is to improve my self-esteem, to look at myself and my own needs. This is my goal and task, and there is noting that is more difficult for me that that."

Night snack: "I am so pissed off that I am not going home this weekend. I feel so full. I finally decided that I want to loose only three kilograms. I really don't want to loose more. Oh god. I am so afraid that if I will start to loose weight again, I won't be able, once again, to stop the process. I will loose control again. Oh, God, I just want to go home for a little while."

3. ***S.A.,*** female, age 16, diagnosed with BN for the past 1.5 years, hospitalized for about two months, with considerable improvement in her ED-related symptoms.

Breakfast: Two slices of bread, cheese, two vegetables, a glass of coffee, ate for 15 minutes. "This is the last day of the week before going home. I can't wait to leave this place. Another girl has irritated me in the dining room. Asked me, in an annoying tone, how I manage to finish two slices of bread in 15 minutes. Five minutes per slice is normal even for a normal person. I have managed to ignore her. This is a big change for me. In the past I would have just kicked this ugly individual. The most important thing for me is that I have managed to overcome my anger. I am very proud of myself. I know that I eat OK, and that I can serve as a model for normal eating for all girls, and even for some of the staff."

Morning snack: one pudding with bran flakes, ate for 15 minutes. "Now it's time for the physical activity class. I have a problem on Thursdays, being irritated form the movement therapy group. I do not have patience for this group. It's boring. This is the group that I hate most from all groups in the department. During the movement group, I fantasize about the physical activity class afterwards. I do not want to miss even a second from my beloved sports group. There I can take everything out. I need this detachment from everything, to run wild, to sweat."

Lunch: Chicken, one glass of rice, two vegetables, ate for 20 minutes. "The sports activity made me feel released, and much calmer. I felt good with myself. Felt tired. Wanted to finish eating and go to sleep. I spoke with my psychiatrist. She was nice. I spoke with her about what I felt about the hospitalization and my progress. She agreed with me about most of the things. I left the meeting with her feeling great.

Afternoon snack: Three biscuits, 3 plums, and a cup of coffee with half milk half water, ate for 15 minutes. "I did not manage in the end to sleep today, and feel ever so tired. I am waiting for my Dad to come to the department. I hope that my hospitalization will not continue for long. I have made such a great progress since being admitted. I am not bulimic anymore. Bulimic – such a disgusting word.

Supper: Three slices of bread, one egg, cheese, three vegetables, ate for 25 minutes. "I am fed up with the department. Only one meal left, and then I can finally rest my head on the pillow. I am in love with my tennis trainer (SA is a gifted tennis player). I don't know what to do. He is 23 years old, and extremely cute and handsome. But he has a girl-friend, and I have a boy-friend. I know that he is fond of me. We talk about everything. Once we even went to eat together after practice. He told me that he does not want to be with me. He likes me as a trainer likes a gifted player, but not more. It's hard to be all the time with someone you're in love with, but that is not in love with you. Now I feel that I have humiliated myself when telling him how I feel, but I could not have done otherwise. I am tired of interpreting things wrong. I wish it would not have happened. Now I feel ashamed and humiliated."

Night snack: Three plums, one glass of pudding with bran flakes, ate for 20 minutes. "During the entire meal I only thought about my trainer. What will happen, what should I do now? After supper I have discovered a very important thing, that my relations with my trainer and all my heartaches have nothing to do with my eating disorder. For the first time it looks as if I have a problem that is not part of an eating disorder. On the one hand I am happy because I feel as if a door is being opened towards living a normal life. On the other hand, it is still a problem, and it hurts real badly."

Feedback

Many feedback reactions demonstrate the identification of the group members with the presenter, likely because they themselves are troubled with ED-related preoccupations as the first girl and with problematic relationships with their parents as the second girl. For example, some girls have commented that the eating-related demands of the department in the case of the AN-R girl overshadow any efforts towards assisting her with issues of autonomy and overall functioning, or that the department should have allowed the AN-P girl to go home in the weekend although she has not gained weight. Nevertheless, other types of feedback reactions also occur. The BN girl, for example, has expressed utter disbelief that the AN-R girl really wishes to live the way she does. Other members have tried to show the AN-R girl that her problematic eating behaviors actually limit her personal freedom, rather than encouraging it as she claims, and offered to encourage and support her before problematic meals. Along the same line, some group members have commented to the AN-P girl that her preoccupation with eating and weight does not allow her to be connected with her feelings towards her mother, and that she retreats to maladaptive eating when being overwhelmed by her emotions. In the case of the BN girl, participants have noted that her current condition stands in contrast to their own, in that she is connected to her life much more than to her eating, even when there are problems. Some girls note that that they are jealous of her, others do not understand why she is still hospitalized. Still others comment that in her present self-monitoring, as compared to her previous one, she is connected not only to positive, but also to deep negative emotions.

The feedback of the group coordinators can involve a host of psychoeducational and/or cognitive interventions. For example: 1. Noting that for many patients, self-monitoring can serve as a means to release strong negative emotions that would have otherwise been regulated by disordered eating. 2. Discussing why a pattern of restricting eating can induce in one girl an" anorectic" breakdown and in the other a "bulimic" crisis (Melchior, 1998). 3. Discussing with the AN-P patient the cognitions that have led her to believe that it will be easier for her to drink high calorie beverages than eat regularly when feeling emotionally overwhelmed. 4. Highlighting, according to the example of the BN girl, the advantages of separating emotions from ED-related preoccupations for a more favorable handling of interpersonal difficulties. The feedback may relate in addition to many other relevant issues, for example issues related to self-esteem, associated in the AN-R girl with her physical appearance, in the AN-P girl with her guilt feelings towards her mother, and in the BN patient with her being rejected by her trainer.

Discussion

In the present chapter we describe a CBT group model carried out in an adolescent ED inpatient department. As shown with the three vignettes, the group includes participants of all gamut of the ED spectrum. Only a few clinical studies have yet described the use of a mixed AN/BN group model. These studies usually support the use of this model, claiming that the benefits of mixing membership by diagnoses outweigh the concerns related to learning new maladaptive eating-related behaviors (Hartman-McGilley, 2006). Thus, AN-R patients, as our first presenter, may slowly begin to understand and experience in the group that being in normal weight range as is her BN peer, is not necessarily associated with the experience of loosing ones most important goals. Adolescent BN patients, by contrast, often feeling like "failed anorexics", can grasp, not only from a cognitive, but also from an experimental perspective, the price that AN patients have to pay to maintain their thin body ideal. Moreover, the inclination of BN patients to openly share their feelings with group members and coordinators may be a new experience to AN-R adolescents who often tend to refrain from talking in treatment and shun their inner world from their therapists (Bachar, 2001). Lastly, the interchange between the rigid, constricted, but organized thought pattern of restricting AN patients, and the rich, experiential, but sometimes chaotic thought pattern of some BN patients, can be of merit for both populations in gaining better understanding as to why they have such a different lifestyle despite sharing many similar concerns and experiences (Lopez et al, 2008).

The ability to gain new understandings and insights that enables cooperation with CBT stems from the premise that most adolescents are not only generally open to new ideas, but are also capable to observe their experiences, build theories with respect to those experiences, and continuously reflect on their thinking (Weisz & Hawley, 2002). Such a process can be found even in those AN patients inclined towards rigid modes of thinking, if their change-related fears can be modified (Schmidt & Treasure, 2006). A CBT group format may be of specific merit both for the evolvement of new thinking modes, and for increasing the motivation for change (Schmidt & Treasure, 2006).

The idea to combine the treatment of restricting and bingeing/purging ED patients has a sound theoretical basis. Patients with any ED subtype may have 1st degree relatives of the other spectrum (Stein et al, 1999), and a significant minority of recovered BN patients show a personality configuration that is remarkably similar to recovered AN-R patients (Kaye et al, 1998). This raises the possibility of a transmission of some shared vulnerabilities among the two spectrums (Kaye et al, 1998). Moreover, between 50-60% of AN-R patients may develop bingeing/purging behaviors within several years from the onset of their illness (Eddy et al, 2008).

There is also a firm theoretical basis to combine the two ED spectrums from a treatment-related perspective. Fairburn et al (2003), in their "transdiagnostic" theory and treatment model, emphasize that basic maladaptive core cognitions are not markedly different in restricting and bingeing/purging type ED patients. Waller and his group, in their extensive studies of dysfunctional cognitions in EDs, have similarly found that underlying core beliefs that are not related to food, weight, or shape, are, with a few exceptions, comparable in the different ED spectrums (Leung et al, 1999).

The shared vulnerabilities and underlying commonalities of the two spectrums do not overshadow the significant attitudinal differences found between acutely-ill restricting and bingeing/purging patients that necessitate different therapeutic considerations. In line with Fairburn et al's (1993) paradigm, CBT can assist our BN patients to become aware of their automatic bingeing/purging behaviors, to identify those cognitive distortions likely increasing the risk of those behaviors, and to better organize not only their chaotic eating, but their overall chaotic lifestyle as well.

The treatment implications of group CBT for restricting AN adolescents are markedly different. Most AN patients are aware and unhappy of their condition, but fear that renunciation of their ego-syntonic symptoms will cause them even greater distress (Garner et al, 1997). The fact that weight gain is achieved, but against the patients' will, has to be repeatedly acknowledged. Other group members can identify with, empathize, and appreciate the AN patients, who have to deal with their most basic fears in the face of unwanted weight change.

From a different perspective, the sharing of experiences with BN group members might render AN-R patients to develop some doubts as to the absolute nature of their dichotomous perception. Thus, the belief of AN patients that gaining weight is the most important factor interfering with self-esteem, may be challenged by the understanding and experience of BN patients that their bingeing and purging behaviors might hamper their well-being even more.

Thus to quote one BN girl: " I am beginning to see that I feel particularly worthless whenever fearing that once again I am going to fail with my dieting; sometimes I do not know anymore what is more important for me: to loose weight or to stop this horrible vicious circle". The expansion of one's choices, combined with the emergence of doubt whether pursuit of thinness does indeed bring about the expected results, stand in sharp contrast to the basic standpoint of restricting AN patients that fear and resist any change (Schmidt & Treasure, 2006). The chance given to discuss these issues with one's peers in the supportive atmosphere of the CBT group might putatively represent the first step towards achieving this change.

The development of doubt can also be encouraged by feedbacks of group members that acknowledge a sense of cognitive dissonance: For example,"can AN and normal, gratifying functioning concomitantly exist?" or "are control and choice mutually exclusive?" It is our opinion that the most important aim of CBT in AN-R patients is to assist them in realizing that although having control over their eating and keeping low weight may improve their self-esteem in the short run, it interferes with age-specific developmental processes that are of importance to adolescents in general, although not yet to them, e.g., to be able to go out with friends, to drink alcohol without being afraid of the calories consumed, or to be able to fall in love. In this respect, we agree with Garner et al (1997), that whereas the treatment of AN should focus on both "specific" ED-related obsessionality and core psychological perspectives, the optimal aim is to disentangle the two. If that happens, and patients become preoccupied not only with their ED, they can begin to identify their cognitions and be in touch with some of their emotions. Again, sharing the experiences and recognizing the cognitions of their BN peers can be of great merit to AN-R patients to increase the scope of non ED-related issues that can become of relevance (Garner et al, 1997).

Both Fairburn et al (1993) and Waller (see Leung et al, 1999), suggest that non-ED core beliefs in both AN and BN represent primarily unconditional negative representations of the self. At the start, adolescent AN-R patients perceive their control over their eating and weight as the one means that can increase their self-esteem (Goodsitt, 1997; Bachar et al, 1999). In the group CBT process that they are undergoing, some AN patients can slowly learn from the experience of their BN peers that change is a possibility but not an unconditioned requirement (this because some BN participants are ready to reconsider their pursuit towards thinness, others are not), that it is possible to overcome their most basic fear of completely losing control (by understanding the difference between lapse and relapse), and that non-ED related issues can indeed become meaningful even for them.

CONCLUSION

The application of a multimodal treatment protocol, as is usually the case in inpatient settings, does not enable to disentangle the effect of group CBT from that of other interventions. We have been nevertheless interested in the patients' satisfaction with this treatment, assessing it by generating group discussions aiming towards continuous eliciting of the members' feedback.

Among the items considered beneficial in these feedbacks, patients note the potential of the procedure to reduce distress, the interactive sharing of experiences with their peers, and that CBT can be meaningful for them in enabling the consideration of new options. Most patients have noted that the intervention has not increased their preoccupation with eating, as they have feared before treatment. Among the detrimental aspects, patients have noted that daily food monitoring can be a hassle and overbearing, specifically following discharge, and that they may not be able, or wish, to continue with the treatment in its present form following discharge.

In conclusion, this chapter suggests that group CBT can be beneficiary to adolescent ED inpatients not only in improving ED-related symptoms, but also in fostering issues that are of relevance for normal adolescent development. Patients can be included in the group when considered to have some control over their illness, a process that, not surprisingly, takes longer in AN. Inclusion of both AN and BN patients in this group is perceived, by both inpatients and therapists, as fruitful and meaningful. The CBT group format fosters the modification of cognitive distortions precisely because it is carried out amidst a framework that allows for developmental considerations and group interactions, but at the same time is structured and task-oriented.

References

Agras, W. S. (1987). *Eating Disorders: Management of Obesity, Bulimia, and Anorexia Nervosa*. Oxford, UK: Pergamon.

American Psychiatric Association (APA) (2006). *Practice Guidelines for the Treatment of Patients with Eating Disorders, 3rd ed.* Washington, DC: APA:.

American Psychiatric Association (APA) (1994). *Diagnostic and Statistical Manual of Mental Disorders, 4th ed. (DSM-IV).* Washington DC: APA.

Anzai, N., Lindsay-Dudley, K., & Bidwell, R.J. (2003). Inpatient and partial hospital treatment for adolescent eating disorders. *Child and Adolescent Clinics of North America. 11*, 279-309.

Bachar, E. (2001). *The Fear of Occupying Space*. The Hebrew University Magnes Press. Jerusalem.

Ball, J., & Mitchell, P.A. (2004). A randomized controlled study of cognitive behavior therapy and behavioral family therapy for anorexia nervosa patients. *Eating Disorders, 12*, 303-314

Channon, S., de Silva, P., Hemsley, D., Perkins, R. (1989). A controlled trial of cognitive-behavioral and behavioral treatment of anorexia nervosa. *Behavior Research and Therapy, 27,* 529-235.

Chen, E., Touyz, S. W., Beumont, P. J., Fairburn, C. G., Griffiths, R., Butow, P., Russell, J., Schotte, D. E, Gertler, R., & Basten, C. (2003). Comparison of group and individual cognitive- behavioral therapy for patients with bulimia nervosa. *International Journal of Eating Disorders, 33*, 241-254.

Crisp, A. H., Norton, K., Gowers, S., Halek, C., Bowyer, C., Yeldham, D., Levett, G., Bhat, A. (1991). A controlled study of the effect of therapies aimed at adolescent and family psychopathology in anorexia nervosa. *British Journal of Psychiatry, 159*, 325-333.

Dare, C., Eisler, I., Russell, G., Treasure, J., & Dodge, L. (2001). Psychological therapies for adults with anorexia nervosa: randomized control trial of out-patient treatments. *British Journal of Psychiatry, 178*, 216-221.

Eddy, K. T., Dorer, D. J., Frankom D. L., Tahilani, K., Thompson-Brenner, H., & Herzog, D. B. (2008). Diagnostic crossover in anorexia nervosa and bulimia nervosa: implications for DSM-V. *American Journal of Psychiatry, 165*, 245-250.

Fairburn, C. G., Cooper, Z., & Shafran, R. (2003). Cognitive behavior therapy for eating disorders: a "transdiagnostic" theory and treatment. *Behavior Research and Therapy, 41*, 509-528.

Fairburn, C. G., Jones, R., Peveler, R. C., Hope, R. A., & O'Conner, M. E. (1993). Psychotherapy and bulimia nervosa: the longer-term effects of interpersonal psychotherapy, behavior therapy, and cognitive behavior therapy. *Archives of General Psychiatry, 50*, 419-428.

Fairburn, C. G. (2005). Evidence-based treatment of anorexia *International Journal of Eating Disorders, 37*, 26-30.

Fassino, S., Piero, A., Daga, G., Leombruni, P., Mortara, P., & Rovera, G. (2002). Attentional biases and frontal functioning in anorexia nervosa. *International Journal of Eating Disorders, 31*, 274-283.

Fernández-Aranda, F., Bel, M., Jimenez, S., Vinuales, M., Turon, J., Vallejo, J. (1998). Outpatient group therapy for anorexia nervosa: a preliminary study. *Eating and Weight Disorders, 3*, 1-6.

Fossati, M., Amati, F., Painot, D., Reiner, M., Haenni, C., & Golay, A. (2004). Cognitive-behavioral therapy with simultaneous nutritional and physical activity education in obese patients with binge eating disorder. *Eating and Weight Disorders, 9*, 134-138.

Garner, D. M. (1997). Psycho-educational principles in treatment. In D. M., Garner & P. E., Garfinkel (Eds.), *Handbook of Treatment for Eating Disorders*. New York-London: Guilford, pp. 145–177.

Golden, N. H., Katzman, D. K., Kreipe, R. E., Stevens, S. L., Sawyer, S. M., Rees, J., Nicholls, D., & Rome, E. S. (2003). Eating disorders in adolescents: position paper of the Society for Adolescent Medicine. *Journal of Adolescent Health, 33*, 496-503.

Goodsitt, A. (1997). Eating disorders: a self-psychological perspective. In D. M. Garner & P. E. Garfinkel (Eds.), *Handbook of Treatment for Eating Disorders*. New York, The Guilford Perss, pp. 205-228.

Hartman-McGilley, B. (1990). Group therapy for adolescents with eating disorders. *Group, 20*, 28-30.

Herpertz-Dahlmann, B., & Salbach-Andrae, H. (2009). Overview of treatment modalities in adolescent anorexia nervosa. *Child and Adolescent Psychiatric Clinics of North America, 18*, 131-145.

Jacobi, C., Dahme, B., Dittman, R. (2002). Cognitive-behavioral, fluoxetine and combined treatment for bulimia nervosa: short- and long-term results. *European Eating Disorders Review, 10*, 179-198.

Kaye, W. H., Bailer, U. F., Frank, G. K., Henry, S., Price, J., Meltzer, C., Becker, C., Ziolko, S., Mathis, C., Wagner, A., Barbarich-Marstellar, N., & Putnam, K. (2008). Serotonin*Psychopharmacoloy, 3*, 1558-1564.

Leung, N., Waller, G., & Thomas, G. (1999). Core beliefs in anorexic and bulimic women. *Journal of Nervous and Mental Diseases, 187*, 736-741.

Lock, J., Agras, W. S., Bryson, S., & Kraemer H. C. (2005). A comparison of short- and long-term family therapy for adolescent anorexia nervosa. *Journal of the American Academy of Child and Adolescent Psychiatry, 44*, 632-639.

Lopez, C., Roberts, M., Tchanturia, K., & Treasure, J. (in press). Using neuropsychological feedback therapeutically in treatment for anorexia nervosa: Two illustrative case reports. *European Eating Disorders Review.*

McIntosh, V. V., Jordan, J., Carter, F. A., Luty, S. E., Mckenzie, J. M., Bulik, C. M., Frampton, C. M., & Joyce, P. R. (2005). Three psychotherapies for anorexia nervosa: a randomized controlled trial. *American Journal of Psychiatry, 162*, 741-747.

Melchior, J. C. (1998). From malnutrition to refeeding during anorexia nervosa. *Current Opinion in Clinical Nutrition and Metabolic Care, 1*, 481-485.

Mitchell, J. E., Pyle, R. L., Pomeroy, C., Zollman, M., Crosby, R., Stein, H., Eckert, E. D., & Zimmerman, R. (1993). Cognitive-behavioral group psychotherapy of bulimia nervosa: importance of logistical variables. *International Journal of Eating Disorders, 14*, 277-287.

Nevonen, L., & Bromberg, A. G. (2006). A Comparison of Sequenced Individual and Group Psychotherapy for Patients with Bulimia Nervosa. *International Journal of Eating Disorders, 39,* 117-127.

Nichols, S., & Gusella, J. (2003). Food for thought: Will adolescent girls with eating disorders self-monitor in a CBT group? *Canadian Child and Adolescent Psychiatric Review, 12,* :37-39.

Nye, S., & Cash, T.F. (2006). Outcomes of manualized cognitive-behavioral body image therapy with eating disordered women treated in a private clinical practice. *Eating-Disorders: The Journal of Treatment and Prevention, 14*, 31-40.

Oesterheld, J. R., McKenna, M. S., & Gould, N. B. (1987). Group psychotherapy of bulimia: a critical review. *International Journal of Group Psychotherapy, 37*, 163-184.

Openshaw, C., Waller, G., & Sperlinger, D. (2004). Group cognitive-behavior therapy for bulimia nervosa: statistical versus clinical significance of changes in symptoms across treatment. *International Journal of Eating Disorders, 36,* 363-375.

Peterson, C., Wimmer, S., Ackard, D.M., Crosby, R., Cavanagh, L.C., & Mitchell, J.E. (2004). Changes in body image during cognitive-behavioral treatment in women with bulimia nervosa. *Body-Image, 1*, 139-153.

Pike, K. M., Walsh, B. T., Vitousek, K., Wilson, G. T., & Bauer J. (2001). Cognitive behavioral therapy in the post-hospitalization treatment of anorexia nervosa. *American Journal of Psychiatry, 160*, 2046-2049.

Quiroga, S., Cryan, G., & Fontao, M. I. (2002). Comparative study on the therapeutic efficacy for eating disorders. *Psicoterapia e Istituzioni: Review of Psychoanalytical Methodological Research and Clinical Experiences, 9*, 37-62.

Robin, A. L., Gilroy, M., & Dennis, A. B. (1998). Treatment of eating disorders in children and adolescents. *Clinical Psychology Review, 18*, 421-446.

Schapman-Williams, A. M., Lock J., Couturier, J. (2006). Cognitive-behavioral therapy for adolescents with binge eating syndromes: a case series. *International Journal of Eating Disorders, 39*, 252-255.

Schmidt, U. (2009). Cognitive behavioral approaches in adolescent anorexia. *Child and Adolescent Psychiatric Clinics of North America, 18*, 147-158.

Schmidt, U., & Treasure, J. (2006). Anorexia nervosa: valued and visible. A cognitive-interpersonal maintenance model and its implications for research and practice. *British Journal of Clinical Psychology, 45*, 343-366.

Schmidt, U., & Treasure, J. (2006). Anorexia nervosa: valued and visible. A cognitive-interpersonal maintenance model and its implications for research and practice. *British Journal of Clinical Psychology, 45*, 343-366.

Schmidt, U., Lee, S., Beecham, J., Perkins, S., Treasure, J., Yi, I., Winn, S., Robinson, P. Murphy, R., Keville, S., Johnson-Sabine, E., Jenkins, M., Frost, S., Dodge, L., Berelowitz, M., Eisler, I. (2007). A randomized controlled trial of family therapy and cognitive behavior therapy guided self-care for adolescents with bulimia nervosa and related disorders. *American Journal of Psychiatry,164*,591-598.

Stein, D., Lilenfeld, L. R., Plotnicov, K., Pollice, C., Rao, R., & Kaye, W.H. (1999). Familial aggregation of eating disorders: results from a controlled family study of bulimia nervosa. *International Journal of Eating Disorders, 26*, 211-215.

Stein, D., Orbach, I., Shani-Sela, M., Har-Even, D., Yaroslavsky, A., Roth, D., Meged, S., & Apter, A. (2003). Suicidal tendencies and body image and experience in suicidal and anorexia nervosa female adolescent inpatients. *Psychotherapy and Psychosomatics, 72*, 16-25.

Strober, M., Freeman, R., & Morrell, W. (1997). The long-term course of severe anorexia nervosa in adolescents: survival analysis of recovery, relapse, and outcome predictors over 10-15 years in prospective study. *International Journal of Eating Disorders, 22*, 339-360.

Thompson-Brenner, H., Glass, S., & Westen, D. (2003) A Multidimensional Meta-Analysis of Psychotherapy for Bulimia Nervosa. *Clinical Psychology: Science* and *Practice,* 10, 269–287.

Treasure, J., Tchanturia, K., & Schmidt, U. (2005). Developing a model of the treatment for eating disorder: using neuroscience research to examine the how rather than the what of change. *Counselling and Psychotherapy Research, 5*, 187-190.

Weisz, J.R., & Hawley, K.M. (2002). Developmental factors in the treatment of adolescents. *Journal of Consulting and Clinical Psychology, 70,* 21-43.

Wifley, D. E. (2002). A Randomized Comparison of Group Cognitive Behavioral Therapy and Group Interpersonal Psychotherapy for the Treatment of Overweight Individuals with Binge Eating Disorder, *Archives General Psychiatry, 59*, 713-722.

Wifley, D. E. et al (1993). Group Cognitive Behavioral Therapy and Group Interpersonal Psychotherpay for the Non-purging Bulimic Individual. *Journal of Consulting and Clinical Psychology, 61,* 296-305.

Wilson, G. T., & Sysko, R. (2006). Cognitive-behavioral therapy of for adolescents with bulimia nervosa. *European Eating Disorders Review, 14*, 8-16.

In: Cognitive Therapy of Eating Disorders...
Editors: S. Sassaroli and G.M. Ruggiero
ISBN: 978-1-60876-617-8

Chapter 9

FAMILY-BASED PROGRAM FOCUSED ON PARENTS IN OUTPATIENT ED CARE: COGNITIVE BEHAVIORAL METHODS COMBINED WITH A PSYCHODYNAMIC APPROACH IN GROUP SETTINGS

Eynat Zubery[1*], Yael Latzer[2] and Daniel Stein[3]

[1]Eating Disorders Unit, Davidson (Hanotrim) Clinic, Raanana, Shalvata Mental Health Center, Clalit Health Services, affiliated with the Sackler Faculty of Medicine, Tel Aviv University, Israel

[2]Eating Disorders Clinic, Psychiatric Division, Rambam Medical Center, Haifa, and the Faculty of Social Welfare and Health studies, Haifa University, Israel

[3]The Pediatric Psychosomatic Department, Safra Children's Hospital, The Chaim Sheba Medical Center, Tel Hashomer, affiliated with the Sackler Faculty of Medicine, Tel Aviv University, Tel Aviv, Israel

ABSTRACT

This chapter describes a family-based therapeutic program focused on parents in outpatient care for eating disorders (ED) which combines a cognitive behavioral methods with a psychodynamic approach in group settings. The treatment includes three phases. Phase I includes evaluation and immediate intervention and is aimed at improving the patient's physical condition with parental involvement in symptom reduction during the crisis phase. The latter is accomplished through enrolling parents in a six session psycho-educational group. Phase II consists of separate and concurrent psychodynamic therapy for both patients and for parents preferably in a group framework. Phase III includes conjoint group sessions and triad meetings between children and parents when dialogue is feasible. In addition, the chapter reviews scientific literature regarding treatment modalities, interventions and family patterns in ED.

* Correspondence to: Eynat Zubery
Eating Disorder Unit, Davidson(Hanotrim) Clinic, Raanana, Shalvata Mental Health Center, Israel
Phone: 972-09-7712249, Fax: 972-3-5470761
E-mail: Eynat@dr-Zubery.co.il

> "The existence of the eating disorder in most of the families seems to lead to fixed patterns of interaction around it. Just as an eating disorder becomes a baffling and impenetrable autonomous condition within the individual, so also the organization of the family around the individual and her behavior has a life of its own." (Colahan & Senior, 1995).

INTRODUCTION

Over the past twenty-five years, out-patient family-based treatment has gradually become established, as a leading therapeutic approach in the successful management of adolescent Anorexia Nervosa (AN). (Minuchin, 1975; Minuchin, 1978; Le Grange, 2005; Eisler, 2000; Latzer & Gaber, 1998; Latzer et al., 2002; Latzer et al., 2003; Latzer et al. 2006). There is increasing evidence that demonstrates families in which one member is suffering from an eating disorder (ED) represent a heterogeneous group in regards to socio-demographic factors, relationships within the family, its emotional climate and patterns of family interaction (Vanderycken, 2002).

Independent of the question as to whether the family plays a significant role in the etiology of the ED, the subsequent familial problems are more than emotional in nature. Due to the severity of the illness, family dynamics are strongly influenced by concerns for the patient's health. This can trigger strong emotional reactions leading to dysfunctional coping, such as parents blaming themselves for not having recognized the disease soon enough or for having delayed seeking professional help.

Cognitive behavioral therapy (CBT) is one of the most utilized treatment models for ED patients. Until recently, CBT and dynamic psychotherapy were considered to be widely divergent, competitive and diametrically opposed conceptual worlds. CBT focuses on the symptoms but it does not enable a deeper exploration of the underlying conflict. By contrast, the dynamic model attempts to explore the inner world and underlying causes, but does not offer immediate relief for the symptoms. The existing gap between these approaches must be bridged before any kind of internal integration can truly be achieved.

To our knowledge, no one has presented a combined model of CBT and dynamic therapy that utilizes a group approach that contains a strong component of psycho-education for both parents and patients. Psycho-educational treatment seems to be an effective component of cognitive –behavioral therapy and has become an integral and standard component of individual and group approaches to ED adult patients, (Garner, 1997) although relatively few studies have been conducted to investigate the effect of family or parent-based psycho-education, and even fewer have examined this approach with the families of ED patients.(Uehara et al., 2001; Holtkamp et al. 2005) (Van Vreckem & Vanderycken, 1989; Jeammet, 1984; Verbeek & Verbeek, 1977; Jeammet & Gorge, 1980; Perednia et al., 1989; Nicholls& Magagna, 1997; Vanderycken, 2002;). These studies described the powerful effect of group interventions on parents yet did not examine the combined impact of cognitive behavioral methods along with psychodynamic approach. As far as we know, other studies have not yet examined the intersection between the cognitive-behavioral and dynamic approaches, either on a theoretical or clinical level, in regards to parent-based interventions with.ED

The Family-based program focused on parents (FB-FP) model developed at Davidson ("Hanotrim) Outpatient Eating Disorder Treatment Center, has sought to integrate these two different conceptual treatment approaches, as well as promote parental efficacy. In order to achieve this, a strong psycho- educational component is provided along with teaching motivational communication skills designed to help parents manage the illness andreduce any inter-personal dynamics which can inadvertently maintain the illness. Parental psycho-education seems to be crucial for the treatment outcome at all ages until ED behavior is under control. In order to maintain recovery, there is a need to address the underlying issues through psychotherapy for both patients and parents, preferably in a group setting.

This chapter seeks to highlight the effectiveness of intensive interventions with parents. It will present a brief literature review of family patterns, family therapy models and family-oriented treatments of eating disorders, presentation of the FB-FP model, i.e. psycho-education group for parents at the initial phase, psychodynamic group of parents during the second phase when weight and related behaviors are controlled, and conjoint sessions with parents and patient during the third phase (Zubery, 1993; Zubery et al., 2005).We shall discuss the importance of engaging parents in the therapeutic process, and the importance of the father's role in enabling the daughter's recovery. The case study will illustrate how we implement the FB-FP model throughout the various stages of treatment.

A Literature Review: Treatment Modalities, Interventions and Family Patterns

As early as the 19th century, Gull (1874) and Lasegue (1873) recognized the need to separate anorexics from their family environment in order for recovery to occur. When psychoanalytic theories on the origin of eating disorders became established in the 1960's, the pathology of the mother-daughter dyad was emphasized. Bruch (1974), one of the earliest and most important writers in the field of eating disorders, described the problem as the young girl's difficulty in separating from her mother. Bruch's ideas, based largely upon Winnicott's (1965) theory of the false self, were highly influential. Bruch (1974) argued the need for weight restoration before commencement of therapy, i.e. that therapy during the initial stages of the treatment should primarily remain supportive, while helping the patient deal with the primary goal of ameliorating her physical condition. Bruch strongly recommended: "Conjoint family sessions in fairly young patients who are relatively healthy emotionally. In those with severe deficiencies in personality development...the chief work needs to be done through individual psychotherapy. When parents are well informed and not too defensive, they will make treatment arrangements on their own decision." (Bruch, 2001, p.116). Later, the importance of engaging parents and motivating them to participate in the same treatment setting became evident, as did the importance of the father's role in family dynamics (Van Vreckem & Vanderyecken, 1989; Verbeek & Verbeek, 1977; Jeammet & Gorge, 1980; Perednia et al., 1989).

In the 1970's Selvini-Palazzoly (1974) and Minuchin (1975; 1978) were among the most renowned theorists to write about families with anorexia nervosa. They attempted to construct a comprehensive theory that would provide an answer to the familial etiology as well as explain the role of family therapy. Minuchin et al (1975; 1978) and the Philadelphia group developed a theoretical framework that referred to “psychosomatic families”, characterized by enmeshment, over-protectiveness, rigidity and lack of conflict resolution. Anorexia nervosa was thought to be a prime illustration of this kind of family. Selvini-Palazzoli and the Milan group (Selvini-Palazzoly, 1974) developed a model referring to "the three way matrimony" i.e. the daughter is trapped within the parent’s relationship. In the 1980’s, Humphrey (1991) and others described the “bulimic family”. It was portrayed by many theorists as a family with multiple conflicts and excessive criticism. Humphrey (1991) suggested that "the holding environment in bulimic families fails them in nurturance, soothing and tension regulation, empathy and affirmation of separate identities. Parents and children alike are ‘starving’ for nurturance.” (Humphrey, 1991, p.324). Later, researchers in the family therapy field came to consensus that no specific family structure can be cited as prone to develop one type of disorder or another (Colahan & Senior, 1995; Vanderycken , 2002; Dare & Eisler, 1995; Eisler, 1995). This is due partly to the fact that research and clinical observations bring us into contact with the families only after the symptoms appear. Due to the acuteness of the illness, family dynamics are strongly influenced by concerns for the patient’s health, making it impossible to distinguish between antecedents of the illness and its consequences. In addition, a dichotomous separation between anorexic and bulimic family types cannot be valid, in view of the transition of many patients from one state to another.

Four large controlled clinical trials at the Maudsley Hospital in London, compared the effectiveness of conjoint family therapy, parent counseling and individual therapy (Dare & Eisler, 1995; Eisler, 1995; Russell, et al., 1992). The results indicated the effectiveness of conjoint family therapy in the treatment of anorexia nervosa in adolescents with a short history of illness (up to 3 years), and supported the need for parent counseling, either as a couple or in group settings. The researchers were surprised to find that parental counseling only was more effective than conjoint family therapy, regardless of the patient’s age. This was especially true for patients with severe eating disorder symptomatology, whose parents expressed a high level of criticism. (Squire-Dehouk, 1993). Eisler et al (2000) showed that treatment of parents and their daughters in separate rather than joint sessions produced better outcomes especially in cases where mothers had expressed many critical comments toward their daughters. Family sessions which are prone towards producing a large number of critical remarks, are difficult to conduct and run the risk of intensifying conflicts within the family, as well as increasing feelings of anger, guilt and shame. This is supported by findings showing the apparent difficulty of families, for various reasons, to provide the adolescent with the necessary impetus towards separateness, which also coincides with the adolescent’s own fears of separateness (Zubery, 1993, 2005; Latzer et al., 2002). This finding pointed to the need to understand the family-system dynamics in conjunction with the intra-psychic and interpersonal elements of each member of the family (Humphrey, 1991 Latzer 2002).

Behavioral Family System Therapy (BFST) was modeled after the Maudsley approach (Le Grange, 2005), although it differed in some important, albeit subtle, ways. Robin et al (1999) defined the adolescents in their study as "out of control" and not able to take care of themselves, while the parents were coached to implement a behavioral weight gain program. This differs somewhat from the Maudsley approach, in which parents were encouraged to explore, and with the help of the therapist, find an optimal way to restore healthy weight in their adolescent with AN. Secondly, Robin et al (1999) broadened the focus of treatment to include cognitions and problems in "family structure" while the parents were still in charge of the re-feeding process. By contrast, the Maudsley approach typically would refrain from "distractions" i.e. general adolescent and family issues were deferred until ED behavior was under control. Both BFST and the Maudsley approach would return control over eating to the adolescent when the target weight was achieved, and the final stage of treatment then focused on adolescent issues such as individuation, sexuality and career (Le Grange, 2005).

The importance of psycho-education for parents of patients with psychiatric disorders has been increasingly emphasized in recent years. Treasure et al (2001, 2003) found significantly higher levels of psychological distress in the relatives and caretakers of adult patients with AN than in relatives and parents of patients with psychotic illnesses. Lilenfeld (1992) reported an increased incidence of various forms of mental health problems, such as depression and anxiety disorders in mothers and other first-degree relatives of ED patients. Psycho-education for parents is conducted in various formats including groups only for relatives, single-family meetings and multi-family groups (MFG) with the frequency ranging from weekly to monthly sessions. McFarnel et al (1995, 1997) Uehara (2001) reported that MFG's are significantly more effective in extending remission than the single-family format. Geist et al (2000) compared the effects of four months of two family-oriented treatments, (family therapy and a family psycho-educational group), on female adolescents in inpatient care with newly diagnosed ED's. Weight restoration was achieved in both groups within the same timeframe of inpatient treatment but no significant change was reported in the psychological functioning of either adolescents or parents.

Uehara et al (2001) conducted five two-hour sessions once a month of multi-family psycho-education group of relatives of adult female patients. They showed decreased rates of high Expressed Emotions (EE). In particular, the study demonstrated less emotional over-involvement and improved family assessment of symptoms. The intervention encouraged positive interactions within the family and lowered distress (Uehara, 2001). Whitney et al (2005) using a qualitative analysis of 40 care-giver narratives, concluded that part of the distress of living with anorexia nervosa may be explained by unhelpful assumptions and maladaptive responses to the illness (self-blame, patient blame, helplessness, over-protective and over-anxious responses). They reported gender differences, e.g. primarily a tendency for mothers to express greater anxiety, whereas fathers produced more detached accounts, with a greater use of cognitive and avoidant coping strategies. They developed a conceptual framework to promote parental efficacy through providing psycho-education and teaching motivational communication skills to manage the illness and reduce any interpersonal factors contributing towards maintaining the ED.

The Aachen program described by Holtcamp et al (2005) is based on a psycho-education group for parents of both inpatient and out-patient children. They conducted five 90 minutes sessions once a week with five "booster sessions" per year for former participants. They found that providing parents with relevant information about ED and the treatment plan during the early phase of treatment reduced uncertainty towards therapeutic interventions and helped minimize conflicts between patients, parents and therapist. It also minimized the drop-out rates which are common in the treatment of ED. The program did not address parental requests for practical advice or on how to deal with problematic eating-related situations at home. They subsequently concluded that a home-based treatment should be added to their treatment protocol for better results.

Group psycho-education is focused on providing information and is therefore, more leader-oriented and directive. Therapy–oriented parent groups address the psychological issues and "offer a network of helping relationships within which the parents unburden themselves, obtain guidance and advice from other parents and in turn experience the gratification of having something to offer to others" (Van Vreckem & Vanderyecken 1989, p.361). They also generally address the role of fathers in facilitating recovery "Fathers are encouraged to intervene more directly, to make closer contact and to accept conflicts with their daughters in order to set and maintain limits". Nicholls & Magagna (1997) stressed that group psychotherapy is an opportunity for parents to share knowledge and skills, as well as to learn from and provide support to each other (Nicholls & Magagna, 1997, p.568). Peredenia et al (1989) in their article "Parent Counseling: From Guidance to Treatment" expressed the need to integrate psycho-education elements with psychodynamic treatment.

In conclusion, certain types of therapies are associated with particular disorders and serve as paradigms for the development of the therapeutic model: "As hysteria was the paradigm for psychoanalysis and phobias were the paradigm for the development of behavioral therapy, anorexia nervosa was largely a paradigm for family therapy" (Dare & Eisler, 1995, p.333). Over the last three decades, the literature has supported the concept of conjoint family therapy for eating disorder patients. However, more recently researchers have indicated greater success by treating parents and their daughters separately rather than in joint sessions. This development emerged from the need for immediate behavioral change and the repetitive patterns of interactions around food, alongside typical adolescent separation issues and the need to understand the unconscious dialogue between parents and daughter as expressed through the eating disorder symptom. Consensus emerged that the family is one of the most important treatment resources. Empowering parents and lowering of family stress--preferably in a group setting, has proved beneficial to patients, especially in the early phases of crisis management. The power of a group can reduce feelings of shame and failure that parents may experience when faced with a single therapist. Parent psycho-education appears to be a crucial element in successful treatment outcomes at all ages, until ED behavior is under control. In order to maintain recovery, there is a need to address the underlying issues through psychotherapy for both patients and parents, preferably in a group setting.

The Davidson (Hanotrim) Model: Family Based Program Focused on Parents (FB-FP)

The Family Based Program Focused on Parents (FB-FP) approach has been utilized in the ED outpatient center since 1992 with modifications over the years, primarily by adding psycho-educational components (Zubery, 1993; Zubery et al., 2005*)*. The program grew out of the need to address acute physical and mental conditions in the hope of preventing the need for hospitalization. Treatment outcome has been evaluated since 1998 by administering eating disorders and co-morbidity questionnaires. In the last decade, out of 120 yearly ambulatory ED patients, 80 patients' parents have participated in the program. Sixty percent of FB-FP participants are adolescents (12-17 years old) and 40 percent adults (18 and older), of whom 10 percent are males. Sixty percent of patients are in home-based treatment following admission. Approximately 75 percent of the program's personnel have remained consistent since its establishment.

The FB-FP team includes the following: adult and child psychiatrists, nurses, dieticians, physical therapists, clinical social workers, psychologists, mentors, family, dance, art and bibliotherapists. The team works simultaneously in adjacent rooms in order to provide a "holding environment" for the patient, parents and the team. Frequent communication is maintained between staff members from different disciplines, starting with the evaluation phase in order to block manipulation, promote shared and up-to-date information, continuity of treatment and minimize potential burn-out among staff. Our treatment protocol consists of three major components:

- Phase I **Evaluation and immediate intervention** to improve the patient's physical condition with parental involvement in symptom reduction during the crisis phase. The latter is accomplished through enrolling parents in a six session psycho-educational group.
- Phase II **Separate** and concurrent **psychodynamic therapy** for both patients and for parents preferably in a group framework. Approximately twenty group sessions occur over the course of a year. This is followed by couples therapy (when needed) aimed at addressing the underlying issues.
- Phase III **Conjoint group sessions and triad meetings** between children and parents when dialogue is feasible.

Phase I: Evaluation and Immediate Intervention

Patient Evaluation

The patient is first interviewed by a multi-disciplinary team after filling out questionnaires designed to assess the presence and severity of the eating disorder and co-morbid symptoms. This is followed by a semi-structured Eating Disorder Examination Questionnaire. The interview encourages the patient to figure out the trigger for her illness and the current reasons for seeking help. Both the information given and the reaction of the patient to our suggested treatment plan provide an indication of the degree of resistance to change.

Parents' Evaluation

The team interviews the parents to evaluate the family system, possible family triggers and the timing for seeking help, along with assessing their ability to take an active role in the treatment process. Parents of patients over 18 years old are also encouraged to participate depending upon the medical and psychiatric needs (This is conditional upon the patient's agreement.) The parents' capability to function as a supportive system and the patient's evaluation is crucial to the decision on the degree of care needed, and whether or not the intervention can occur in an outpatient setting. In cases where home-based treatment is indicated we assess the parents' anxiety levels. If their anxiety is seen as potentially undermining the progress, mentorship will be advised as an alternative for hospitalization.

Treatment Plan

Patient and parents are invited to participate in establishing a treatment contract that highlights a clear division of responsibilities among patient, parents and the treatment team. In highly motivated patients--especially bulimic patients, parental involvement in behavioral change, is not required. However, with AN patients, parents are asked to help with regular mealtimes and ensuring adequate food is available at home, yet asked to avoid any discussions with their child about food-related behavior. In cases where parents are coached to implement a behavioral weight gain, the team will stress that the eating disorder is now controlling the patient. Therefore, the parents will be temporarily responsible of the feeding process until weight or purging behavior is improved. Other adolescent needs of control and autonomy in areas other than weight must be respected. The patient signs a written contract and is informed of the consequences if progress is not satisfactory. In that case, the treatment will become more intensive (including hospitalization). Establishing a setting in which the re-feeding can take place is more important than the details of what to feed. Joint sessions only focused on symptom reduction are held on weekly basis until the patient is stabilized. The patient is expected to change the following behaviors: eating, body checking and avoidance, excessive exercise, and self-mutilation. This is conducted through various forms of cognitive behavioral therapy along with medication if needed. During this initial stage, the parents are required to participate in a psycho-educational group.

Description of Phase I Psycho-Education Group- Format and Content

The group is comprised of parents whose children (ages 13-30) are living in the same household and who are suffering from all kinds of eating disorders, since heterogeneity has a therapeutic power. It is limited to ten couples and six sessions, which occur weekly during the initial phase of treatment when the crisis is most acute. We insist on the participation of both parents—even when divorced, since engaging the father is therapeutically valuable. As mothers are more often available, the father's participation is a clear sign of his involvement, and as such, it is practically always appreciated by his daughter, as well as by his wife. In most cases, the need to empower fathers and reinforce the importance of the paternal authority function toward their daughters even following treatment remains important and is emphasized.

Each session consists of a combination of educational material and therapeutic strategies to enhance the family's knowledge of ED along with their communication and coping skills. The first half of the session consists of didactic information and during the second half the role of parents in eating-related situations is addressed. This varies from one family to another, depending on the severity of symptoms and family interaction patterns. Participants are given copies of all the lectures and presentations.

(*Exclusion Criteria: Severe psychiatric disorders of either parent and/or patients; or a high level of conflict that cannot be contained in an out-patient setting. These patients are referred for hospitalization.*)

Session I

Parents are asked to introduce themselves and may raise two urgent issues that he or she feels needs immediate attention. Parents' experiences vary from emotional turmoil, ranging from self-blame to blaming others (the child, society, or the therapists). They may vacillate between a need for over involvement to a wish to abandon the entire situation. The need for advice from other parents coping with ED children is central at first. It is important to raise parental anxiety and concern while simultaneously reducing guilt in order to facilitate appropriate action. The state of disorientation frees them from their usual patterns and allows them to take the therapist's lead and experiment with moving towards new patterns of behavior. The crisis of possible hospitalization, motivates some families to think differently and thus to act differently.

We stress that for some adolescents and young adults eating and the relationship to one's body becomes a "battleground" for the separation-individuation conflict. The "battle" is about who controls the body. Since our goal is to help facilitate the patient's growth process--but not at the expense of the body, parents are asked to follow three guidelines when home-based treatment is indicated: a) parents are expected to prepare and serve the precise amount of food prescribed by the dietician, in order to build a trusting relationship; b) they are requested to sit at the table during meals with their daughter but eating is her sole responsibility; and c) they are advised to avoid discussions about food. In cases of BN or BED, we recommend not to take responsibility for preventing binge eating and vomiting by their child.

Session II

The DSM IV 1994 eating disorders classifications of AN, BN and BED are elucidated along with core behavioral, cognitive and psychological symptoms. For example, in AN, the irrational fear concerning weight gain is compared to phobias that cannot be countered by rational argument nor reduced by psychotherapeutic interventions in the short term. The vicious cycle of hunger, binge attacks, compensatory behavior and somatic changes are described in order to help parents understand the possible advantages their children gain by these behaviors, and why they are often afraid of gaining weight or are afraid of stopping binge-purging behavior.

Session III

The multidimensional etiological model is demonstrated through interactions among biological, genetic, socio-cultural, individual and familial factors. Families can play an important but unpredictable role with no causal link, yet we demonstrate how dysfunctional interactions maintain and intensify symptoms. Co-morbidity such as depression, anxiety, OCD, impulsivity--including self-mutilation behaviors, are major therapeutic challenges. If we recognize major co-morbidity in parents, they are referred for further evaluation. Some parents share with the group their own ED history. We stress the risks of dieting behavior during childhood and the teen-age years are stressed, along with the need to respect genetic determinants on body size.

Session IV

The three stages of the FB-FP model are delineated and the participants are informed about the various dimensions of the multi-disciplinary treatment. These consist of 1) nutritional counseling including the a specific protocol for treating AN, BN and BED respectively, along with the use of food diaries and defined nutritional rehabilitation targets 2) psychiatric medication when necessary and depending upon the severity of the ED and co-morbidity, and 3) a description of the various forms of psychotherapy. In the initial stage our approach entails CBT for ED symptoms, including body checking and body avoidance, tackling the problem of excessive exercise in AN patients and conversely, encouraging exercise in BN and BED. Under the guidance of a physical therapist exercise also serves as a component of mood regulation. Dynamic or expressive therapy including group psychotherapy for parents commences during the second stage, while triad therapy begins only in the third stage if feasible.

Session V

This session focuses on informing participants about potential medical complications and the possible long-term effects of nutritional deficiency. This includes a description of the physical consequences of starvation along with promoting an understanding of the interaction between physical, psychological and cognitive processes in the overall context of eating disorders.

Session VI

During the final session, parents report on their progress in symptom reduction and in coping skills and future treatment options are reviewed. Parents are encouraged to start "living again", e.g. inviting friends over, returning to having family meals, and paying attention to the effect of the situation on the patient's siblings. We emphasize maintaining boundaries for chaotic families and flexibility for rigid ones. If home-based treatment is still indicated, we address how to cope with long term changes in the family's daily routine. Strategies of relapse prevention are discussed and the necessity of long-term maintenance and treatment is emphasized.

Phase II: Individual Psychodynamic Therapy for Patients and Group Therapy for Parents

Patient Treatment Plan

After terminating the crisis phase (1-6 meetings) and ensuring that she is medically stable, the patient receives psychotherapy or expressive therapy while parents participate in a psycho-dynamic therapy group or in couples' therapy. Beyond creating a "holding environment" for parents and daughters, the separate treatments create a space that enables the adolescent to examine the role of the "food object" in her dialogue with her parents, freeing-up the parents to examine their own issues. When an adolescent strongly opposes psychotherapy, she is only required to participate in physical and dietary supervision.

Parent Psychodynamic Groups

The psychodynamic group sessions are limited to ten participating couples and up to twenty sessions. Upon completing the initial six session psycho-educational group, the parents are now more motivated to address underlying issues. All of us exist as subjects in our parents' mind even before birth. Parents have expectations, desires and wishes about each of their children before they are born, related to the circumstances of their individual lives and their relationship with each other. Through the therapeutic process parents begin to identify "what" they nurtured in each child with, even before birth. Many times the history of the symptom and the eating disorder is bound up the past. Parents gradually begin discussing what their child was like before the ED, what reactions she elicited in them. They share the dreams, expectations and disappointments they experienced through parenting and begin to take responsibility for those aspects of interaction belonging to them and their family of origin that may have been projected onto their daughters. This process enables the beginning of separateness.

A great deal of attention is paid to the role of the father and specifically his importance in relation to his daughter's development. Many parents describe changes in the relationship since their child became of teenager. From our experience, father daughter relationships are characterized in polarities e.g. a negative attitude toward the father sometimes to the extent that the patient will not stay in the same room with him, while at the same time the adolescent may be in a symbiotic relationship with mother. However, the opposite too may exist as the contact between father and daughter may become eroticized. Parents may need to change this interactive pattern in order to impose any rules and set boundaries. References to marital issues are limited, although we do highlight the point that sometimes the illness could be a symptom reflecting the marital relationship, and we encourage further couple's therapy if needed when group therapy ends.

(Exclusion Criteria: Although the psycho-educational groups are a requirement, parents who may have a psychiatric disorder or are assessed as potentially binge disruptive to the group process are not referred to group psychotherapy.)

Phase III- Conjoint Sessions

Five sessions are added to the parental group for joint meetings of parents and daughters. A recovered patient is invited to the first session to speak about her journey, including the process with her own parents and their contribution to her recovery, as well as to answer any questions of emanating from either parents or daughters. . The recovered patient functions as a bridge enabling a dialogue between parents and their children. . Starting with the second session, parents and children are divided into small groups- for the first part of the meeting. Families are separated so that children are not in the same group as their parents. During the second part of the session an open dialogue is held. The parents' need to question other children about their feelings is evident. They always share their struggle for a way to get through to their child, almost always asking the other children for advice on what to do. The timing that we choose for the therapeutic encounter between parents and their own child is when dialogue has become more feasible. By this time, it is easier to identify meanings such as "for whom" or "what" the child is eating, and "who" the parents are feeding. For closure, a final session is held only with parents, where they have the opportunity to reflect upon what they've learned during the treatment.

Case Presentation: Sara's Assessment and Treatment Plan

In presenting Sara's case, we will describe the full course of Sara's family's experience at our clinic over the course of approximately 18 months.) It illustrates the many challenges inherent in working with resistant patients and parents. The goal in the initial stage of Sara's treatment was to enable her to begin eating and to attain more flexibility in her rigid eating habits. Sara was strongly opposed to treatment in general and psychotherapy in particular. She was brought to treatment against her will and remained steadfast in her silence. The case will demonstrate how her insistence on silence compelled us to confront the parents' resistance to any kind of counseling, as represented mainly by the father. This family was unable to sit together and talk due to paralyzing anxiety, stemming from the father's domination. Sara was the only one "speaking", which she did pathologically through her body.

Phase I. Developing the Treatment Plan and Psycho-Educational Groups for Parents

Sara arrived at our clinic when she was 15 years old, having suffered from AN-R since she was ten years old. The youngest of three children, Sara came from a family with a high socio-economic status. Her older sister had previously suffered from Bulimia Nervosa. Sara was admitted to our clinic following six months of hospitalization. Her weight after being discharging from the hospital was: 45 kg, Height: 1.58, BMI: 18. She had never menstruated. and suffered from severe osteoporosis. During intake, her stubbornness was apparent as she put up a determined struggle to maintain a particular number (45 kg) on the scale. Alongside her father's concern, his appreciation for the resolute side of her character could be discerned.

Mr. A. had very strict eating habits, acquired during childhood, when his father's chronic illness led all members of the family to eat a very limited diet on a very rigid schedule. Mr. A is obsessively neat about his appearance with a domineering and critical personality. He criticized his wife about her appearance, her lack of attention to order, organization and economy, and he tended to interfere in every detail of home life. Mrs. A. lived in his shadow throughout the years, never standing up for herself and often crying in response to his criticisms. In many ways she seemed typical of women who have been battered, although Mrs. A was not physically abused.

Sara began dietary supervision, psychiatric treatment and psychotherapy against her will. She was told that the goal was to restore menstruation and the target weight was evaluated at approximately 50 kg. In the first stage of treatment her parents refused to join our groups. During Sara's short therapy, she stated the only issue bothering her was her mother's weakness and inability to stand up for herself. After two months, she refused to continue psychotherapy. We decided to release her from psychotherapy and required her to be in dietary supervision with the support of SSRI's, and later to participate in five sessions of the parent-child group. It was clear that no change would be attained without the involvement of her parents in the treatment. Sara, in her determined opposition guided us in insisting upon engaging her father in the treatment despite his own resistance.

Sara's parents were required to participate in a psycho-education group. Home-based treatment was partially indicated enabling Sara to attend school for the first in three months. Mr. A. joined the group against his will, saying, "I don't believe in this, but I'm willing to do anything to help her recover". Both parents barely spoke throughout the six meetings, only asking occasional questions regarding how best to coach Sara, in order implement the behavioral weight gain. Sara's case provides a glimpse into the complex role of the dietician working with eating disorder patients in an outpatient setting as it represents a case bordering on a chronic condition. In these instances, the dietician tries to minimize physical damage as much as possible. Despite the treatment's demands, it took Sara a year to achieve her target weight and to receive her first spontaneous period. Due to her extreme fear of losing control, she was preparing her own food in her parent's presence. During the first stage of treatment, she was allowed to choose the texture of her food, since she insisted on putting everything into the blender. Like an infant learning to eat, Sara went from soft food to chunky food and only later to regular food, in a long and exhausting process. Sara's rigid eating was experienced as identification with her father's Spartan patterns.

Phase II and Phase III. Parental Group Psychotherapy, Ongoing Treatment Regime for Sara and Conjoint Sessions

Sara's parents were also quite resistance to participating in the psycho-therapy group and although they reluctantly agreed to attend, rarely spoke throughout the entire course of group treatment. A surprising turning point finally occurred in the joint sessions. In one of the joint sessions, Mr. A. had the opportunity to hear another girl talk about her relationship with her father, and he surprisingly, responded with tears. Mrs. A. and Sara saw him express weakness for the first time. In response to one of the other parents' direct question towards her, Sara replied, "I know why I eat this way". Her father addressed her, a rare moment for this family, and asked, "What is the reason?" Sara answered, "I know the psychologists think it's because of you, but it's because I need everything to be under control". By her response she continued to unconsciously protect her parents, but the change was the dialogue itself, which had become possible for the first time.

In the last session, with parents only, Mr. A. recalled this conversation with Sara and said that what frightened him was her determination and lack of doubts. Slowly, it became clear to him that he usually had no doubts either. "I always had clear ideas about what I was doing. Now I have to start asking myself questions". A conversation ensued in which the fathers spoke about their complex encounter with their daughters' maturation. This discussion created the possibility for Mr. A. to participate and be present. It was hard for him to identify with the feelings of rejection that some of the fathers expressed towards their bulimic daughters. He said, "What I feel is helplessness. I see everything and notice every detail, and I say what I see. My children know that. But I haven't said a thing to Sara since she got sick". One of the fathers responded, in a humorous, gentle tone: "By shutting her mouth, Sara was the only one who managed to shut yours". When the group terminated, a decision was made that Sara's parents would continue in couples' therapy. Sara would not continue psychotherapy due to her continued refusal to talk. She was only required only to eat, with the help of SSRI medication, against which she also struggled.

CBT Treatment for Sara and Couples Therapy for her Parents

Sara's symptoms were an expression of her parents' relationship. For her, the knowledge that they were coming in and talking was a release from the unconscious responsibility of maintaining and mediating their relationship. Mrs. A. appeared unable to speak in her husband's presence, and rarely spoke in the group. However, she heard her husband speak and saw him cry for the first time in her life and felt the softening in him.

About two months after the conclusion of the group, Mrs. A. began to speak in couples' therapy and to assert herself. On one occasion, Sara overheard her father telling her mother about a significant investment of time that had allowed him to save a minute sum of money. She turned to her mother and asked, "Would you have done the same thing**?**" Mrs. A. said "No" and Sara said, "I agree with you". The therapeutic holding environment encouraged self-expression and tolerance of differences as first steps toward separation. At this point .Sara finally agreed to start CBT in order to loosen her attachment to the symptoms, as well as work on control issues in other areas of her life.

Case Summary

A genuine dialogue is still impossible between Sara and her parents but there are several indications of positive and healthy changes in her. Her question to her mother demonstrated that she has doubts as to whether her father's way is always right and her behavior gradually became more flexible and less Spartan. Sara began to allow herself enjoy leisure time, movies and parties that she had previously denied herself, and bought new, flattering clothes enjoying the compliments she received. Sara's sister, who suffered from Bulimia Nervosa, had told her father in the past, "You never hit us, but your looks were worse than beatings". Sara now told her mother and sister that she perceived a great change in her father. After gaining 5 kg with a great deal of difficulty, Sara began having regular menstrual periods for the first time in her life.

The clinic setting of meetings with all concerned every six weeks, helped set the stage for discussing Sara's emotional condition and determining whether it was possible to devise a reasonable compromise that would enable us to continue to work with her. This was born out of Sara's refusal to participate in any kind of therapy. Sara ended her treatment at the clinic when the time came for her to begin her compulsory military service. Although her treatment had not been completed, we believe Sara could easily have gone down in the statistics as a chronic anorexic in constant mortal danger, had it not been for her parents' engagement in both groups as well as the complicated, creative path her dietician took with her. We believe that after 8 years of pre-pubertal anorexia nervosa her journey can be seen as an achievement.

CONCLUSION

The FB- FP model has proven effective in facilitating changes in parental behavior and psychological functioning which help reduce ED symptoms. Additional findings have been a significant transition from over or under involvement to more appropriate involvement levels--particularly by fathers, who may express greater empathy towards their daughters, no longer perceived a "troublesome rival". Therefore, the mother and daughter are often released from the symbiotic relationship, which is not uncommon in ED. We believe the success of FB-FP is also due to the impact and power of the group format. The group enables parents who are more reserved or passive, to listen to others without being required to speak, and may evoke motivation for subsequent individual, couples or conjoint therapy. Parental change can also positively effect interactions with the other siblings as well, and strengthen the functioning of the entire family unit.

In approaching the treatment of a family system, it is important to recognize the differences between families and among each individual within the family. In order to develop an effective treatment plan, it is crucial to diagnose the dynamics of each family along with identifying what resources are needed and can be mobilized to aid in their child's recovery.

REFERENCES

American Psychiatric Association (APA) (2006). *Practice Guidelines for the Treatment of Patients with Eating Disorders, 3rd ed.* Washington, DC: APA:.

American Psychiatric Association (1994). *Diagnostic and Statistical Manual of Mental Disorders (DSM-IV) (4th ed.).* Washington, DC: APA.

Bruch, H. (1973). *Eating Disorders: Obesity, Anorexia Nervosa and the Person Within.* New York: Basic Books.

Bruch, H. (1982). Anorexia nervosa: Theory and therapy. *American Journal of Psychiatry, 139*, 1531-1538.

Bruch, H. (2001). Family disengagement. In: *The golden cage: the enigma of anorexia nervosa.* US: Harvard University Press, pp. 106-120.

Colahan, M., & Senior, R. (1995). Family patterns in eating disorders: going round in circles, getting nowhere fasting. In: G. Szmukler, C. Dare & J. Treasure (Eds.), *Handbook Of Eating Disorders: Theory, Treatment and Research.* London: John Wiley & Sons Ltd., pp. 243-257.

Dare, C. & Eisler, I. (1995). Family therapy. In: G. Szmukler, C. Dare & J. Treasure (Eds.), *Handbook Of Eating Disorders: Theory, Treatment and Research.* England John Wiley & Sons Ltd., pp. 334-349.

Eisler, I. (1995). Family models of eating disorders. In: G. Szmukler, C. Dare & J. Treasure (Eds.), *Handbook Of Eating Disorders: Theory, Treatment and Research.* England: John Wiley & Sons Ltd., pp. 155-176.

Eisler, I., Dare, C., Hodes, M., Russell, G., Dodge, E., & le Grange, D. (2000). Family therapy for adolescent anorexia nervosa: The results of a controlled comparison of two family interventions. *Journal of Child Psychology and Psychiatry, 41*, 727–736.

Garner, D. M. (1997). Psycho-educational principles in treatment. In D. M., Garner & P. E., Garfinkel (Eds.), *Handbook of Treatment for Eating Disorders.* New York-London: Guilford, pp. 145–177.

Geist, R., Heinmaa, M., Stephens, D., Davis, R., & Katzman, D. K. (2000). Comparison of family therapy and family group psychoeducation in adolescents with anorexia nervosa. *Canadian Journal of Psychiatry, 45*, 173–178.

Gull, W. W. (1874). Anorexia nervosa (apepsia hysterica, anorexia hysterica). *Transactions of the Clinical Society of London, 7*, 222-228.

Holtkamp, K., Herpertz-Dahlmann, B., Vloet, T. & Hagenah, U.(2005) Group Psychoeducation for Parents of Adolescents with Eating Disorders. *The Aachen Program. Eating Disorders, 13*, 381-390.

Jeanmet, P. (1984). La groupe de parents: sa place dans le traitement de l'anorexie mentale [The parents' group: its place in the treatment of anorexia nervosa.]. *Neuropsychiat Enfan , 32,* 299-303.

Jeanmet, P., & Gorge, A. (1980). Une forme de therapie familiale: le groupe de parents [A form of family therapy: the parent group]. *Psychiatrie Enfant, 23,* 587-636.

Latzer, Y., & Gaber, L. B. (1998). Pathological conflict avoidance in Anorexia Nervosa: Family perspective. *Contemporary Family Therapy, 20*, 539-551.

Latzer, Y., Ben-Ari, A. & Galimidi, N. (2002). Anorexia nervosa and the family: Effects on younger sisters to anorexia nervosa patients. *International Journal of Adolescent Medicine and Health, 14,* 275-281.

Latzer, Y., Gaber, L.B. & Nadler, S. (2006). Pathological conflict avoidance in Anorexia Nervosa: *Family perspective. Clinical nutrition, 2*, 72-77.

Latzer, Y., Hochdorf, Z., Bachar, E., & Conetti, L. (2003). The treatment as a "secure base": family therapy as a secure based attachment in eating disorders. *Sihot , 3*, 1-9.

Latzer, Y., Hochdorf, Z., Bachar, E., Conetti, L. (2002). Attachment style and family functioning as discriminating factors in eating disorders. *Contemporary Family Therapy, 24*, 581-599.

Le Grange, D. (1999). Family therapy for adolescent anorexia nervosa. *Journal of Clinical Psychology, 55,* 727-739.

Le Grange, D. (2005). The Maudsley family-based treatment for adolescent anorexia nervosa. *World Psychiatry Association, 4*, 142-146.

McFarlane, T. L., Olmsted, M. P., & Goldbloom, D.S. (2005). Beliefs and Expectations Regarding Etiology, Treatment and Outcome in Bulimia Nervosa. *Eating and Weight Disorders, 10*, 187-192.

McFarlane, W.R. (1997). Fact: integrating family psycho - education and assertive community treatment. *Administration and Policy in Mental Health and Mental*, 25, 191-198.

McFarlane, W. R., Lukens, E., Link, B., Dushay, R., Deakins, S. A. & Newmark, M. et al. (1995). Multiple-family groups and psychoeducation in the treatment of schizophrenia. *Archives of General Psychiatry, 52*, 679-687.

Minuchin, S., Baker L., Rosman, B.L., Liebman, R., Milman, L., & Todd, T.C. (1975). A conceptual model of psychosomatic illness in children. *Archives of Genetics Psychiatry, 32*, 1031-1038.

Minuchin, S., Rosman, B.L. & Baker, L. (1978). *Psychosomatic Families: Anorexia Nervosa In Context.* Cambridge, Mass: Harvard University Press.

Nicholls, D., & Magagna, J. (1997). A group for the parents of children with eating disorders. *Clinical Child Psychology and Psychiatry, 2*, 565–578

Perednia, C., VanVreckem, E. Wanderyecken, W. (1989). Parent counseling: from guidance to treatment. In W. Vanderyken, E. Kog, & J. Vanderlinden (Eds.). *The Family Approach to Eating Disorders: Assesment, and Treatment of Anorexia Nervosa and Bulimia*. New York: PMA Publishing, pp. 249-62.

Robin, A. L., Siegel, P. T., Moye, A. W., Gilroy, M., Dennis, A. B., & Sikand, A. (1999). A controlled comparison of family versus individual therapy for adolescents with anorexia nervosa. *Journal of the American Academy of Child and Adolescent Psychiatry, 38*, 1482–1489.

Russell, G. F. M., Dare, C., Eisler, I.. & Le Grange P. D. F.(1992). Controlled trials of family treatments in anorexia nervosa. In K. A. Halmi (Ed.), *Psychobiology and treatment of Anorexia Nervosa and Bulimia Nervosa.* Washington, D.C. :American Psychiatric Press.

Selvini-Palazzoli, M. S. (1974). *Self Starvation: From the Intrapsychic to the Transpersonal Approach*. London: Chaucer.

Squire-Dehouk, B. (1993). *Evaluation of Conjoint Family Therapy Vs. Family Counseling in Adolescent Anorexia Nervosa Patients: A Two Year Follow-Up Study* [dissertation]. Institute of Psychiatry and University of Surrey.

Treasure, J., Murphy,T., & Szmukler, T. (2001). The experience of care giving for severe mental illness: a comparison between anorexia nervosa and psychosis. *Social Psychiatry and Psychiatric Epidemiology, 36*, 343-347.

Treasure, J., Tchanturia, K., & Schmidt, U. (2005). Developing a model of the treatment for eating disorder: using neuroscience research to examine the how rather than the what of change. *Counselling and Psychotherapy Research, 5*, 187-190.

Treasure, J., Todd, G., Brolly, M., Tiller, J., Nehmed, A., & Denman, F. (1995). A pilot study of a randomized trial of cognitive analytical therapy vs. educational behavioral therapy for adult anorexia nervosa. *Behavior Research and Therapy, 33*, 363-367.

Treasure, J.,Gavan, K., Todd,G., et al (2003). Changing the environment in eating disorders: working with carers/families to improve motivation and facilitate change. *European Eating Disorder Review, 11*, 25-37

Uehara, T., Kawashima, Y., Goto, M., Tasaki, S. I., & Someya, T. (2001). Psychoeducation for the families of patients with eating disorders and changes in expressed emotion: A preliminary study. *Comprehensive Psychiatry, 42*, 132–138.

Van Vreckem, E., & Vanderyecken, W. (1989). Counseling groups for parents of eating disorder patients. In W. Vanderyecken, E. Kog & J. Vanderlinden (Eds), *The Family Approach to Eating Disorders: Assesment and Treatment of Anorexia Nervosa and Bulimia*. New York: PMA Publishing, pp. 347-62.

Vanderycken, W. (2002). Families of patients with eating disorders. In C. G. Fairburn & K. D. Brownell (Eds.), *Eating Disorders and Obesity: A Comprehensive Handbook*. The Guilford Press. New York, London, pp. 215-229.

Verbeek, N., & Verbeek, E. (1977). Anorexia nervosa: karakteristiek en therapie van de drie-hoeksrelatie in het ouderlijk gezin [Anorexia nervosa: characteristics and treatment of the triangular relation in family]. *Tijdschr Psychiat, 19*, 685-703

Whitney, J., Murray, J., Gavan, K., Todd, G., Whitaker, W. & Treasure, J. (2005). Experience of caring for someone with Anorexia Nervosa: qualitative study. *The British Journal of Psychiatry, 187*, 444-449.

Winnicott, D. (1951). *Through Pediatrics to Psycho-analysis*. London: Karnac.

Winnicott, D.W. (1965). *The Maturation Process and the Facilitating Environment*. New York: International University Press.

Zubery, E. (1993). Eating disorders: A Psycopathology of the individual, family and society. *Bamishpah'a Journal of the Israeli Association for Marital and Family Therapy and Family Life Education, 37*, 24-33.

Zubery, E., Binsted, N. Zifman, N. & Jeczmien, P. (2005). Adolescents Resisting Treatment: Exploring the resistance in Eating Disorder Patients to treatment within *The Family System. Israeli Journal of Psychiatry, 42*, 146-153.

In: Cognitive Therapy of Eating Disorders...
Editors: S. Sassaroli and G.M. Ruggiero

ISBN: 978-1-60876-617-8

Chapter 10

AN INTEGRATIVE APPROACH TO THE TREATMENT OF BULIMIA NERVOSA: COGNITIVE BEHAVIOR THERAPY WITH A DYNAMIC APPROACH

Yael Latzer[1], Tamar Peretz[2], Sarit Kreutzer[3], Eynat Zubery[4] and Daniel Stein[5]

[1] Director, Eating Disorders Clinic, Psychiatric Division, Rambam Medical Center, Haifa, Israel, and the Faculty of Social Welfare and Health studies, University of Haifa, Haifa, Israel

[2] Clinical Psychologist, Eating Disorders Clinic, Psychiatric Division, Rambam Medical Center, Haifa, Israel

[3] Clinical Psychologist and Supervisor, Eating Disorders Clinic, Psychiatric Division, Rambam Medical Center, Haifa, Israel

[4] Eating Disorders Unit, Davidson Clinic, Shalvata Mental Health Center, Clalit Health Services, affiliated with the Sackler Faculty of Medicine, Tel Aviv University, Israel

[5] The Pediatric Psychosomatic Department, Safra Children's Hospital, The Chaim Sheba Medical Center, Tel Hashomer, affiliated with the Sackler Faculty of Medicine, Tel Aviv University, Tel Aviv, Israel

ABSTRACT

The present chapter aims to describe an alternative treatment model for bulimia nervosa (BN), integrating cognitive behavioral and short-term dynamic therapies. Referred to as conflict-oriented Cognitive Behavioral Therapy (CO-CBT), this model focuses on the underlying emotional and dynamic aspects of BN more than does traditional CBT. The need for such an integration emerges from the necessity to focus more on the underlying conflicts attached to the disorder, which do not receive sufficient consideration in the traditional existing CBT model.

The chapter briefly reviews the basics of cognitive behavioral treatment, as well as the short-term dynamic treatment for patients with BN and then describes the development and characteristics of the suggested integrated treatment model. A case study is presented followed by discussion on the strength and importance of the proposed model as compared to traditional existing treatments for BN and their efficacy.

INTRODUCTION

Bulimia Nervosa (BN) is an eating disorder characterized by recurrent uncontrollable episodes of binge-eating that lead to the rapid consumption of large amounts of food within a short period of time, followed by purging through vomiting, use of laxatives or diuretics, compulsive exercise, or prolonged fasts (APA,1994). This is a complex disorder whose etiology most likely represents and interplay between social, psychological, and biological forces (Williamson, Martin, & Stewart, 2004).

Because of the multifaceted nature of the illness, BN is often treated through the use of multiple therapeutic approaches, including behavioral, interpersonal (IPT), pharmacological, psychodynamic, dialectic behavioral (DBT) and cognitive behavioral therapies (CBT) (Mitchell et al., 2002). According to Fairburn et al (1993), the most effective approach for the treatment of Bulimia Nervosa is the CBT approach (Freeman, 1995). Wilson (1999), however, argues that although CBT offers considerable assistance in reducing symptoms it does not meet the needs of the entire population suffering from BN. Another intervention, described by Ryle and associates (Ryle, 1995; Ryle & Beard, 1993; Ryle & Golynkina, 2000), is that of time-limited cognitive analytic therapy (CAT), which has been used successfully in the treatment of borderline personality disorder patients.

To our knowledge, no one has yet explored a model integrating both cognitive behavioral and dynamic therapies for the treatment of BN. Until recently, dynamic psychotherapy and CBT were considered to be widely different conceptual worlds that were competitive and diametrically opposed to one another. However, Hamilton (2001) has raised the question as to whether these two approaches are entirely different, or if they share a common denominator.

According to Hamilton (2001), the cognitive-behavioral model is centrally-focused on the symptoms and on the accompanying emotional experience of the illness, but it does not enable a deeper exploration of the underlying conflict. In contrast, the dynamic model attempts to uncover and resolve the underlying conflicts that are involved in the development of the illness. While a dynamic approach does not offer immediate relief of symptoms, as does the CBT, the concept behind the dynamic model is that a deep understanding of the underlying mechanisms of the illness leads to an eventual reduction in symptoms. Integrating techniques from both approaches may lead to a more comprehensive treatment for patients with BN.

The present chapter presents the authors' preliminary attempt to integrate these two approaches in the treatment of females suffering from BN by combining short-term dynamic treatment with CBT in a group setting. The authors' refer to this approach as conflict oriented-CBT treatment "Conflict-Oriented CBT" (CO-CBT). The uniqueness of this model is its deep and focused exploration of the psychopathological basis of BN's underlying conflict, combined with a focus on the immediate treatment of symptoms.

The chapter begins by presenting a brief literature review on the theory and research pertaining to cognitive-behavioral and short-term dynamic treatments as applied to BN, followed by a delineation of a clinical application of the proposed treatment model and a case example. The discussion at the end of the chapter addresses the dilemmas that arise from combining these two approaches and provides recommendations for future research. (Monteleone, Castaldo, Di Filippo, & Maj, 2006; Triosi, DiLorenzo, Alcinic, Nanni, Di Pasquale, & Siracusano, 2006; McFarlane, Olmsted, & Goldbloom, 2005; Williamson, Martin, & Stewart, 2004).

An Overview of the Use of CBT for Treating BN

The cognitive-behavioral model, was first developed by Beck for individuals suffering from depression,(1963). This approach focuses on cognitive components, such as the modification of negative thoughts and accompanying behavior, by challenging the automatic thoughts that arise in the event of a threatening situation. The treatment is conducted by having the patient act as a scientific observer of his/her own thoughts from a cognitive-behavioral perspective. .

The central theme of this model for individuals suffering from eating disorders is that dysfunctional thoughts and beliefs about food, weight, and body image along with inadequate problem solving skills, and flawed interpersonal relationships play an essential role in the development and maintenance of the illness.

The application of the cognitive-behavioral model to the treatment of BN was first developed in the early 1980'ss by Fairburn (1981) and was implemented in several eating disorder treatment centers in the US and in England. CBT was subsequently found to be one of the most effective approach in the treatment of BN (Fairburn, 2003). Research conducted by Wifley, Agras, Telch, Rossiter, Schneider, Cole, et al., (1993) identified interpersonal psychotherapy (IPT) as an equally successful treatment model for BN. Both treatments are found to have the same level of efficacy, however IPT does not focus on the eating habits and symptoms of the illness, and treatment is conducted over a one-year period. CBT in contrast, is a short-term therapy and focuses on changing eating habits and behavior (Fairburn et al., 1993, 1995).

While a large percentage of patients do improve with CBT or IPT not all individuals with BN can be helped with these approaches. Treatment is particularly unsuccessful in those individuals with borderline personality disturbances, women with a history of sexual abuse and those with severely low levels of self-esteem(Fairburn, 1993; Mitchell et al., 2002).

An Overview of Dynamic Treatment for BN

The dynamic view of Bulimia Nervosa tries to understand the intra-psychic meaning of the disorder, Certain psychodynamic theories consider Bulimia Nervosa as reflecting a lack of basic self-control, while the symptoms are seen as helping to regulate internal tension and self-determination (Johnson, 1995).

The self-psychology approach views eating disorders as representing a deficit of the self.. The essence of such disorders is that those with EDs cannot rely on others to meet their needs, and subsequently turn to food to meet them (Goodsitt, 1997 Bachar et al., 1999).

Bruch interprets bulimic symptoms are a final attempt to assert oneself and to reach autonomy (Bruch, 1973).

Britton (1992) speaks about the great difficulty in seeing one's parents as sexual partners who have a relationship that excludes the patient. Failing to cope with this reality may have pathological ramifications, including the emergence of eating disorders. Patients with BN derive satisfaction through the intake of food, experiencing it as an all-powerful force that supplies tranquility, warmth and safety, while also serving as a regulator for painful emotions, such as anger, shame, guilt, depression, and anxiety (Sands, 1991). Since the eating and the ritual connected with it are a main source for fulfilling one's own needs, it is protected with great strength.

The binge and purge pattern of Bulimia Nervosa has been described as a "no entry" mechanism to protect against the fantasies projected by the mother (Williams, 1997). Laurence (2001) considers the symptoms as emerging from the desire to rule the introverted parents. Through bulimic symptoms, one can attack the introverted parents, swallow them through binge eating, and kill them through vomiting. That way, the patient tries to achieve a command over her inner world. Ogden (1991) sees the urge to eat as a way of blocking unpleasant feelings, which individuals with BN have difficulty identifying.

The numerous psychoanalytic interpretations of BN and their subsequent treatment techniques make it difficult to assess their efficiency. Johnson (1995) claims that despite the results of comparative research, which point to an advantage of CBT over the dynamic approach, the use of dynamic psychotherapy is most effective after patients are relieved from the symptoms of BN.

To the best of our knowledge, the only treatment approach that aims to combines CBT with dynamic analytic therapy was used by Ryle (2000) in the treatment of patients with borderline personality disorders (BPD). Nevertheless, case histories (Ryle & Bread, 1993; Ryle, 1995; Ryle & Golynkina, 2000) demonstrate that despite the effectiveness of dynamic CBT with borderlines, challenges remain in treating severe cases of BPD.

Our proposed model which will be discussed below, aims to combine CBT and short-term dynamic therapy. Short-term dynamic psychotherapy was first developed by Mann (1964), and later by Sifenos (1966) on the basis of the psychodynamic approach. The treatment is very short and limited to twelve to thirty sessions with the therapist playing a very active role. The treatment focuses around a central conflict, identified by the patient. The dynamic treatment aims to deepen the understanding of this conflict, focusing on its origin and its implications for the present situation. At the same time, emphasis is placed on dealing with the process of ending treatment and separation from the therapist. According to this model, change can be achieved through insightful experiences (Sifneos,1966; Malan,1963; Davanloo,1979).

To the best of our knowledge, there is no report in the literature of short-term dynamic treatment being used among a population suffering BN.

CO-CBT: The Proposed Integrative Model

Treatment Structure and Setting

Our model integrates a dynamic component into a structured CBT within a group setting, which raised several concerns. The primary concern was that the inclusion of a dynamic component in the group might create an unstructured element, which could lead to an "open" group dynamic. This could lend itself to competition among patients and creates a risk of patients hurting each other emotionally.. It could also cause the patients to feel overwhelmed, and frustrated. Subsequently, the groups were structured as a psycho-educational group which combined a psychodynamic approach within the existing structure of CBT.(Riess, Helen, 2002).

Group therapy is a common feature found in treatment models for eating disorders. (Moreno, 1994, Wifley et al, 2002). The popularity of group treatment may be due to a combination of economic factors, as well as the fact that groups tend to quickly facilitate growth by reducing feelings of isolation, low self-esteem, difficulty identifying feelings, and trouble communicating, which are all characteristics of bulimic patients (Hendren, et al, 1987). In addition, the group reduces the shame factor, in part because individuals feel that they are not alone in their suffering (Barth & Wurman, 1986; Levine & Mishna, 2007).

The group setting creates an environment in which the patients are able to support each other, and creates an internal social network that the patients can rely upon, reach out to, and benefit from. This setting highlights the differences between patients and invites positive comparison analysis between core conflicts and coping mechanisms, which differ from patient to patient. This creates a learning environment instead of a competitive one. (Rorty, Yager, Buckwalter, & Rossotto, 1999; Moreno, Furhirman, & Hileman, 1996: Nevonen & Borberg, 2006; Moreno, 1994). The CBT model was adapted for use with patients in Israel, being treated in two centers for ED's under the management of Prof. Danny Stein and Prof.Yael Latzer.

THE PROPOSED CO-CBT MODEL

Treatment Criteria

Prior to acceptance into the program, all patients had an individual interview.. Groups consisted of thirteen, weekly, ninety-minute sessions. The group was led by clinical psychotherapists, trained in both CBT and dynamically-oriented psychotherapies, as well as a dietitian. For the first meeting time is divided equally among participants. In subsequent sessions one individual is given proportionately more time to discuss their issues and receive feedback and the remaining time is divided equally between group members.

All patients were committed to fulfilling the entire CBT protocol requirements (Fairburn et al., 1997). CBT programs include strict selection criteria regarding the suitability of patients for treatment. The proposed model included a treatment contract, whereby patients agreed to maintain their present body weight, follow a diet plan, keep a food diary during the entire period of treatment and attend all treatment sessions (Fairburn, 1993, 1995, 2003: Lacey, 1983).

The main purpose of the food diary is to identify the patterns and connections between the patients' underlying emotional conflicts and binge/purge behaviors. Patients are instructed to write exactly what, where, and the time that they ate, and who was present. Individuals must also report if they experienced an urge to or actually had a binge/purge episode, if laxatives or diuretics were used, and if and for how long they exercised. In addition, they are asked to record any special events that occurred during the day. Finally, they are required to report any thoughts and feelings associated with the urge to engage in binge/purge behaviors. This activity enables patients to identify and understand the relationship between their pathological eating patterns and their emotional world.

The patients are required to keep the diary with them 24 hours a day and write about the aforementioned issues in real time. In this way, the diary also serves as a "transitional object" by fostering a sense of connection to themselves and knowing that the therapist will be reviewing the diary on a daily basis, which also helps to reduce destructive behaviors. Maintaining a balanced diet and writing in the diary dramatically reduces binge-eating episodes. Patients begin to understand that their binge/purge behaviors are a reaction to their emotions. The diary, the diet and the group all serve to help them understand the underlying conflict between eating behaviors and actions. The contract also requires patients to attend meetings with the dietician once a week which takes place prior to the therapeutic group meetings.

The First Meeting

The main objective of the first meeting is to acquaint patients with the treatment plan in order to achieve control over their symptoms. Individuals first accept the treatment contract which emphasizes the structured nature of the treatment approach.. The stages of treatment are then reviewed in conjunction with the tools they will acquire to cope with and reduce symptoms. At this point each member shares the history and current status of their eating disorder.

The Second through Fourth Meetings: Reviewing the Food Diary

The next several meetings are devoted to reviewing the food diary and learning to use it as a tool to identify emotional patterns associated with binge/purge episodes At these meetings members review their observed emotional and behavioral patterns and one member does so in depth and receives feedback from the rest of the group.

Attention is first given to whether patients are maintaining their required structured and balanced meal plans in spite of binge/purge episodes. This is followed by examining the accompanying thoughts that the patients report having while eating. Once individuals' emotional patterns are identified alternative coping strategies are recommended to replace binge/purge behaviors.

The Fifth through Twelfth Meetings: Identifying of the Underlying Central Conflict

The fifth meeting is dedicated to the identification of underling central conflicts generating binge/purge symptoms. At this stage of treatment, each patient, with the assistance of the group therapist, is encouraged to use their previously identified emotional patterns to elucidate the main conflict underlying their ED symptoms. The remaining meetings are focused on broadening each patient's understanding of her own conflicts and finding alternative healthier ways of coping with these stressful situations.. Examples of these may include journaling, sharing thoughts and feelings with supportive others, listening to music or watching TV. Group members are continually encouraged to serve as a support system for each other.

The Thirteenth Meeting: A Conclusion

For the final meeting, patients are required to prepare and share a summary of their treatment process. This includes a description of their emotional and behavioral journey and the subsequent changes they have made throughout treatment. They were asked to write about the identified emotional patterns connected to their ED symptoms as well as underlying related conflicts and the alternative coping mechanisms that they found helpful. This is an opportunity for every patient to evaluate their current condition, and the issues on which the patient would like to focus thereafter.

Case Example: "Craving for Mommy"

Natasha (name has been changed), is a 22-year-old female patient who has suffered from acute Bulimia Nervosa for the last five years, since her arrival to Israel from Russia. She was one of five females who participants in the group, whose ages ranged from 19-22.

Natasha was born in Russia, and immigrated alone to Israel as an adolescent, while her parents stayed behind in Russia. She referred herself to the Eating Disorder Clinic where she was diagnosed with BN. She reported having three uncontrolled binge episodes per day, which terminated with self-induced vomiting. She said that since her immigration to Israel she has suffered from this problem and only recently had the courage to ask for help.

Since finishing high school she has worked at various jobs. A few weeks prior to her self-referral to the clinic, she moved in with her with boyfriend. All her attempts to overcome and solve the problem on her own were unsuccessful. She was desperate, yet highly motivated for treatment to succeed, to the extent that she was not resistant when told that weight gain often occurs during treatment as a result of the balanced meal plan that individuals are assigned.

During the first meetings, when she reviewed her food diary, she described multiple daily binge episodes that were accompanied by numerous rituals surrounding food. Her preparation for her binges began with a "shopping journey" in which she would purchase roughly nine lbs of assorted baked goods, such as croissants, pizza, donuts, etc. Afterwards she would return home and wait for the "perfect moment" when she would be alone and able to "unite with her forbidden foods". She describes how the first moments of the eating rituals were very pleasant and gave her feelings of fullness and relaxation. However, within a short period of time, she would experience feelings of anxiety which led to extreme food cravings and a subsequent loss of control. During these episodes she reports feeling like a "monster", inhaling all her food without any sense of control. Her anxiety and loss of control were accompanied by feelings of guilt, low self-esteem, self-hatred, and self-disgust. The food, which initially felt like a "good object" that nurtured and relaxed her soon, became a bad object of aggression, requiring immediate elimination. At this moment she would rush to the toilet, and induce vomiting by putting her finger down her throat, all the while sitting in the bathroom feeling helpless, empty, and that her life was meaningless.

The thoughts which she documented in her diary following the binge episodes included memories which related to her ambivalent relationship with her mother who stayed in Russia, as well as an ambivalent feeling towards her boyfriend, with whom she currently resided. The conflict, which became apparent during the therapy, was a cyclical battle in which she missed her mother and wished to unite with her, but at the same time she would become angry at herself for needing her. Natasha told the group, that when she was a child she felt that her mother disliked her, and was disappointed in her and wished that she did not exist. She reported that her decision to immigrate to Israel on her own was an expression of this internal conflict relating to her relationship with her mother. She said, that by leaving the country she suppressed her need to be near to and supported by her mother. Subsequently, food provided, the necessary soothing, nurturing, and calming that she did not receive from her mother. However, at the same time, the food became her enemy, destroying her own body. As a result of the sessions she came to understand that the binge episodes were her attempts to reduce the pain experienced from her ambivalent feelings towards her mother whom she missed but was angry with.

Subconsciously, her desire to immigrate to Israel, at such a vulnerable young age, was fueled by the fantasy that she would find an idealized mother within the State of Israel, which would compensate for the mother that rejected her. However, this fantasy was quickly shattered and the need for a new mother reappeared. Meeting her boyfriend partially fulfilled her need to be nurtured, loved and accepted.. According to her therapist's explanation, the fact that she moved in to live with him reawakened her fear of loss and rejection, while at the same time allowing her the strength and support to come seek help.

The patient viewed the main conflict as her desiring intimacy and closeness but at the same time being afraid of being rejected. She understood that the binge episodes were a safe way to be close to a non-human object, which could never reject her, thereby replacing the need for human closeness She also came to understand that her guilt was associated with the fact that her relationship with food was more intimate than that with her boyfriend.

Understanding this conflict and identifying it on an emotional level enabled her to view the connection between her eating disorder and her feelings of deprivation. At this stage of treatment, the patient was given a behavioral assignment in which she was asked to offer alternative coping behaviors for this conflict, rather than binging and purging. From a variety of suggested behaviors she chose to write an essay to herself in which she gave herself permission to experience her needs without feelings of guilt. She was further asked to create a list of some other areas, other than eating, which allow her to feel satisfaction in her life. Additionally, she was instructed to eat one "forbidden" food each day, which she usually allowed herself only during binges. Another assignment was to take initiative in interacting with others and establishing interpersonal relationships.

Natasha, like the other members in the group, expressed great fear of exposing herself in front of the other group members at the beginning of the treatment. The structure of the group, which allowed each member an equal time to share their thoughts and behaviors, enabled her to overcome this difficulty and slowly open up. The group members supported her and by sharing their stories, enabled her to feel that her problems were shared by others and therefore were not as embarrassing as she had always perceived them. The highly structured nature of the program was a source of comfort, which provided a context in which she felt safe and secure.

As the therapy progressed, she shared her newly acquired coping mechanisms for stopping her urge to binge with the group. The group served as the family that she lacked and provided her with the strength to make meaningful life changes. Natasha reported that she used to have close to four binge episodes a day which were now down to one in the last four weeks. She was attuned to her drive towards binging and immediately was able to connect it to her painful conflict. She began showing an interest in studying at the University and talked about feeling closer to her boyfriend. Although she was aware of the conflict underlying her symptoms, facing the pain of deprivation was very difficult for her and she needed more support and treatment. It was recommended that she continue treatment privately, with a focus on addressing this conflict.

The case of Natasha illustrates the process by which patients give up eating disorder symptoms through, the maintenance of a balanced diet, an identification of emotional patterns associated with binge eating and finally an understating of the underlying dynamic conflict generating these patterns. This case also demonstrates the process of separation from and replacement of from the maladaptive coping mechanism with a new one targeting the fulfillment of the underlying need in an adaptive manner. In this case, the group setting enabled her to work on both intrapersonal understanding and interpersonal skills because of interaction with and feedback from group members.

INTERVENTION'S OUTCOME

The proposed model describes three groups of seven women each ranging in age from 20-35. The three groups were conducted successively for about 40 weeks. Seventy percent of women interviewed were accepted for participation in the program.

Of the three BN group receiving the CO-CBT intervention in the ED clinic, 60% of the women completed the full course of treatment. The remaining 40% left the clinic during the course of their treatment because they felt that the treatment was too difficult. This dropout rate is similar to attrition rates described in the literature in the treatment of CBT for BN, both in group and individual settings (Mitchell et al, 2002). A high level of motivation for treatment and low level of resistance to weight gain was found to be a good predictor of fitness for undergoing the treatment.

Follow up interviews were conducted with members who dropped out of treatment. In general, these patients lacked sufficient motivation and readiness to give up their ED symptoms at this stage in their lives. This predictor was similar to those reported by Fairburn, Cooper and Shafran (2003) in classical CBT. They indicated that those patients, who had difficulty lowering the number of binge-purge episodes during the first few weeks of treatment, had lower predictive rates of success and would most likely drop out. Additionally other factors that were not observed in our treatment model, including depression, impulsivity, and severe bulimic symptoms as predicting future drop-outs from group CBT therapy have been reported (Agaras, Crow, Halmi, Mitchell, Wilson & Kraemer, 2000, Steel, Jones, Adcock, Clancy, Bridgford-West, & Austin, 2000).

According to both self-reports and clinical impressions, it appears that all women who completed the treatment, without exception, experienced an improvement in their symptoms as well as in their emotional condition. As of yet, this data has not been empirically or qualitatively measured. Efficacy was evaluated according to self-reports of the participants and the objective measurements of their symptoms and emotional, and functional status which wer conducted pre and post treatment by the multidisciplinary staff at the ED clinic (According to DSM-IV, Psychiatric Evaluation, Clinical Evaluation, Nutrition Evaluation). This evaluation was done immediately after the treatment, and again six months and one year post treatment.

These are still very preliminary findings and cannot be used to derive any conclusions regarding the efficacy of the proposed model in comparison with the classic CBT model. In addition it is important to note the small sample size. However, in light of the considerable improvement in the symptoms and in the emotional state of all the patients who completed the treatment, it is important to conduct a controlled empirical examination.

Discussion

BN is an eating disorder characterized by recurrent uncontrolled binge episodes, with the consumption of large amounts of food within a short period of time followed by purging behavior. The physical and emotional effects of BN have engendered a number of treatment modalities that were developed using a variety of theoretical approaches. These approaches were considered in the past as being separate or even contradictory to each other. The questions arising from the various modes of treatment have presented the therapist with a considerable challenge.

CBT was found to be an effective approach for the treatment of BN, however not effective enough, as only about half of BN patients make a full and lasting recovery. (Fairburn, Cooper, & Shafran ,2003), making it necessary to explore more effective treatment options. Though the original CBT model has been lauded in its application in the treatment of BN, it is necessary to consider some of its limitations, which perhaps contribute to the lower than expected success rates. While the model seems to provide an immediate answer for coping with symptoms, it is suitable only for a narrow group of patients who are willing and able to meet the conditions for acceptance to the treatment program. Even among those patients who fit within this narrow parameter, the model still does not provide a satisfactory solution for their spiritual suffering and underlying conflicts. However, in our proposed CO-CBT model, as the treatment progressed and the intensity of the symptoms was reduced, the therapist was able to have access to the emotional needs and conflicts to which they were previously denied. In the beginning of the therapy, it appears that the intensity of the symptoms makes it difficult for both the therapist and the patient to explore deeply the underlying conflicts behind their disorder.

The proposed treatment model, attempted to address the limitations emerged from the literature .by creating and an in-depth intervention to the pre-existing CBT model, focusing on the conflict underlying the BN pathology (Wanlass, Janine, Moreno, Kelly, Thomson, & Hannah, 2005; Hendren, Atkins, Sumner, et al, 1987). Bridging the gap between the immense accumulation of knowledge and the wealth of clinical experience in applying the CBT model by the ED clinic staff has made it possible to create the proposed "Conflict-Oriented CBT" (CO-CBT) model. This model connects the range of cognitive-behavioral techniques and short-term dynamic treatment. This merging of techniques makes it possible to target a wider range of people requiring treatment and to meet a greater variety of needs. Likewise, it makes it possible for therapists of different schools of thought to treat such eating disorders.

Although the proposed model starts similarly to the classical CBT model, it defines the objective not only in terms of the binge/purge symptoms, but also in terms of the frequency of usage of the treatment tool. This alternative definition reduces the tension associated with immediate termination of the symptoms and thereby enables the patients to cope with their symptoms with less anxiety, relieving them of the feeling that they failed in their task. At the same time, when symptoms are alleviated, it is considerably easier to identify and resolv the underlying conflict through the use of cognitive programming and to assign patients appropriate behavioral tasks.

Hamilton (2001) concluded that the success of combining the cognitive and psychodynamic worlds rests on the ability of the therapist to integrate the various theoretical techniques into the treatment process. Likewise, Kogan (1996) claims that in recent years the modern dynamic approach tends to favor short-term dynamic treatment.

This raises the question as to what extent it is possible to bridge the gap between the internal and the external worlds with the use of psychotherapy in general and for the treatment of EDs' in particular. In the classical psychodynamic model, the two worlds were seen in a dichotomous manner, while any attempt from either the therapist or the patient to connect cognitive and dynamic influences was seen as either as resistance or as superficial (Klein, 1950).

Attempts to understand the phenomenon of EDs through dynamic theories have failed to provide a satisfactory explanation. Goodsit (1997) addressed this issue, claiming that in the treatment of AN or BN it is difficult to separate between the inner and the outside worlds, as there is an injury on a very deep level involving deprivation of basic needs. Bachar (2001) strengthens this approach, adding that the therapist must assist the patient in the process of self-awareness by relating to the point of view of the patient, through which eating is conceived as fulfilling the function of self-preservation, and by respecting the importance of the symptoms to the patient. The therapist's primary goal is to provide support for the patient in the process of becoming a separate self-formed person.

It seems that the combination of the physical with the spiritual, of the material with the abstract, and of the outer reality with the inner psyche is essential to treatment. In Freud's writings, we also find recognition of the importance of combining the principle of pleasure with the principle of reality, and the responsibility of the therapist to locate that point of conflict as a means of intervention.

The ability of the therapist to integrate the two worlds in treatment also makes it possible for the patient to follow in the same direction and to relinquish the split between fantasy and reality in favor of belonging socially and culturally, as well as belonging to oneself. Such a combination of therapeutic approaches may act as a "transitional object" (Winnicott, 1951) called it, which is important to the creation of the real self and an inner expanse that will enable the individual to digest the food rather than to swallow and vomit it.

With the development of this integrated proposed model, there are still some clinical and theoretical problems that remained to be solved.. These problems involve the manner in which a meeting between the two treatment approaches can be achieved and maintained. Therapists are inclined, by nature of their training, beliefs and ethical codes, to stick to a single theory and treatment approach.

Thus, there is a need to deepen and enlarge the proposed model on both the theoretical and the research levels; to analyze the effectiveness, and the limitations of CO-CBT with empirical tools, and to develop a training plan for therapists to move in the direction of a more integrated approach to the treatment of eating disorders.

ACKNOWLEDGMENT

We would like to thank Dr. Sarah Weinberger-Litman for her valuable contribution to this chapter

REFERENCES

Bachar, E. (2001). *The Fear of Occupying Space*. The Hebrew University Magnes Press. Jerusalem.

Bachar, E., Latzer, Y., Kreitler, S., Berry, E.M. (1999). Empirical Comparison of two Psychological Therapies: Self psychology and cognitive orientation in the treatment of Anorexia and Bulimia. *The Journal of Psychotherapy Practice and Research, 8*, 115-128.

Barth, D., & Wurman, V. (1986). Group therapy with bulimic women: A self-psychological approach. *International Journal of Eating Disorders. 5*, 735-745.

Beck, A. T. (1963). Thinking and Depression: Idiosyncratic content and cognitive distortions. *Archives of General Psychiatry, 9*, 324-333.

Britton, R. (1992). *The Oedipal Situation and the Depressive Position. Clinical Lectures on Klein and Bion*. London: Routledge, pp. 34-45.

Bruch, H. (1973). *Eating Disorders: Obesity, Anorexia Nervosa and the Person Within*. New York: Basic Books.

Bruch, H. (1982). Anorexia nervosa: Theory and therapy. American Journal of Psychiatry, 139, *1531-1538.*

Bruch, H. (2001). Family disengagement. In: *The golden cage: the enigma of anorexia nervosa*. US: Harvard University Press, pp. 106-120

Davanloo, H. (1979). *Techniques of Short-Term Dynamic Psychotherapy*. New York: Jason Aronson.

Fairburn, C. G. (1981). A cognitive behavioural approach to the management of bulimia. *Psychological Medicine, 11,* 707–711.

Fairburn, C. G., & Harrison, P. J. (2003). Eating disorders. *The Lancet, 361*, 407-416.

Fairburn, C. G., Cooper, Z., & Shafran, R. (2003). Cognitive behaviour therapy for eating disorders: a "transdiagnostic" theory and treatment. *Behavior Reserch and Therapy; 41,*:509-528.

Fairburn, C. G., Jones, R., Peveler, R. C., Hope, R. A., & O'Conner, M. E. (1993). Psychotherapy and bulimia nervosa: the longer-term effects of interpersonal psychotherapy, behavior therapy, and cognitive behavior therapy. *Archives of General Psychiatry, 50*, 419-428.

Fairburn, C. G., Norman, P. S., Welch, S. L., O'Conner, M. E., Doll, H. A. & Peveler, R. C. (1995). A prospective study of outcome in bulimia nervosa and the long term effects of three psychological treatments. *Archives of General Psychiatry, 52*, 304-312.

Fairburn, C. G., Shafran, R., & Cooper, Z. (1999). A cognitive behavioural theory of anorexia nervosa. *Behaviour Research and Therapy, 37*, 1–13.

Freeman, C. (1995). Cognitive therapy. In G. Szmukler, C. Dare, & J. Treasure (Eds.). *Handbook of Eating Disorders: Theory, Treatment and Practice*. John Wiley & Sons, pp. 309 –331.

Goodsitt, A. (1997). Eating disorders: a self-psychological perspective. In D. M. Garner & P. E. Garfinkel (Eds.), *Handbook of Treatment for Eating Disorders*. New York, The Guilford Press, pp. 205-228.

Goodsitt, A. (1986). Self psychology and the treatment of anorexia nervosa. In: Garner D. Garfinkel P. (Eds). *Handbook of Psychotherapy for Anorexia and Bulimia*. New York: Guilford.

Goodsitt, A. (1997). Eating disorders: A self-psychological perspective. In D. M. Garner & P. E. Garfinkel (Eds.), *Handbook of Psychotherapy for Eating Disorders*. New York: Guilford press, pp. 205-228.

Hamilton, J. (2001). Psychoanalysis and cognitive behavior therapy – rival paradigms or common ground? *International Journal of Psychoanalysis, 82,* 431-477.

Hendren, R. L., Atkins, D. M., Sumner, C. R., & Barber, J. K. (1987). Model for the group a treatment of eating disorders. *International Journal of Group Psychotherapy, 37,* 589-603.

Johnson, C. (1995). Psychodynamic treatment of bulimia nervosa. In C. G. Fairburn & K. D. Brownell (Eds.). *Eating disorders and Obesity*). The Guilford Press: New York, pp 349-353.

Lacey, J. H., & Evans, C. D. H. (1986). The impulsivist: a multi-impulsive personality disorder. *British Journal of Addiction, 81*, 641-649.

Lacey, J. H., & Read, T. R. C. (1993). Multi-impulsive bulimia: description of an inpatient eclectic treatment programme and a pilot follow-up study of its efficacy. *Eating Disorders Review, 1*, 22-31.

Lawrence, M. (2001). Loving them to death: the anorexic and her objects. *International Journal of Psychoanalysis, 82*, 43-55.

Levine, D., & Mishna, F. (2007). A Self Psychological and Relational Approach to Group Therapy for University Students with Bulimia. *International Journal of Group Psychotherapy, 57,* 167-185.

Malan, D. H. (1963). *A Study of Brief Psychotherapy*. New York: Plenum Press.

Mann J. J. (1998). Alterations in serotonin activity and psychiatric symptomatology after recovery from bulimia nervosa. *Archives of General Psychiatry, 55*, 927-935.

Mann, J. (1964). The specific limit of time in psychotherapy. *Seminar of Psychiatry, 1*, 375-379.

Mann, J. (1973). *Time-Limited Psychotherapy*. Cambridge: Harvard University Press.

McFarlane, T. L., Olmsted, M. P., & Goldbloom, D. S. (2005). Beliefs and expectations regarding etiology, treatment and outcome in bulimia nervosa. *Eating and Weight Disorders, 10*, 187-192.

Mitchell, J. E., Halmi, K., Wilson, G. T., Agras, W. S., Kraemer, H., & Crow, S. (2002). A randomized secondary treatment study of women with bulimia nervosa who fail to respond to CBT. *International Journal of Eating Disorders, 32*, 271-281.

Mitchell, J. E., Pyle, R. L., Pomeroy, C., Zollman, M., Crosby, R., Stein, H., Eckert, E. D., & Zimmerman, R. (1993). Cognitive-behavioral group psychotherapy of bulimia nervosa: importance of logistical variables. *International Journal of Eating Disorders, 14*, 277-287.

Monteleone, P., Castaldo, E., Di Filippo, C., & Maj, M. (2006). Physiopathology, diagnosis and management. *Minerva Psichiatrica, 47*, 59-78.

Moreno, J. K. (1998). Long-term psychodynamic psychotherapy for eating disorders: A descriptive case report. *Journal for Specialist in Group Work. 23*, 269-284.

Ogden, T. H. (1989). *The Primitive Edge of Experience*. London: J. Aronson.

Riess, H. (2002). Integrative time-limited group therapy for bulimia nervosa. *International Journal of Group Psychotherapy, 52*, 1-26.

Ryle, A., & Beard, H. (1993). The integrative effect of reformulation: cognitive analytic therapy with a patient with borderline personality disorder. *British Journal of Medical Psychology, 66*, 249-258.

Ryle, A., & Golynkina, K. (2000). Effectiveness of time-limited cognitive analytic therapy of borderline personality disorder: Factors associated with outcome. *British Journal of Medical Psychology, 73*, 197-210.

Ryle, A., (1995). Transference and counter-transference variations in the course of the cognitive-analytic therapy of two borderline patients: The relation of the diagrammatic reformulation of self-states. *British Journal of Medical Psychology, 68*, 109-124.

Sands, S. (1991). Bulimia, dissociation and empathy: A self-psychological view. In C. Johnson (Ed.), *Psychodynamic Treatment of Anorexia Nervosa and Bulimia*. New York: Guilford Press. pp. 34-50.

Sifneos, P. (1966). Psychoanalytically-oriented short-term dynamic anxiety provoking psychotherapy for mild obsessional neuroses. *Psychiatry Quarterly, 40*, 271-282.

Triosi, A., DiLorenzo, G., Alcinic, S., Nanni, R. C., Di Pasquale, C., & Siracusano, A. (2006). Body Dissatisfaction in Women with Eating Disorders: Relationship to Early Separation Anxiety and Insecure Attachment. *Psychosomatic Medicine, 68*, 449-453.

Wifley, D.E. & Saelens, B. E. (2002). Epidemiology and causes of obesity in children. In C. G. Fairburn & K. D. Brownell (Eds.). *Eating Disorder and Obesity a Comprehensive Handbook*. New York Guilford Press, pp. 429-432.

Wifley, D.E., Agras, W. F., Telch, C. F., Rossiter, E. M., Schneider, J. A., Cole, A. G. (1993). Group cognitive-behavioral therapy and group intepersonal psychotherapy for the non purging bulimic individual: a controlled comparison. *Journal of Consulting and Clinical Psychology, 61*, 296-305.

Williams, G. (1997). *Internal Landscapes and Foreign Bodies*. London: Duckworth.

Williams, G. J., Chamove, A. S., & Millar, H. R. (1990). Eating disorders, perceived control, assertiveness and hostility. *British Journal of Clinical Psychology, 29*, 327-335.

Williams, G. J., Power, K. G., Millar, H. R., Freeman, C. P., Yellowlees, A., Dowds, T., Walker, M., Campsie, L., MacPherson, F., & Jackson, M. A. (1993). Comparison of eating disorders and other dietary/weight groups on measures of perceived control, assertiveness, self-esteem, and self-directed hostility. *International Journal of Eating Disorders, 14*, 27-32.

Williamson, D. A., Martin, C. K., Stewart, T. (2004). Psychological aspects of eating disorders. *Best Practice & Research in Clinical Gastroenterology, 18*, 1073-88.

Williamson, D. A., White, M. A., York-Crowe, E, & Stewart, T. M. (2004). CBT theories of Eating Disorders. *Behavioral Modification, 28*, 711-738.

Wilson, G. T. (1999). CBT for eating disorders. *Behavioral Research Therapy, 37*, 79-95.

Wilson, G. T., & Sysko, R. (2006). Cognitive-behavioral therapy of for adolescents with bulimia nervosa. *European Eating Disorders Review, 14*, 8-16.

In: Cognitive Therapy of Eating Disorders... ISBN: 978-1-60876-617-8
Editors: S. Sassaroli and G.M. Ruggiero

Chapter 11

PHARMACOLOGICAL TREATMENT OF EATING DISORDERS

***Giovanni M. Ruggiero*[1], *Carmelo Lamela*[2] *and Sandra Sassaroli*[3]**
[1] "Psicoterapia cognitiva e ricerca" Cognitive psychotherapy school and research center, Milano, Italy
[2] "Scuola Cognitiva Firenze", Cognitive psychotherapy school and research center, Florence, Italy
[3] "Studi Cognitivi" Cognitive psychotherapy school and research center, Milano, Italy

ABSTRACT

This chapter is a concise review of the pharmacological treatment of eating disorders. According to Harrison and Fairburn (2003), the empirical state of art of drug treatments recommended for patients with eating disorders involves the use of antidepressants during the acute treatment, of antidepressants during the relapse prevention, of antipsychotics and of appetite suppressants. Of these 4 options, only the use of antidepressant drugs during acute treatment can be considered as having significant weight of supporting evidence and able to show significant magnitude of treatment effects observed. Antidepressant drugs are able to generate a decline in the frequency of binge eating and purging. However, the evidence tells us also that the effect is not sustained and enduring and, more important, that it is lower than that of cognitive behavior psychotherapy. In addition, combining antidepressant drugs and cognitive behavior therapy seems to produce only few significant improvement over cognitive behavior therapy alone (Mitchell et al., 1990; Walsh et al., 1997).

PHARMACOLOGICAL TREATMENT OF BULIMIA NERVOSA

The present state of the evidence based pharmacological treatment of eating disorders can be considered partially satisfactory only for bulimia nervosa. On the one hand, the encouraging and consistent findings of many randomized controlled trials have shown that the pharmacological management of bulimia nervosa is possible. Antidepressant drugs have proved superior to a pill placebo in reducing binge eating and purging in numerous randomized (Devlin & Walsh, 1995). In addition, different classes of antidepressants seem to be equal. However, two uncontrolled studies have suggested that patients failing to respond to an antidepressant drug in an early phase of the therapy may respond to another (Mitchell et al., 1989 ; Walsh, Hadigan, Devlin, Gladis, & Roose, 1991).

Specific antidepressant agents that have demonstrated efficacy among patients with bulimia nervosa in double-blind, placebo-controlled studies include trazodone (Pope Jr., Keck Jr., McElroy, & Hudson, 1989); tricyclic compounds such as imipramine (233, 236), desipramine (234, 237, 238, 240), and amitriptyline (235); the SSRIs fluoxetine (Goldstein, Wilson, Thompson, Potvin, & Rampey Jr., 1995; Fluoxetine Bulimia Nervosa Collaborative Study Group, 1992) and sertraline (Milano, Petrella, Sabatino, & Capasso, 2004) but not fluvoxamine (Schmidt et al., 2004); and several MAOIs (Walsh et al., 1984; Kennedy et al., 1988). Summing up, the therapeutic role of antidepressant in bulimia nervosa seems to be an initial intervention, especially recommended in primary care, which is necessary followed by cognitive behavioral psychotherapy delivered by a professionally trained therapist.

The emergence of cognitive-behavioral therapy (Fairburn, 1981; Fairburn et al., 1995) and of antidepressant medication as leading treatments for bulimia nervosa has raised questions about their comparative efficacy and about the advantages of combining them. The results of some studies examining these issues indicate that cognitive-behavioral therapy alone is generally superior to a trial of a single antidepressant agent and suggest that there may be some advantage to combining cognitive-behavioral therapy with antidepressant medication (Mitchell et al., 1990, Agras et al., 1992; Leitenberg et al., 1994; Fichter et al, 1991).

Mitchell et al. (1990) studied the short-term treatment outcome of a comparison trial of bulimic outpatients and found that the amount of improvement obtained with imipramine treatment combined with a intensive group psychotherapy component was superior to that obtained with antidepressant treatment alone. The addition of antidepressant treatment to the intensive group psychotherapy component resulted in more improvement in the symptoms of depression and anxiety. Walsh et al. (1997) found that bulimic patients receiving medication in combination with psychological treatment experienced greater improvement in binge eating and depression than did patients receiving placebo and psychological treatment. McCann and Agras (1990) found the tricyclic desipramine to be significantly superior to placebo in reducing the frequency of binges, reducing the tendency for disruptive environmental events to precipitate binges (less disinhibition), reducing hunger, and increasing dietary restraint. Another report of the tricyclic imipramine (Alger, Schwalberg, Bigaouette, Michalek, & Howard, 1991) found that although the median decrease in frequency of binges was 90% in the imipramine-treated group, there was no significant difference in response compared with placebo.

In addition, Walsh et al (2000) compared fluoxetine to placebo for patients who had participated in a controlled comparison of cognitive behavior therapy and interpersonal psychotherapy for bulimia nervosa but who had not responded sufficiently or who had relapsed after the end of the psychological intervention and found that fluoxetine may be a useful intervention for patients with bulimia nervosa who did not responded adequately to any psychological treatment. The results of this study extend previous data in demonstrating that fluoxetine is of benefit even to patients with bulimia nervosa who have not responded satisfactorily to psychotherapy.

Pharmacological Treatment of Anorexia Nervosa

On the other hand, the situation for eating disorders other than bulimia nervosa is less encouraging. The little number of randomized controlled studies which have explored the efficacy of the treatment of anorexia nervosa or atypical eating disorders tells us that at the present time the clinical guidelines for these two classes of eating disorders must remain tentative.

As widely known, patients with anorexia nervosa are reluctant to change and to involve in treatment and need to achieve a significant weight restoration as a first step of any kind of treatment. The current therapeutic approach relies on a combination of psychological and behavioral techniques often provided in an inpatient or intensive outpatient setting (American Psychiatric Association, 1993). Although such interventions are generally successful in restoring weight, patients typically remain ambivalent about treatment, and relapse is common (Steinhausen, Rauss-Mason, & Seidel, 1991; Eckert, Halmi, Marchi, Grove, & Crosby, 1995). Pharmacological interventions are useful in the treatment of disorders overlapping with anorexia nervosa, like major depression and bulimia nervosa (Walsh & Devlin, 1993). In addition, antidepressant medications that inhibit serotonin reuptake (SSRIs) are beneficial in obsessive compulsive disorder (Pigott, 1996). However, anecdotal reports have suggested that SSRIs might be valuable in the treatment of underweight patients with anorexia nervosa (Ferguson, 1987, Gwirtsman, Guze, Yager, Gainsley, 1990). Some controlled trials of antidepressant medication compared to placebo confirmed that antidepressants (amitriptyline, clomipramine and fluoxetine) conferred no additional benefit to the inpatient treatment of underweight patients with anorexia nervosa (Lacey & Crisp, 1980; Halmi, Eckert, LaDu, Cohen, 1986; Biederman at al., 1985). Frequent medical complications depending on the severe weight loss make the use of psychiatric drugs difficult. Drugs have not a clear role in the treatment of anorexia nervosa. There is no drug which has shown any significant effect on weight restoration (Mitchell, 2001; Treasure & Schmidt, 2002). The results of trials for fluoxetine (Ricca et al., 1999; Barbarich et al., 2004; Walsh et al., 2006), citalopram (Pallanti, Quercioli, & Ramacciotti, 1997; Fassino et al., 2002), fluvoxamine (Holtkamp et al., 2005), sertraline (Holtkamp et al., 2005), and venlafaxine (Ricca et al., 1999) have been disappointing (Barbarich-Marsteller, 2007). There is only some evidence suggesting that fluoxetine could be helpful in reducing the risk of relapse in patients whose weight has been restored (Kaye et al., 2001; Ruggiero et al., 2003).

More recently, the field of eating disorders has considered the possibility that atypical antipsychotics may be a tool for increasing weight gain and improving symptoms in anorexia nervosa. To date, the most common atypical antipsychotic studied is olanzapine. Olanzapine is thought to exert its mechanism of action through a combination of DA and 5-HT_2 receptor antagonism. Some case studies and open trials of olanzapine have reported efficacy in decreasing anxiety and promoting weight gain and decreasing anorexic worry about fatness and dieting (La Via, 2000; Hillebrand et al., 2005; Mondraty et al., 2005).

In conclusion, anorexia nervosa is a life-threatening disorder, with a complex clinical presentation including high rates of comorbidity and mortality. The chronic effects of starvation on drug metabolism complicate the use of pharmacological treatments during the ill state.

PHARMACOLOGICAL TREATMENT OF BINGE EATING DISORDER

Binge eating disorder, this disorder is characterized by recurrent binge-eating episodes, similar in many ways to those in bulimia nervosa, but without behaviors to prevent weight gain, such as self-induced vomiting. Stunkard et al. (1996) reported that *d*-fenfluramine (an appetite suppressant with serotonin-enhancing properties that has recently been removed from the market) was more effective than placebo in the treatment of binge-eating disorder in an 8-week trial. In addition, two small open-label trials (Prats, Diez-Quevedo, Avila, & Planell, 1994; Gardiner, Freeman, Jesinger, & Collins, 1993) suggested that SSRIs may also be used to treat binge-eating disorder. Hudson et al. (1998) studied fluvoxamine. Compared with placebo, fluvoxamine treatment was associated with a significantly greater rate of reduction in the frequency of binges and a significantly greater rate of global improvement than was placebo. In addition, fluvoxamine was associated with a greater rate of reduction in body mass index than was placebo, and weight loss after 9 weeks of treatment was correlated with reduction in frequency of binges. In conclusion, fluvoxamine was found to be effective according to most outcome measures in the acute treatment of binge-eating disorder. In addition, also variety of other SSRIs, like citalopram (McElroy et al., 2003), fluoxetine (Arnold et al., 2002), and sertraline (McElroy et al., 2000) have been found to be associated with significantly greater decreases in binge frequency than placebo.

REFERENCES

Agras, W. S., Rossiter, E. M., Arnow, B., Schneider, J. A., Telch, C. F., Raeburn, S. D., Bruce, B., Perl, M., & Koran, L. M. (1992). Pharmacologic and cognitive-behavioral treatment for bulimia nervosa: a controlled comparison. *American Journal of Psychiatry, 149*, 82–87.

Alger, S. A., Schwalberg, M. D., Bigaouette, J. M., Michalek, A. V., & Howard, L. J. (1991). Effect of a tricyclic antidepressant and opiate antagonist on binge-eating behavior in normal weight bulimic and obese, binge-eating subjects. *American Journal of Clinical Nutrition, 53*, 865–871.

American Psychiatric Association (1993). Practice guideline for eating disorders. *American Journal of Psychiatry, 150*, 208–228.

Arnold, L. M., McElroy, S. L., Hudson, J. I., Welge, J. A., Bennett, A. J., & Keck, P. E. (2002). A placebo-controlled, randomized trial of fluoxetine in the treatment of binge-eating disorder. *Journal of Clinical Psychiatry, 63*, 1028–1033.

Attia, E., Haiman, C., Walsh, B.T., & Flater, S.R. (1998). Does Fluoxetine Augment the Inpatient Treatment of Anorexia Nervosa? *American Journal of Psychiatry, 155*, 548-551.

Barbarich, N. C., McConaha, C. W., Halmi, K. A., Gendall, K., Sunday, S. R., Gaskill, J., La Via, M., Frank, G. K., Brooks, S., Plotnicov, K. H., & Kaye, W. H. (2004). Use of nutritional supplements to increase the efficacy of fluoxetine in the treatment of anorexia nervosa. *International Journal of Eating Disorders, 35*, 10-5.

Barbarich-Marsteller, N. C. (2007). Neurochemistry and Pharmacological Treatments: Where is the Field of Anorexia Nervosa Heading? *Central Nervous System Agents in Medicinal Chemistry, 7*, 35-43.

Biederman, J., Herzog, D. B., Rivinus, T. M., Harper, G. P., Ferber, R. A., Rosenbaum, J. F., Harmatz, J. S., Tondorf, R., Orsulak, P. J., & Schildkraut. J. J. (1985). Amitriptyline in the treatment of anorexia nervosa: a double-blind, placebo-controlled study. *Journal of Clinical Psychopharmacology, 5*, 10–16

Devlin, M. J., & Walsh, T. (1995). Medication treatment for eating disorders. *Journal of Mental Health, 4*, 459-469.

Eckert, E.D., Halmi, K.A., Marchi, P., Grove, W., & Crosby, R. (1995). Ten-year follow-up of anorexia nervosa: clinical course and outcome. *Psychological Medicine, 25*, 143–156

Fairburn, C.G. (1981). A cognitive behavioural approach to the treatment of bulimia. *Psychological Medicine, 11*, 707–711.

Fairburn, C.G., Harrison, P.J. (2003). Eating disorders. *The Lancet, 361*, 407-416.

Fairburn, C.G., Norman, P.A., Welch, S.L., O'Connor, M.E., Doll, H.A., & Peveler, R.C. (1995). A prospective study of outcome in bulimia nervosa and the long-term effects of three psychological treatments. *Archives of General Psychiatry, 52,* 304–312.

Fassino, S., Leombruni, P., Daga, G., Brustolin, A., Migliaretti, G., Cavallo, F., & Rovera, G. (2002). Efficacy of citalopram in anorexia nervosa: a pilot study. *European Neuropsychopharmacology, 12,* 453-459.

Ferguson, J. M. (1987). Treatment of an anorexia nervosa patient with fluoxetine (letter). *American Journal of Psychiatry, 144*, 1239.

Fichter, M. M., Leibl, K., Rief, W., Brunner, E., Schmidt-Auberger, S., Engel, R. R. (1991). Fluoxetine versus placebo: a double-blind study with bulimic inpatients undergoing intensive psychotherapy. *Pharmacopsychiatry, 24*, 1–7.

Fluoxetine Bulimia Nervosa Collaborative Study Group (1992). Fluoxetine in the treatment of bulimia nervosa: a multicenter, placebo-controlled, double-blind trial. *Archives of General Psychiatry, 49*, 139–147.

Gardiner, H. M., Freeman, C. P. L., Jesinger, K. D., & Collins, S. A. (1993). Fluvoxamine: an open pilot study in moderately obese female patients suffering from atypical eating disorders and episodes of bingeing. *International Journal of Obesity, 17*, 301–305.

Goldstein, D. J., Wilson, M. G., Thompson, V. L., Potvin, J. H., & Rampey, A. H. Jr. (1995). Long-term fluoxetine treatment of bulimia nervosa: Fluoxetine Bulimia Nervosa Research Group. *British Journal of Psychiatry, 166*, 660–666.

Gwirtsman, H. E., Guze, B. H., Yager, J., & Gainsley, B. (1990). Fluoxetine treatment of anorexia nervosa: an open clinical trial. *Journal of Clinical Psychiatry, 51*, 378–382.

Halmi, K. A., Eckert, E. D., LaDu, T. J., & Cohen, J. (1986). Anorexia nervosa: treatment efficacy of cyproheptadine and amitriptyline. *Archives of General Psychiatry, 43*, 177–181

Hillebrand, J. J., van Elburg, A. A., Kas, M. J., van Engeland, H., & Adan, R.A. (2005). Olanzapine reduces physical activity in rats exposed to activity-based anorexia: possible implications for treatment of anorexia nervosa? *Biological Psychiatry, 58*, 651-657.

Holtkamp, K., Konrad, K., Kaiser, N., Ploenes, Y., Heussen, N., Grzella, I., & Herpertz-Dahlmann, B. (2005). A retrospective study of SSRI treatment in adolescent anorexia nervosa: insufficient evidence for efficacy. *Journal of Psychiatric Research, 39*, 303-310.

Hudson, J.I., McElroy, S. L., Raymond, N. C. et al. (1998). Fluvoxamine in the Treatment of Binge-Eating Disorder: A Multicenter Placebo-Controlled, Double-Blind Trial. *American Journal of Psychiatry, 155,* 1756-1762.

Kaye, W.H., Nagata, T., Weltzin, T.E., Hsu, L.K., Sokol, M.S., McConaha, C., Plotnicov, K.H., Weise, J., & Deep, D. (2001). Double-blind placebo-controlled administration of fluoxetine in restricting- and restricting-purging-type anorexia nervosa. *Biological Psychiatry, 49*, 644-52

Kennedy, S. H., Piran, N., Warsh, J. J., Prendergast, P., Mainprize, E., Whynot, C., & Garfinkel, P. E. (1988). A trial of isocarboxazid in the treatment of bulimia nervosa. *Journal of Clinical Psychopharmacology, 8*, 391–396.

La Via, M. C., Gray, N., & Kaye, W. H. (*2000*). Case reports of olanzapine treatment of anorexia nervosa. *International. Journal of Eating Disorders, 27*, 363-366.

Lacey, J. H., & Crisp, A. H. (1980). Hunger, food intake and weight: the impact of clomipramine on a refeeding anorexia nervosa population. *Postgraduate Medical Journal, 56* (suppl. 1), 79–85.

Leitenberg, H., Rosen, J. C., Wolf, J., Vara, L. S., Detzer, M. J., & Srebnik, D. (1994). Comparison of cognitive-behavior therapy and desipramine in the treatment of bulimia nervosa. *Behaviour Research and Therapy, 32*, 37–45.

McCann, U. D., & Agras, W. S. (1990). Successful treatment of nonpurging bulimia nervosa with desipramine: a double-blind, placebo-controlled study. *American Journal of Psychiatry, 147*, 1509–1513.

McElroy, S. L., Casuto, L. S., Nelson, E. B., Lake, K. A., Soutullo, C. A., Keck, P.E. Jr., & Hudson, J. I. (2000). Placebo-controlled trial of sertraline in the treatment of binge eating disorder. *American Journal of Psychiatry, 157*, 1004–1006.

McElroy, S. L., Hudson, J. I., Malhotra, S., Welge, J. A., Nelson, E. B., & Keck, P. E. Jr. (2003). Citalopram in the treatment of binge-eating disorder: a placebo-controlled trial. *Journal of Clinical Psychiatry, 64*, 807–813.

Milano, W., Petrella, C., Sabatino, C., & Capasso, A. (2004). Treatment of bulimia nervosa with sertraline: a randomized controlled trial. *Advances in Therapy, 21*, 232–237.

Mitchell, J. E., Pyle, R. L., Eckert, E. D., Hatsukami, D., Pomeroy, C. & Zimmerman, R. (1989). Response to alternative antidepressants in imipramine nonresponders with bulimia nervosa. *Journal of Clinical Psychopharmacology, 9*, 291-293.

Mitchell, J. E., Pyle, R. L., Eckert, E. D., Hatsukami, D., Pomeroy, C. & Zimmerman, R. (1990). A comparison study of antidepressants and structured intensive group psychotherapy in the treatment of bulimia nervosa. *Archives of General Psychiatry, 47*, 149-157.

Mitchell, J.E. (2001). Psychopharmacology of eating disorders: current knowledge and future directions. In R. Striegel-Moore & L. Smolak (Eds.), *Eating Disorders: Innovative Directions in Research and Practice*. Washington: American Psychological Association, pp. 197-214.

Mondraty, N., et al., (2005). Randomized controlled trial of olanzapine in the treatment of cognitions in anorexia nervosa. *Australasian Psychiatry, 13*, 72-75.

Pallanti, S., Quercioli, L. & Ramacciotti, A. (1997). Citalopram in anorexia nervosa. *Eating & Weight Disorders, 2*, 216-221.

Pigott, T.A. (1996). OCD: Where the serotonin selectivity story begins. *Journal of Clinical Psychiatry, 57*, 11–20.

Pope, H. G. Jr., Keck, P. E. Jr., McElroy, S. L., & Hudson, J. I. (1989). A placebo-controlled study of trazodone in bulimia nervosa. *Journal of Clinical Psychopharmacology, 9*, 254–259

Prats, M., Diez-Quevedo, C., Avila, C., & Planell, L. S. (1994). Paroxetine treatment for bulimia nervosa and binge eating disorder, in *Abstracts of the Sixth International Conference on Eating Disorders*. New York, Montefiore Medical Center, April 1994, abstract number 308.

Ricca V, Mannucci E, Paionni A, Di Bernardo M, Cellini M, Cabras PL, et al.(1999). Venlafaxine versus fluoxetine in the treatment of atypical anorectic outpatients: a preliminary study. *Eating and Weight Disorders, 4*, 10-14.

Ricca, V., Mannucci, E., Paionni, A., Di Bernardo, M., Cellini, M., Cabras, P. L., & Rotella, C. M. (1999): Venlafaxine versus fluoxetine in the treatment of atypical anorectic outpatients: a preliminary study. *Eating and Weight Disorders, 4*, 10-14.

Ruggiero, G.M., Mauri, M.C., Omboni, A.C., Volonteri, L.S., Dipasquale, S., Malvini, L., Redaelli, G., Pasqualinotto, L., & Cavagnini, F. (2003). Nutritional management of anorexic patients with and without fluoxetine: 1-year follow-up. *Progress in Neuro-psychopharmacology & Biological Psychiatry, 27*, 425-30.

Schmidt, U., et al. (2004). Fluvoxamine and graded psychotherapy in the treatment of bulimia nervosa: a randomized, double-blind, placebo-controlled, multicenter study of short term and long-term pharmacotherapy combined with a stepped care approach to psychotherapy. *Journal of Clinical Psychopharmacology, 24*, 549–552.

Steinhausen, H.C., Rauss-Mason, C., & Seidel, R. (1991). Follow-up studies of anorexia nervosa: a review of four decades of outcome research. *Psychological Medicine, 21*, 447–454.

Stunkard, A., Berkowitz, R., Tanrikut, C., Reiss, E., & Young, L. (1996). *d*-Fenfluramine treatment of binge eating disorder. *American Journal of Psychiatry, 153*, 1455–1459.

Treasure, J., & Schmidt, U. (2002). Anorexia nervosa. In S. Barton (Ed.), *Clinical Evidence: Mental Health*. London: BMJ Publishing Group, pp. 13-22.

Walsh, B. T., Stewart, J. W., Roose, S. P., Gladis, M., & Glassman, A. H. (1984). Treatment of bulimia with phenelzine: a double-blind, placebo-controlled study. *Archives of General Psychiatry, 41*, 1105–1109.

Walsh, B.T., & Devlin, M. (1993). Psychopharmacology of anorexia nervosa, bulimia nervosa, and binge eating. In F. E. Bloom & D. J. Kupfer (Eds.), *Psychopharmacology: The Fourth Generation of Progress*. New York, Raven Press, pp. 1581–1589..

Walsh, B.T., Agras, W. S., Devlin, M. J,. et al. (2000). Fluoxetine for Bulimia Nervosa Following Poor Response to Psychotherapy. *American Journal of Psychiatry, 157*, 1332–1334.

Walsh, B.T., Kaplan, A.S., Attia, E., Olmsted, M., Parides, M., Carter, J.C., Pike, K.M., Devlin, M.J., Woodside, B., Roberto, C.A., & Rockert, W. (2006). Fluoxetine After Weight Restoration in Anorexia Nervosa: A Randomized Controlled Trial. *Journal of American Medical Association, 295*, 2605-2612.

Walsh, B.T., Wilson, G.T., Loeb, K.L., et al. (1997). Medication and psychotherapy in the treatment of bulimia nervosa. *American Journal of Psychiatry, 154*, 523-531.

INDEX

A

B

D

G

H

I

N

O

P

Q

R

S

T

U

V

W

Y

Z